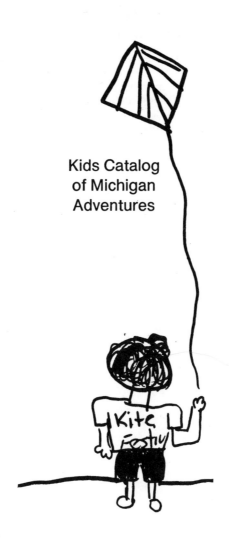

Kids Catalog
of Michigan
Adventures

GREAT LAKES BOOKS

A complete listing of the books in this series can be found at
the back of this volume.

Phillip P. Mason, Editor
Walter P. Reuther Library, Wayne State University

Dr. Charles K. Hyde, Associate Editor
Department of History, Wayne State University

KIDS

CATALOG OF
MICHIGAN ADVENTURES

ELLYCE FIELD

Wayne State University Press
Detroit

97 96 95 94 93   5 4 3 2 1

Library of Congress Cataloging-in-Publication Data

Field, Ellyce, 1951–
    Kids catalog of Michigan adventures / Ellyce
    Field.
        p. cm. — (Great Lakes books)
    Includes index.
    ISBN 0-8143-2463-0 (pbk. : alk. paper)
    1. Michigan—Guidebooks. 2. Family recreation—
Michigan—Guidebooks.   3.   Children—Travel—
Guidebooks. I. Title. II. Series.
F564.3.F54   1993
917.7404′43—dc20   92-39216

Designer: Mary Primeau

Sites listed were chosen by the author. No one paid
to be included in this book. Every effort was taken to
be sure all information in this book was correct when
we went to press. However, hours, exhibits, prices,
and even locations change from time to time. So,
PLEASE CALL AHEAD.

For my husband Steve, my best friend, whose loving support sustained me during this project.

For my parents, Charles and Belle Ruben, who taught me that with hard work anything is possible and supervised my carefree growing up in Detroit.

For my three sons, Jordan, Andrew, and Garrett, who smilingly endured tossed-together dinners, diminished computer time, and school vacations spent zigzagging across Michigan.

CONTENTS

10   Contents

PREFACE

Born and raised in Detroit and its suburbs, I am the consummate Hometown Tourist.

As soon as my children were portable (a backpack for the firstborn, twin strollers for the next two), my husband Steve and I started searching for sites and experiences that our entire family could enjoy. In 1987, I began writing *The Detroit News* "Kid Stuff" column, and so a quest for memorable family experiences that could be shared with a readership began in earnest.

My family and I have crisscrossed Michigan, exploring new sites and revisiting old favorites. With a growing sense of adventure, we have bucked the crowds at popular area attractions, found pleasure in little-known museums, and spent afternoons all by ourselves in nature centers off the beaten track. We have picked apples, strawberries, and pumpkins; listened to jazz and classical concerts; watched puppet shows, light opera, mime, and drama. We have ridden wild waves, tame ponies, and zooming go-carts. We have cheered for our home teams, lounged at the beach, marveled at laser and planetarium shows and witnessed the birth of many Made-in-Michigan products. In short, we have discovered the child's world in Michigan.

Due to the popularity of *Detroit Kids Catalog*, and many readers' requests for additional outstate Michigan information, this second edition, now renamed *Kids Catalog of Michigan Adventures*, has a larger focus. You'll find over 600 new sites, more maps, and a more comprehensive city listing. *Kids Catalog of Michigan Adventures* is a handbook for both adults and children who are ready to explore Michigan and become hometown tourists.

1
FIRST THINGS FIRST

Things to Know

The secret to successful family outings is to PLAN AHEAD. Be sure to CALL AHEAD to verify times, prices, directions, and special events whenever you go anywhere with your kids. This way, you'll minimize disappointment and unnecessary frustration.

This chapter is designed to help you plan ahead and learn how to best use *Kids Catalog of Michigan Adventures*. Listed are: publications that offer calendars of kids' events; telephone information numbers; emergency resources; and information about transportation and tours, Canada and customs, and Michigan's best kid stuff.

Weather and Clothes

Michigan is famous for its changeable weather, its extremes and its surprises. When it isn't doing any of the above, it's safe to say: summer is hot; autumn is cool; winter is snowy cold, and spring is wet. So dress the kids in layers and throw an extra jacket or sweatshirt in the backseat. Take along a sun hat or visor in the summer and carry boots, hats, and mittens in the winter. I always carry a large shopping bag or a backpack to hold the layers as they are peeled off.

Publications

The Detroit News "Kid Stuff" column highlights family entertainment and sites and includes a calendar of kids' events for the coming weekend and week. 313-222-2300.

The Detroit Free Press offers a "Family Fare" column and a "Seeing & Doing" calendar. 313-222-6583.

Detroit Monthly, the monthly city magazine, includes a very brief listing of kids' events in its monthly calendar. 313-446-6000.

metroPARENT, a monthly parenting newspaper available by subscription, offers a monthly calendar of kids' events. 313-352-0990.

How To Use This Book

I wrote this book for busy parents who, like myself, enjoy traveling around town with their kids, but have very little time to plan out a detailed adventure and would rather have all the information at their fingertips, with all the suggestions and pitfalls mentioned.

Chapters are arranged around a specific theme, for example, museums or parks. Sites are listed in alphabetical order. The most important information (address, phone, location, hours, admission, ages, plan, parking, lunch, and facilities) is listed. A short annotation describes the site and gives you its flavor.

Here are some important facts to remember:

The age designation of a particular site is based on my experience with my children, who are often very mature, cooperative travelers, but at other times are very reluctant, irritable travelers! No one knows your children's needs, interests, and attention span better than you do, so use the age designation as a suggested guideline. However, please respect a specific age requirement for admittance to a site or performance.

Plan refers to how long you should plan on the visit taking. I've indicated *approximate* amounts of time by: "all day visit" (6+ hours), "half day visit" (4+ hours), "short visit" (2+ hours) and "under one hour." Keep in mind that the best laid plans often go awry. If your baby needs a nap, your guest has to get to the airport, or your children become cranky and hungry, your half day visit could turn into a short visit. Come back on a more relaxing day.

Lunch tells you where you can find food on the premises or nearby. If you're going out for the day, it doesn't hurt to pack a snack or a picnic lunch just in case the kids get hungry, which they always do, when you're lost or driving on the expressway.

Facilities includes information about stroller rental, bathrooms, and gift shops.

Chapters 8, 9, 13, and 15 group sites by type or location. Because the sites in chapters 5, 6, 7, 10, 11, 12, 14, and 16 are so various, a brief description of the site or its activities—for instance, "Petting Farm" or "Music & Dance"—appears above the entry in these chapters.

Michiganians love their cars. Most of us have sturdy wheels and are not afraid to drive from here to there. For this reason, the chapters include sites in Southeastern Michigan, plus cities that are within a 2-hour drive (approximately 120 miles) from Detroit, such as Ann Arbor, Ypsilanti, East Lansing, Lansing, Jackson, Flint, and Port Huron. Sites more than 2 hours away are listed geographically in the Regional Adventures chapter. Families who are planning Michigan vacations will find Chapter 2—City Listing, and Chapter 3—Maps, as well as Chapter 15—Regional Adventures, very helpful.

Enjoy traveling with your kids. With each excursion, you'll develop a core of family memories and a love for Michigan.

Telephone Information

General Information

Detroit Visitor Center: 313-567-1170

Detroit Convention and Visitor Center Main Office: 313-259-4333 (open Monday-Friday)

Michigan Regional Tourist Associations:
Upper Peninsula: 906-774-5480, 1-800-562-7134
West Michigan: 616-456-8557

Michigan Travel Bureau: 1-800-543-2937

Michigan Travel Bureau: TDD 1-800-722-8191 (for the hearing impaired)

Michigan State Chamber of Commerce: 517-371-2100 (for the name, address, and phone of a specific city's chamber of commerce)

Sterling Heights Special Recreation Services (programs for children with disabilities): 313-977-6123, ext. 200

Sell Ticket Service (Ticket Broker): 313-262-1555
Time: 313-472-1212
Ticketmaster: 313-645-6666
Windsor Convention and Visitors Bureau: 519-255-6530

Emergency Numbers

Babysitting—Hourly Drop-Off:
My Place: 313-737-5437 (West Bloomfield), 313-540-5702 (Birmingham)
Dental Referral Service: 313-871-3500, 313-559-7767
Doctor's Referral Service: 313-567-1640
Hospitals:
Beaumont Hospital, Royal Oak:
1-800-633-7377, Emergency 313-551-2000
Bon Secours of Michigan, Grosse Pointe:
313-343-1000, Emergency 313-343-1605
Children's Hospital of Michigan, Detroit:
313-745-5437, Emergency 313-745-5206
Henry Ford Hospital, Detroit:
313-876-2600, Emergency 313-876-1545
North Oakland Medical Center, Pontiac:
313-857-7200, Emergency 313-857-7257
Oakland General Hospital, Madison Heights:
313-967-7000, Emergency 313-967-7670
Providence Hospital, Southfield:
313-424-3000, Emergency 313-424-3331
St. Joseph Mercy Hospital, Ann Arbor:
313-572-3456, Emergency 313-572-3000
St. Joseph Mercy Hospital, Pontiac:
313-858-3000, Emergency 313-858-3100,
Pediatric After Hours Center 313-858-3493
Sinai Hospital, Detroit:
313-493-5713, Emergency 313-493-5555
University of Michigan Medical Center,
Ann Arbor:
313-936-4000, Emergency 313-936-6662,
Pediatric Walk-In Clinic 313-936-4230
Medical Societies:
Oakland County Medical Society: 313-646-5400
Macomb County Medical Society: 313-790-3090
Wayne County Medical Society: 313-567-1640
Police, Fire, EMS: 911 in Wayne, Oakland, Macomb, Washtenaw and Livingston Counties.

Frequently Used Box Office Numbers

The Ark, Ann Arbor: 313-761-1451
Attic Theatre, Detroit: 313-875-8285

Birmingham Theatre, Birmingham: 313-644-1096

Boarshead Theatre, Lansing: 517-484-7800

Bonstelle Theatre, Detroit: 313-577-2960

Cobo Arena, Detroit: 313-396-7600, 313-645-6666 (use Ticketmaster for orders)

Detroit Symphony Orchestra, Detroit: 313-833-3700

Fisher Theatre, Detroit: 313-872-1000

Fox Theatre, Detroit: 313-396-7600 (office), 313-645-6666 (use Ticketmaster for orders)

Gem Theatre, Detroit: 313-963-9800, 313-396-7600

The George Burns Theatre for the Performing Arts, Livonia: 313-422-8200, 1-800-589-8000 (theatre hotline)

Hilberry Theatre, Detroit: 313-577-2972

Joe Louis Arena, Detroit: 313-396-7600, 313-645-6666 (use Ticketmaster for orders)

Lydia Mendelssohn Theatre, Ann Arbor: 313-763-1085

McMorran Place Theatre, Port Huron: 313-985-6166

Macomb Center for the Performing Arts, Mount Clemens: 313-286-2222, 313-286-2268

Magic Bag Theatre, Ferndale: 313-544-3030

Marquis Theatre, Northville: 313-349-8110

Masonic Temple, Detroit: 313-832-7100

Meadow Brook Theatre, Rochester: 313-377-3300

Meadow Brook Music Festival, Rochester: 313-396-7600, 313-645-6666 (use Ticketmaster for orders)

Michigan Opera Theatre, Detroit: 313-874-SING

Michigan Theater, Ann Arbor: 313-668-8397

Michigan Union Ticket Office, Ann Arbor: 313-763-TKTS

Music Hall, Detroit: 313-963-7680

Orchestra Hall, Detroit: 313-833-3700

The Palace, Auburn Hills: 313-377-8600, 313-377-0100, 313-645-6666 (use Ticketmaster for orders)

Pine Knob, Clarkston: 313-377-8600, 313-377-0100 (office), 313-645-6666 (use Ticketmaster for orders)

Pontiac Silverdome, Pontiac: 313-456-1600

Power Center, Ann Arbor: 313-763-3333

Ticketmaster (Order tickets by phone using credit card): 313-645-6666

Youtheatre, Detroit: 313-963-7680

Transportation and Tours

Unlike other major cities, Detroit is an automobile town. It is almost impossible to get around town without a car, unless you are staying downtown and visiting only downtown, uptown, and Cultural Center sites. Then you can hop on the People Mover, trolley, and a Woodward bus.

Driving is easy around Metro Detroit. We are a town with well-marked, easy-to-follow freeways. I-75, I-275, and US-10 are the major north-south highways, I-94, I-696, and I-96 are the east-west highways.

Traffic tends to be heavy going downtown during morning rush hour, generally 7:30-9 a.m., and leaving downtown in afternoon rush hour, 4:30-6 p.m. On Friday afternoon during the summer, northbound I-75 is quite dense. Ditto Sunday evening on southbound I-75. This is "Up North" traffic. Be sure to buckle up!

Bus Lines

People Mover: 313-962-7245
50 cents a ride. Token machines selling 50-cent coupons for dollar bills are in all stations but Greektown. Monthly, semi-annual, and annual passes are available. Hours are 7 a.m.-11 p.m., Monday-Thursday. 7 a.m.-midnight, Friday. 9 a.m.-midnight, Saturday. Noon-8 p.m., Sunday. *See* Best Rides in Town for more information about the People Mover as a tourist attraction.

SMART: 313-962-5515
The Suburban Mobility Authority for Regional Transportation provides commuter service between Detroit and the suburbs and between suburbs. There are also "connector" buses that provide curb-to-curb service and are useful for the handicapped. Fares vary with routes.

D-Dot: 313-933-1300
Detroit Department of Transportation has many bus routes throughout the city. Fare is $1 in change only, plus 10 cents for a transfer.

A mini-bus service connecting major downtown hotels with the business district costs 45 cents.

A doubledecker red trolley operates daily from Grand Circus Park to the Renaissance Center. 7:10 a.m.-5:40 p.m., Monday-Friday. 10 a.m.-5:40 p.m., Saturday, Sunday, and holidays. Fare is 45 cents. Trolley drivers do not give change.

Greyhound Lines: 313-963-9840
Detroit-Canada Tunnel Bus: 313-567-4422

Taxis

You'll have the best luck with cabs if you call for one and wait. Some cabs hang around the major downtown hotels, but rarely cruise near attractions. Cabs operate on a meter system. Basic charge is approximatey $1.10 per mile. Meters start at $1.10.

The city's major cab companies are City Cab 313-833-7060, Checker Cab 313-963-7000, Blue Eagle Cab 313-934-2000, and Detroit Cab 313-841-6000.

Railroads

Amtrak: 1-800-872-7245 or 313-964-5335
Detroit's station at 2601 Rose Street, and Dearborn's station at 16121 Michigan Avenue, provide service to various parts of the country.

The one-hour train ride to Ann Arbor from Dearborn is a great way to introduce the kids to rail travel. Have a family member drive the family car to Ann Arbor and meet you at the station so you can explore Ann Arbor by car.

Canadian National Railroad: 1-800-387-1144

Air Travel

Detroit City Airport: 313-267-6400
Detroit Metropolitan Airport: 313-942-3685 (airport operations), 313-942-3550 (lost and found). Call individual airlines for departure and arrival information.
Windsor Airport: 519-969-2430
Northwest Airlines: Detroit's largest carrier 1-800-225-2525 (reservations), 1-800-441-1818 (arrival, departure information) or 313-962-2002 (Detroit office, incoming flight information)
Limousine Service: Commuter Transportation Co. 313-946-1000. This is the major shuttle service between the airport and downtown hotels. A booth is located in the airport baggage claim area. They also have scheduled pickups from hotel to airport.

Rental Car Agencies

Detroit's largest and best-known national companies are Avis 1-800-331-1212, Hertz 1-800-654-3131, and National 1-800-227-7368.

Organized Tours

Charter Bus Unlimited: 313-272-5000
Classic Trolley: 313-945-6100
Detroit Department of Transportation: 313-935-3808
Detroit Historical Society: 313-833-7934
D-Tours: 313-647-6022
Kirby Tours: 313-278-2224

Canada and Customs

For a quick trip abroad, take the Detroit-Windsor Tunnel or the Ambassador Bridge into Canada. Traveling through the tunnel and across the bridge will be a great adventure for children. There's plenty to do across the border, and the kids will marvel at the colorful Canadian currency

You can also drive into Canada across the Blue Water Bridge that connects Port Huron to Sarnia, Ontario. Lake Huron is on one side of the bridge; the St. Clair River is on the other.

U.S. citizens should carry with them a driver's license or proof of car ownership, personal identification, and birth certificate or naturalization papers. Landed immigrants should carry their passport. Foreign nationals should consult immigration officials for details on border crossing.

U.S. citizens are permitted to bring back duty-free up to $25 of personal or household merchandise per person. After 48 hours in Canada, the customs' exemption is $400 per person, including children.

There is a toll collected at each side of the Detroit River. It is $1.50 U.S. and $1.75 Canadian for passenger cars at the Detroit-Windsor Tunnel; $1.50 U.S. and $1.75 Canadian for passenger cars at the Ambassador Bridge. The Blue Water Bridge toll is 75 cents in either Canadian or U.S. currency.

U.S. Customs: 313-226-3138
U.S. Immigration: 313-226-3290
Canadian Customs: 519-973-8506
Canadian Immigration: 519-253-3006.

Be sure the kids are buckled up. Both Michigan and Ontario have a seatbelt law.

Michigan's Best Kid Stuff

No guidebook is complete without a list of the area's best attractions. These sites have a proven track record and have been family favorites for many years. I offer this list knowing full well that when my children were small, they sometimes enjoyed the neighborhood playground more than a visit to Michigan's best children's sites. Apply your discretion in using this list. As your children grow, your family favorites will change. Check the index for a more complete listing.

Alfred P. Sloan Museum, Flint
Ann Arbor Hands-On Museum, Ann Arbor
Belle Isle Aquarium, Detroit
Children's Museum, Flint
Cranbrook Institute of Science,
   Bloomfield Hills
Curious Kids Museum, St. Joseph
Denoss Museum, Traverse City
Detroit Historical Museum, Detroit
Detroit Institute of Arts, Detroit
Detroit People Mover, Detroit
Detroit Science Center, Detroit
Detroit Symphony Orchestra Young
   People's Concerts, Detroit
Detroit Zoological Park, Royal Oak
Ella Sharp Museum, Jackson
Fort Malden National Historic Park,
   Amherstburg
Gerald R. Ford Museum, Grand Rapids
Great Lakes Shipwreck Museum,
   Paradise
Greenfield Village and Henry Ford
   Museum, Dearborn
Impression 5 Museum, Lansing
Jesse Besser Museum and Planetarium,
   Alpena
Michigan Historical Museum, Lansing
Michigan Space Center, Jackson
Midland Center for the Arts, Midland
Pictured Rocks National Lakeshore,
   Munising
Tahquamenon Falls, Paradise
University of Michigan Exhibit Museum
Youtheatre

During the summer:
Boblo Island, Detroit
Crossroads Village/Huckleberry Railroad,
Flint
Four Bears Water Park, Utica
Hartwick Pines, Grayling
Iron Mountain Iron Mine, Iron Mountain
Mackinac Island

**Meadow Brook Music Festival,
    Rochester**
Penny Whistle Place, Flint
Pine Knob Music Theatre, Clarkston
Sleeping Bear Dunes National Lakeshore
White Pine Village, Ludington

Just For Toddlers

The following sites are geared for preschoolers
through second grade. For maximum enjoyment,
be sure to visit while the kids are still small.
Check the index for a more complete listng.

Belle Isle Zoo, Detroit
Bumper bowling
Children's Museum, Flint
**Deer Acres Storybook Amusement Park,
    Pinconning**
**Dinosaur Gardens Prehistoric Zoo,
    Ossineke**
**Discovery Room, Jewish Community
    Center, West Bloomfield**
**Farmington Hills Library Children's
    Room play structures**
Huron-Clinton Metroparks Tot Lots
Junction Valley Railroad, Bridgeport
**Maybury State Park Petting Farm,
    Northville**
Penny Whistle Place, Flint
**Pine Knob Music Theatre Children's
    Series, Clarkston**
Prehistoric Forest, Irish Hills
Saginaw Children's Zoo
Youtheatre's Wiggle Club

Just For Teens

For a family outing with teens, take my foolproof
advice: have your teenager invite along a friend,
then the two can pretend they aren't really with
you. Most teens won't even mind having the family tag along to the following sites. Check the index for a more complete listing.

Batting cages, go-carts, miniature golf
Big Boy Warehouse Tour, Warren
Boblo
Buick City Tour, Flint
**Concerts at Joe Louis Arena, The Palace
    or Pine Knob**

(you can wait for them in the
"Parent Holding Area,"
known as the Quiet Room)
**Cranbrook Institute of Science laser
shows, Bloomfield Hills**
Phaserland, Farmington Hills
**Red Oaks Golf Dome and Sports Village,
Madison Heights**
Studio Audiences
**U-pick berries, apples, pumpkins and
Christmas trees**
**Veteran's Park skateboard ramp,
Ann Arbor**
Wave pools/waterslides
**Whirly Ball, Ann Arbor, Mount Clemens,
West Bloomfield**

Family Memberships

Many Michigan institutions offer yearly family memberships ranging from $25-$75. Here's your chance to support your favorite museum and become a V.I.P. at the same time. Family members enjoy free admission, newsletters, special parties, activities, and gift shop discounts. With a Family Membership, you'll be able to drop in on an institution for a short visit and not worry about staying long enough to "get your money's worth." Think of these institutions when holidays and birthdays roll around. Here's a sampling:

Alfred P. Sloan Museum, Flint: 313-760-1169
Ann Arbor Hands-On Museum: 313-995-5439
Children's Museum, Flint: 313-238-6931
Cranbrook Academy of Art Museum: 313-645-3312
Cranbrook Institute of Science: 313-645-3203
Detroit Historical Society: 313-833-7934
Detroit Institute of Arts: 313-833-7971
Detroit Science Center: 313-577-8400
Detroit Zoological Society: 313-541-5505
Henry Ford Museum/Greenfield Village, Dearborn: 313-271-1620
Impression 5 Museum, Lansing: 517-485-8815
Museum of African American History, Detroit: 313-833-9800

2
A CITY LISTING
OF SITES

Here is a listing of all the sites and programs described in this book, arranged by the city in which they are located. You'll find over 1,000 sites in over 250 cities in Michigan and southwestern Ontario. Plan on browsing through this chapter often to plan your day trips and overnight adventures. You might even be surprised to find what's available in your own hometown.

MICHIGAN CITIES

Acme
American Spoon Foods Kitchen
Music House

Ada
Amway Corporation
Coopersville and Marne Railroad Company

Adrian
Croswell Opera House

Allen Park
Allen Park Arena
Allen Park Bowling
Law Fair

Almont
Brookwood Fruit Farm

Alpena
Besser Company
Jesse Besser Museum

Ann Arbor
Ann Arbor Art Fair
Ann Arbor Community Education and Recreation
    Junior Theatre
Ann Arbor Community Education and Recreation
    Mini-Matinee Club
Ann Arbor Farmers' Market
Ann Arbor Hands-On Museum
Ann Arbor Pow Wow
Ann Arbor Skate Company
Ann Arbor Summer Festival
Ann Arbor Symphony Orchestra
Argo Park Livery
The Ark
Barbara Schutz-Gruber
Buhr Park Ice Rink

CHAMPS - U. of M. Museum of Art
Cobblestone Farm
Colonial Lanes
Country Christmas
Delhi Metropark
Gallup Canoe Livery
Gemini
Goodtime Players
Huron Hills Ski Center
Kerrytown Plaza
Leslie Science Center
Little Dipper Shoppe
Michigan Theater
Mixer Playground
Museum of Art
O.J. Anderson
Performance Network
Peter Madcat Ruth
Phoenix Memorial Laboratory
Power Center
Project Grow
Scrap Box
The SongSisters
Stearns Collection of Musical Instruments
T.J.'s Cages
T.J.'s Sports World
University of Michigan Exhibit Museum
University of Michigan Exhibit Museum
    Planetarium
University of Michigan Matthaei Botanical
    Gardens
University of Michigan Museum of Art
University of Michigan Wolverines
Veterans Park
Whirly Ball Ann Arbor
Wild Swan Theatre
WUOM - Michigan Public Radio
Yost Ice Arena
Young People's Theater

Armada
Blake's Big Apple Orchard
Blake's Orchard and Cider Mill
Coon Creek Orchard

Auburn Heights
Michigan Humane Society-North

Auburn Hills
Detroit Pistons Basketball
Oakland County Animal Care Center
The Palace
Palace Summerfest

Augusta
Kellogg Bird Sanctuary

Baldwin
Wolf Lake Ranch

Bangor
Kalamazoo Toy Trains

Battle Creek
Battle Creek International Balloon Championship
Binder Park Zoo
Kingman Museum of Natural History
McCamly Place

Bay City
Historical Museum of Bay County
Jennison Nature Center
St. Laurent Brothers

Bellaire
Shanty Creek/Schuss Mountain

Belleville
Belleville Strawberry Festival
Boughan's Tree Farm
Lower Huron Metropark
Pumpkin Factory
Sandy Acres Blueberry Farm
Thornhollow Tree Farm

Benton Harbor
Sarett Nature Center

Berkley
Berkley Ice Arena
Hartfield Lanes

Berrien Springs
Historic Courthouse Square
Lemon Creek Fruit Farm and Winery
Love Creek County Park and Nature Center

Bessemer
Big Powderhorn Mountain Ski Corporation
Blackjack Ski Resort

Beulah
Homestead Sugar House Candies

Beverly Hills
Beverly Hills Village Park

Birmingham
Art in the Park
Baldwin Public Library
Birmingham-Bloomfield Symphony Orchestra
Birmingham Community House
Birmingham Ice Sports Arena
Birmingham Theatre

Birmingham YMCA
Children's Halloween Ball
Crown Coach, Inc.
First Night
The Puppet Connection
Shaine Park Concerts
Temple Beth El
The Townsend Hotel

Blissfield
Adrian and Blissfield Railroad
Santa Train

Bloomfield Hills
Autumn Fest
Charles L. Bowers Farm
Cranbrook Academy of Art Museum
Cranbrook House and Garden
Cranbrook Institute of Science
Cranbrook Institute of Science Planetarium
Cranbrook Summer Children's Theatre
E.L. Johnson Nature Center
Excellent Electrical Event
Native American Activity Day

Boyne Falls
Boyne Mountain

Bridgeport
Amigo Mobility, Inc.
Junction Valley Railroad

Brighton
Huron Meadows Metropark
Island Lake Recreation Area
Leah Gold, Ltd.
Mt. Brighton Ski Area
Warner's Orchard and Cider Mill
Warren's Tree Farm
Wenzel's Tree Farm

Brooklyn
Arend Tree Farms
Michigan International Speedway
Walker Tavern Historic Complex

Brown City
Frank Industries, Inc.

Burton
For-Mar Nature Preserve and Arboretum
Michigan Balloon Corporation

Cadillac
Caberfae Ski Resort
Four Winns Boat Company
Johnny's Wild Game and Fish Park

Calumet
Coopertown U.S.A. Mining Museum

Canton
Canton Softball Center Complex
Lower Rouge Parkway
Skatin' Station

Carleton
Calder Brothers Dairy Farm

Caspian
Iron County Museum

Cedar
Sugar Loaf Resort

Charlevoix
American Spoon Foods Kitchen

Chelsea
Waterloo Geology Center

Clarkston
Bellair's Hillside Farm and the Sheep Shed
Cherry Hill Lane
Independence Oaks
Indian Springs Metropark
Pine Knob Music Theatre
Pine Knob Ski Resort
Starlab

Clawson
Clawson Parks & Recreation Children's Series
Stevens and Associates

Clinton
Shores Skateland
Southern Michigan Railroad

Clio
Runyan's Country Tree Farm

Cohoctah
Cohoctah Tree Works

Coloma
Deer Forest

Colon
Abbott's Magic Get-Together
Abbott's Magic Manufacturing Company

Commerce Township
Hazen's Blueberries
Roy Long

Copper Harbor
Brockway Mountain Drive
Delaware Copper Mine
Fort Wilkins State Park

Croswell
Croswell Swinging Bridge

Davisburg
Davisburg Candle Factory
Oakland County 4-H Fair
Springfield Oaks

Davison
Masters Orchard and Cider Mill
Uptegraff's Orchard

Dearborn
Adray Ice Arena
Arab Folk Heritage Museum
Cherry Hill Lanes
Children's World at Christmas
Christmas Past at Greenfield Village
Classic Trolley Company
Dearborn Historical Museum: McFadden Ross
    House and Exhibit Annex
Dearborn Rollerdome
The Fun Factory
Greenfield Village
Greenfield Village Theatre Company
Henry Ford Estate-Fairlane
Henry Ford Museum
Lower Rouge Parkway
Martinsville Cider Mill
Middle Rouge Parkway
The Ritz-Carlton Hotel
Santa's Workshop
Time Travelers
University of Michigan-Dearborn Arena
University of Michigan-Dearborn Environmental
    Study Area

Dearborn Heights
Canfield Ice Arena
Warren Valley Golf Course

Detroit
Adams Ice-Skating Arena
African Heritage Cultural Center
Ambassador Bridge
Ami D.
Anna Scripps Whitcomb Conservatory
Art and Scraps
Atlantis Expedition
Attic Theatre
Belle Isle
Belle Isle Aquarium
Belle Isle Nature Center
Belle Isle Zoo

Blue Pigs
Bonstelle Theatre
Channel 4 WDIV
Chene Park
Children's Museum
Children's Museum Planetarium
Christmas Carnival
Clark Park
Cobo Arena
Cobo Hall
Day of Puppetry
Detroit A Glow
Detroit Center for the Performing Arts
Detroit Compuware Ambassadors
Detroit Drive!
Detroit Edison-School Safety Coordinator
Detroit Festival of the Arts
Detroit Fire Department Historical Museum
Detroit Grand Prix
Detroit Historical Museum
Detroit Institute of Arts
Detroit Kennel Club Dog Show
Detroit Mini Grand Prix
Detroit People Mover
Detroit Police Horse Stables
Detroit Public Library-Children's Library
Detroit Red Wings
Detroit Rockers
Detroit Science Center
Detroit Symphony Orchestra
Detroit Thanksgiving Festival
Detroit Thunderfest
Detroit Tigers
Detroit Trolley
Detroit Turbos
Detroit Water Department-Springwells Water
    Plant
Detroit-Windsor Tunnel
The Detroiter
Dossin Great Lakes Museum
Downtown YMCA
Eastern Market
Eastside YMCA
East Warren Lanes
The Fabricators
Festival of Trees
Fisher Building
Fisher Mansion/Bhaktivedanta Center
Fisher Theatre
Fox Theatre

Garden Bowl
Gem Theatre
GM Building
Great Lakes Indian Museum
Greektown
Hart Plaza
Hilberry Theatre
Historic Fort Wayne
Holiday in Lights
International Freedom Festival
International Institute
Joe Louis Arena
Madame Cadillac Dancers
Masonic Temple
Michigan Opera Theatre
Michigan Sports Hall of Fame
Michigan State Fair
Michigan Taste Fest
Miller Lite Montreaux/Detroit Jazz Festival
Motown Museum
Museum of African American History
Music Hall
Naim Abdur Rauf
National Museum of Tuskegee Airmen
Noel Night
North American International Auto Show
Northland Roller Rink
Northside YMCA
Northwestern YMCA
Nsoroma Institute
Oakwood Blue Jackets Bowl
Officer Ollie and Friends
Omni Arts in Education
Orchestra Hall
Palmer Park
Paper Bag Productions
Pewabic Pottery
Pippin Puppets
Puppets at the DIA
Redford Bowl
Renaissance Center
Renaissance Christmas
Renaissance City Storyfest
River Place Athletic and Croquet Club
Roller-Cade
St. Aubin Park
Santa's at the People Mover
Sesame Street Live!
Spirit of Detroit Thunderfest
Splat Ball City Playing Field

State Fairgrounds
Story Peddlar
The Storytellers
Trapper's Alley (The Alley)
Underground Railroad-Second Baptist Church
United States Post Office-General Mail Facility
University of Detroit Titans
Wayne State University Tartars
Western YMCA
Winterfest
Your Heritage House
Youtheatre at Music Hall

Dexter
Coldsprings Farm
Dexter Area Museum
Dexter Cider Mill
Dexter-Huron Metropark
Frank's Orchard
Hudson Mills Metropark
Lakeview Farm and Cider Mill
Mosher Tree Farm
Spring Valley Trout Farm
Zabinsky Blueberry Farm

Drayton Plains
Children's Theatre of Michigan
Drayton Plains Nature Center

Dryden
Heritage Harvest Days
Seven Ponds Nature Center

East Jordan
Crazy Richard the Madd Juggler

East Lansing
Abrams Planetarium
Horticultural Gardens
Kresge Art Museum
Michigan Festival
Michigan State University Museum
Michigan State University Spartans
Michigan State Veterinary School Vet-A-Visit
Red Rug Puppet Theatre

Empire
Sleeping Bear Dunes National Lakeshore

Erie
Erie Orchards and Cider Mill
Langenderfer Farm

Farmington
Bel Aire Lanes
Farmington YMCA
Mark Thomas

Phazer Land

Farmington Hills
Bonaventure Roller Skating Center
The Community Center of Farmington and
    Farmington Hills
Drakeshire Lanes
Farmington Hills Branch Library
Farmington Hills Library Play Structure
Glen Oaks
Karaoke-Wing Hong's Tokyo Japanese Steak
    House
Langans Northwest Lanes
Marvin's Marvelous Mechanical Museum and
    Emporium
Mercy Center Pool
Parkey's Series
Putt-Putt Golf and Games
Scheer Magic Productions
Summer Fun Series
Youtheatre at Mercy High School

Fayette
Historic Fayette Townsite

Fenton
Capt. Phogg
Fenton Riding Academy
Hilltop Orchards and Cider Mill
Preiss Sod and Strawberry Farm
Spicer Orchards Farm Market and Cider Mill
Tom Walker's Grist Mill

Ferndale
Magic Bag Theatre
Storybuilders

Flat Rock
Flat Rock Speedway
Oakwoods Metropark

Flint
AC Spark Plug Tour
Alfred P. Sloan Museum
Buick City Tour
Children's Celebration
Children's Museum
Christmas at Crossroads
Crossroads Village Cider Mill
Crossroads Village/Huckleberry Railroad
Flint Institute of Arts
Flint Youth Theatre
Harvest Jubilee
Longway Planetarium
Michigan Human Society-Genesee County
Mott Farm

Penny Whistle Place

Flushing
Almar Orchards
Chaprnka Tree Farm
Koan's Orchards
McCarron's Orchard
R.L.B. Tree Farm

Frankenmuth
Antique Auto Village
Bronner's Christmas Wonderland
Frankenmuth Bavarian Festival
Frankenmuth Brewery, Inc.
Frankenmuth City Tours
Frankenmuth Flour Mill and General Store
Frankenmuth Pretzel Company
Frankenmuth Riverboat Tours
Holz-Brucke and Woodcarvers' Pavilion
Michigan's Own Inc. Military and Space Museum

Franklin
Franklin Cider Mill

Fraser
Fraser Hockeyland
Liberty Bowl

Freeland
Bintz Apple Mountain

Fremont
Gerber Products Company

Garden City
Ford Road Miniature Golf
Garden City Ice Arena
Maplewood Family Theatre

Gaylord
Bavarian Falls Park
Call of the Wild Museum
El Rancho Stevens
Michaywe Slopes
Treetops Sylvan Resort
Tyrolean Ski Resort

Glen Arbor
The Homestead

Goodells
Jeffery's Blueberries
Pampered Pines

Goodrich
Porters Orchard and Cider Mill
Symanzik's Berry Farm

Grand Blanc
Trim Pines Farm

Grand Haven
Harbor Steamer

Harbor Trolley
Tri-Cities Museum
Waterfront Stadium

Grand Marais
Pictured Rocks National Lakeshore

Grand Rapids
Becky Goodspeed
Bissel, Inc.
Blandford Nature Center
Carol Johnson
Fish Ladder Sculpture
Gerald Ford Museum
Grand Rapids Art Museum
Grand Rapids Public Museum
Grand Rapids Zoological Gardens
Gypsum Mine Tour
Roger B. Chafee Planetarium
Splash - Family Water Park

Grass Lake
Arend Tree Farms
Christmas Tree Lane
Fodor's Christmas Tree Farm

Grayling
Civilian Conservation Corps Museum (North Higgins Lake State Park)
Hartwick Pines State Park
Noel Tree Company

Gregory
DeGroot's Strawberries

Grosse Ile
Westcroft Gardens

Grosse Pointe Farms
Brunch with Santa
Concerts for Kids
Grosse Pointe Children's Theatre

Grosse Pointe Shores
Edsel and Eleanor Ford House
Showtime at the Playhouse

Hamtramck
Paczki Day
Veterans Memorial Park

Hancock
Arcadian Copper Mine Tours, Inc.
Quincy Mine Hoist No. 2

Harbor Springs
Boyne Highlands
Chief Blackbird Museum
Nub's Nob Ski Area

Harrisville
Cedarbrook Trout Farm

Hastings
Charleton Park Historic Village

Hazel Park
Hazel Park Raceway
Mauro's Miniature Golf

Highland
Broadview Christmas Tree Farm
Huff Tree Farm
Ridgemere Berry Farm

Holland
Brooks Beverages Plant
DeGraaf Nature Center
Deklomp Wooden Shoe and Delftware Factory
  and Veldheer Tulip Garden
Dutch Village
Windmill Island
Wooden Shoe Factory

Holly
Diehl's Orchard and Cider Mill
Groveland Oaks Waterslide
Michigan Renaissance Festival
Mt. Holly, Inc.

Houghton
Isle Royale National Park

Howell
Art Hazen
Howell Nature Center
Pleasant Knoll Tree Farm
Waldock Tree Farm

Huron Township
Willow Metropark

Ida
Marlin Bliss Tree Farm
Matthes Evergreen Farm
Stotz's Pumpkin Farm

Independence Township
Waterford Hills Road Racing

Indian River
The Cross in the Woods
Sturgeon and Pigeon River Outfitters, Inc.

Inkster
Inkster Civic Arena

Interlochen
Fun Country
Interlochen Center for the Arts

Iron Mountain
Cornish Pump and Mining Museum
Iron Mountain Iron Mine
Menominee Range Historical Foundation
  Museum

Pine Mountain Lodge

Iron River
Ski Brule/Ski Homestead

Ironwood
Black River Drive
Copper Peak Ski Flying Hill
Hiawatha, World's Tallest Indian
Mt. Zion Overlook

Ishpeming
National Ski Hall of Fame

Jackson
Ella Sharp Museum
Illuminated Cascades
Jackson Harness Raceway
Michigan Space Center

Kalamazoo
Gilmore Classic Car Museum
Kalamazoo Aviation History Museum
Kalamazoo Institute of Arts
Kalamazoo Nature Center
Kalamazoo Public Museum and Planetarium
Mad Hatters
Scott's Mill Park
Train Barn

Kearsage
Delaware Copper Mine

Lake Orion
Bald Mountain Recreation Area
Brad Lowe
Goodison Cider Mill
Willow Creek Miniature Golf

Lakeport
Lakeport State Park

Lansing
Boarshead Theatre
Carl F. Fenner Arboretum
Impression 5 Museum
Lorann Oils, Inc.
Michigan Historical Museum
Michigan Women's Historical Center and Hall of
    Fame
Potter Park Zoo
R.E. Olds Transportation Museum
State Capitol
Woldumar Nature Center
Young Entomologists Society

Lapeer
Candy Cane Christmas Tree Farm

Leland
Good Harbor Vineyard
Leelanau Scenic Railway
Lennon
Asplin Farms
Leonard
Addison Oaks
Lexington
Lexington Marina
Lincoln Park
Fantasyland
Lincoln Park Community Center
Litchfield
Harvard Clothing Company
Livonia
Devon-Aire Arena
Eddie Edgar Arena
Friendly Merri-Bowl Lanes
The George Burns Theatre for the
    Performing Arts
Greenmead Museum and Historical Village
Ladbroke Detroit Race Course
Linda Day
Livonia YMCA
Mobile Ed Productions
Observer and Eccentric Newspapers
Riverside Roller Arena
Woodland Lanes
Your Creation!
Ludington
Great Lakes Visitor Center
Rose Hawley Museum
S.S. Badger Ferry Service
White Pine Village
Macinac Island
Old Fort Mackinac
Mackinaw City
Colonial Michilimackinac and Mackinaw Maritime
    Park and Museum
Old Mill Creek State Historic Park
Revolutionary War Sloop *Welcome*
Teysen's Woodland Indian Museum
Madison Heights
Astro Lanes
Madison Heights Civic Center
Red Oaks Golf Dome and Sports Village
Red Oaks Waterpark
Manchester
Alber Orchard and Cider Mill
Manistique
Kitch-iti-kipi Spring and Raft

Siphon Raft and Bridge

Marine City
Lucy's Livery

Marquette
Presque Isle Park
United States Olympic Training Center Tours

Marshall
American Museum of Magic
Cornwell's Turkey House

Mason
Adventures Aloft

Mass City
Windmill Farms

Mattawan
Michigan Fisheries Interpretive Center

Mears
Mac Wood's Dune Rides
Silver Queen Riverboat Rides

Melvindale
Melvindale Ice Arena

Memphis
Belle River Farms

Midland
Automotive Hall of Fame
Chemistry is Fun
Chippewa Nature Center
Dow Gardens
Dow Visitor's Center
Midland Center for the Arts

Milford
Alpine Valley
Heavner's Canoe and Cross Country Ski Rentals
Highland Recreation Area
Kensington Metropark
Kensington Nature Center and Farm Center
Proud Lake Recreation Area
Snacks with Santa

Monroe
Monroe County Historical Museum
Monroe Farmers' Market
Navarre-Anderson Trading Post and Country
    Store Museum
Navarre Strawberry Farm
River Raisin Battlefield Visitor's Center
September Productions
Sterling State Park
Weier's Cider Mill

Montrose
Montrose Orchards

Mount Clemens
C.J. Barrymore's Sports Center
Crocker House
Daren Dundee Entertainer
Friendly Frontier Lanes
Great Western Riding Stables
Lionel Trains Visitor Center
Macomb Center for the Performing Arts
Macomb YMCA
Marino Sports Center, Inc.
Metro Beach Metropark
Metropolitan Beach Putt-Putt
Morley Candy Makers, Inc.
Mount Clemens Farmers' Market
Mount Clemens Train Ride
Recreation Bowl
Rick's Puppet Theater
Selfridge Military Air Museum
Whirly Ball of Michigan
Youtheatre at the Macomb Center for the Performing Arts

Mount Morris
Wolcott Orchards

Munising
Pictured Rocks Boat Cruises
Pictured Rocks National Lakeshore

Muskegon
E.Genevieve Gillette Nature Center
Hackley and Humes Historic Site
Michigan's Adventure Amusement Park
Muskegon County Museum
Muskegon Museum of Art
Muskegon Race Course
Muskegon Sports Complex (Muskegon State Park)
Muskegon Trolley Company
Pleasure Island Water Fun Park
Port City Princess
U.S.S. Silversides
Waterfront Centre

Negaunee
Michigan Iron Industry Museum

New Baltimore
Stahl's Bakery

New Boston
Apple Charlie's and South Huron Orchard and Cider Mill
Davies Orchard and Cider Mill
Green Tee
Huron Christmas Farm
Pumpkin Patch

Newport
Fermi 2 Power Plant

Niles
Fernwood Nature Center and Botanic Gardens
Fort St. Joseph Historical Museum

Northville
Foreman Orchards and Cider Mill
Guernsey Farm Dairy
Marquis Theatre
Maybury State Park Petting Farm
Meyer Berry Farm
Middle Rouge Parkway (Edward Hines Park)
Mill Race Historical Village
Northville Downs
Obstbaum Orchards and Cider Mill
Parmeter Cider Mill
Victorian Festival

Novi
Chilly Willy Winter Festival
Ella Mae Power Park
Festival of Bands
Grand Slam U.S.A.
Living Science Foundation
Novi Bowl
Tollgate 4-H Center

Oakland
Middleton Berry Farm

Oak Park
Compuware-Oak Park Arena
David Shepherd Park
Jewish Community Center
Oak Park Family Entertainment Series
Oak Park Fun Fest
Oak Park Mini-Golf

Omer
Russell Canoes and Campgrounds

Onsted (Irish Hills)
Eisenhower Presidential Car
Prehistoric Forest
Stagecoach Stop, U.S.A.

Orchard Lake
Orchard Lake Boats and Windsurfing
Pine Lake Marina

Ortonville
Ashton Orchards and Cider Mill
Cook's Farm Dairy
Possum Corner
Silver Saddle Hay and Sleigh Rides
Silver Saddle Riding Stable

Oscoda
Au Sable River Queens
Paul Bunyan Statue

Ossineke
Dinosaur Gardens Prehistoric Zoo

Otisville
Smiths Farm

Owosso
Curwood Castle
Shiawassee Valley Railroad Company

Oxford
Baldwin Road Tree Farm
Camp Oakland
Candy Cane Christmas Tree Farm
In Cahoots
The Junior World Game
Upland Hills Ecological Center
Upland Hills Farm
Upland Hills Pumpkin Festival

Paradise
Great Lakes Shipwreck Museum
Tahquamenon Falls State Park

Paw Paw
St. Julian Winery
Warner Champagne Cellars and Bistro

Petoskey
American Spoon Foods Kitchen
Kilwins Candy Kitchens, Inc.
Little Traverse Historic Museum
Pirate's Cove Adventure Golf

Pinckney
Hell Creek Ranch
Hell Survivors, Inc.

Pinconning
Deer Acres Storybook Amusement Park

Plymouth
Oasis Golf/Tru-Pitch Batting Cages
Plymouth Community Family YMCA
Plymouth Farmer's Market
Plymouth Historical Museum
Plymouth Ice Rink
Plymouth Ice Sculpture Spectacular
Plymouth Orchards and Cider Mill

Pontiac
Detroit Lions, Inc.
Lakeland Ice Arena
Pine Grove Historical Museum
Pontiac Farmers' Market
Pontiac Lake Recreation Area
Pontiac Silverdome

Pontiac West-Division of General Motors
Sun and Ski Marina
Waterford Oaks Wave Pool and Waterslide

Port Austin
Huron City Museum
Sanilac Petroglyphs

Port Huron
Blue Water Festival
Blue Water International Bridge
Fort Gratiot Lighthouse
Huron Lightship Museum
London Farm Dairy Bar
McMorran Place Complex
McMorran Place Theatre
Mary Maxim, Inc.
Museum of Art and History
Tollander Tree Farm

Port Sanilac
Port Sanilac Historical Museum

Presque Isle
Old Lighthouse and Museum

Ray Township
Wolcott Mill Metropark

Redford
Bell Creek Park and Lola Valley Park
Crossroads Productions
Lekotek
Mayflower Lanes
Redford Arena

Richmond
Pankiewicz Farms Cider Mill

River Rouge
River Rouge Arena

Riverview
Riverview Highlands Ski Area

Rochester
Bloomer State Park
Detroit Lions Training Camp
Dinosaur Hill Nature Preserve and Den
Eisenhower Dance
Leader Dog for the Blind
Meadow Brook Hall and Knole Cottage
Meadow Brook Music Festival
Meadow Brook Theatre
Meadowbrook Village Mall Puppet Theatre
North Oakland County YMCA
Oakland University Department of Music, Theater
    and Dance
O'Neill Pottery
Paint Creek Mill

Reasonable Facsimile
Rochester Cider Mill
Saturday Fun for Kids
Story Time with Santa and the Animals
Wondrous Christmas at Meadow Brook Hall
Wright and Filippis, Inc.
Yates Cider Mill

Rochester Hills
The Mime Ensemble
Rochester Hills Museum at Van Hoosen Farm
Rochester Hills Winter Festival

Rockford
Wolverine World Wide, Inc.

Rockwood
Lake Erie Metropark Wave Pool

Rogers City
Ocqueoc Falls

Romeo
Bowerman's Westview Orchards
Hy's Cider Mill
Miller's Big Red
Romeo Horse Drawn Hayrides
Stony Creek Orchard and Cider Mill
Verellen Orchards

Roseville
Emerald Greens
The Great Skate
Rose Bowl Lanes

Rothbury
Double JJ Ranch/Resort

Royal Oak
Bluewater Michigan Chapter - National Railway
    Historical Society
Captain's Cove Adventure Golf
Detroit Audubon Society
Detroit Zoological Park
Grand Slam Baseball Training Center
John Lindell Ice Arena
Royal Oak Farmers' Market
Royal Oak Grand National
South Oakland YMCA
Stagecrafters Youth Theatre
Starlight Archery Co.
Starr-Jaycee Park Train
Superior Fish Co., Inc.
Wagner Park

Ruby
Ruby Farms
Ruby Tree Farm

Saginaw
Andersen Water Park
Green Point Nature Center
Historical Museum for Saginaw County
Japanese Cultural Center and Tea House
Marshall Fredericks Sculpture Gallery
Saginaw Art Museum
Saginaw Children's Zoo
Saginaw Harness Raceway
Saginaw Rose Garden
Saginaw Trolley Company
Saginaw Water Works
St. Clair Shores
Great Lakes Yachts
Harbor Lanes
Home Plate Sports Center
Lakeshore Family YMCA
St. Clair Shores Civic Center
St. Ignace
Deer Ranch
Father Marquette Memorial and Museum
Marquette Mission Park and Museum of Ojibwa
    Culture
St. Johns
Uncle John's Cider Mill
St. Joseph
Curious Kid's Museum
Saline
Morton's Strawberry Farm
Sun Tree Farms
William Lutz
Windy Ridge Orchard and Cider Mill
Saugatuck
Saugatuck Dune Rides
Star of Saugatuck Boat Cruises
Sault Ste. Marie
Soo Locks
Soo Locks Boat Tours
Soo Locks Train Tours
S.S. Valley Camp and Marine Museum
Tower of History
Sawyer
Warren Dunes State Park
Shelby Township
Deneweth's Pick Your Own Strawberry Farms
Shingleton
Iverson Snowshoe Factory
Smyrna
Double R Ranch
Southfield
Actor's Alliance Theatre Company

Autumn Fest
BABES
Beech Woods Recreation Center
Chamber Music for Youth
Channel 50 WKBD
Channel 7 WXYZ
Channel 2 WJBK
Dolls for Democracy
Fire Safety House
Judy Sima
Kids Koncerts, Southfield Parks and Recreation
Kids On The Block
Law Fair
Old World Market
Plum Hollow Lanes
Southfield Civic Center-Evergreen Hills
Southfield Sports Arena
Southgate
Southgate Ice Arena
Ted's Southgate Golf Center
South Haven
Lake Michigan Maritime Museum
South Lyon
Depot Days
Driver's Berry Farm
Erwin Orchards
Greenock Mills
Hock Acres
Washburn One-room Schoolhouse
Witch's Hat Depot Museum
Stanton
Howell's Apple Ranch
Sterling Heights
Freedom Hill
Friendly Ark Sterling Lanes
Plaster Playhouse
Sterling Heights Nature Center
Stockbridge
Dewey School
Pioneer Days
Skyhorse Station Evergreen Plantation
Waterloo Area Farm Museum
Taylor
Midway Golf Range
M.V. Trampoline Center
Vinson's Golf Range
Tecumseh
Chocolate Vault
Southern Michigan Railroad Fall Colors Tour
String Puppet Theatre
Thompsonville
Crystal Mountain Resort

Tipton
Hidden Lake Gardens
Hillside Farm

Traverse City
Amon Orchard Tours
Candle Factory
Clinch Park Zoo
Denoss Museum
Grand Traverse Balloons
Leelanau Wine Cellars, Ltd.
McManus' Southview Orchards
Pirate's Cove Adventure Golf
Ranch Rudolf
Underwood Orchards and Farm Market

Trenton
Belmar II
Country Christmas
Elizabeth Park
Kennedy Ice Rink
Trenton Historical Museum
War of 1812 Battle Re-enactments

Troy
Art Castle
Bowl One
Firefighters' Park
Hanging of the Greens
Harvest Home Festival
Lloyd A. Stage Outdoor Education Center
Skateworld of Troy
Troy Family Playhouse
Troy Museum and Historic Village Green
Troy Parks and Recreation Family Playhouse

Union Lake
Plaster Playhouse

Utica
Four Bears Water Park
Middleton Cider Mill
The Rink, Inc.

Wakefield
Indianhead Mountain Resort

Walled Lake
Coe Rail
Wallace Smith Productions

Warren
Big Boy Warehouse
Friendly Bonanza Lanes
Friendly Bronco Lanes
Pampa Lanes
Regal Lanes
Starlight Archery Co.
Universal Lanes

Van Dyke Sport Center
Warren Area Family YMCA

Washington
Altermatt's Farm
Finley Stables
Stony Creek Metropark

Waterford
Dodge No. 4 State Park
Mary Klever Kreations
Rolladium
Waterford Hills Road Racing

Wayne
Wayne Ice Arena

West Bloomfield
Detroit Archers Club
Discovery Room
Fun with Plaster
Holocaust Memorial Museum
Jewish Community Center
The Matzoh Factory
Puppets in the Park
West Bloomfield Lanes
West Bloomfield Parks and Recreation Concerts
West Bloomfield Youtheatre
Whirly Ball West

Westland
Michigan Humane Society-West
Skateland West
Sport-Way
Wayne/Westland YMCA
Westland Multi-Purpose Arena
William P. Holliday Forest and Wildlife Preserve

White Lake Township
Hidden Ridge Stables
Kelley's Frosty Pines
White Lake Oaks

Woodhaven
Skateworld of Woodhaven

Wyandotte
Boblo Island
Downriver YMCA
Yack Arena

Ypsilanti
Depot Town Caboose
Makielski Berry Farm
Quirk Theatre
Ray Schultz Farm
Rolling Hills County Park
Rolling Hills Water Park
Rowe's Produce Farm

Wasem Fruit Farm
Wiard's Orchards
Yankee Air Force Museum
Ypsi-Arbor Lanes
Ypsilanti Farmers' Market
Ypsilanti Heritage Fair
Ypsilanti Historical Society and Museum
Ypsilanti Putt-Putt

SOUTHERN ONTARIO CITIES

Amherstburg
Fort Malden National Historic Park
Navy Yard Park
North American Black Historical Museum
Park House Museum

Essex
John R. Park Homestead
Southwestern Ontario Heritage Village

Kingsville
Jack Miner Bird Sanctuary
Pelee Island Cruises
Pelee Island Winery

Leamington
Pelee Island Cruises
Point Pelee National Park

Maidstone Township
John Freeman Walls Historic Site

Ruthven
Colasanti's Tropical Gardens

Sandwich
MacKenzie Hall Children's Concert Series -
   "The Peanut Gallery"

Sarnia
Kiwanis Children's Farm

Tecumseh
Sports Afield 2

Windsor
Art Gallery of Windsor
Carrousel of Nations
Chrysler Theatre at Cleary International Centre
Coventry Gardens and Peace Fountain
Hiram Walker Historical Museum
International Freedom Festival
Ojibway Park and Nature Center
Queen Elizabeth II Gardens
Willistead Manor
Windsor City Market
Windsor Raceway
Windsor Symphony Orchestra

3
MAPS

The maps in this chapter are intended as general guides to the area. Maps of the cities of Detroit, Windsor, Ann Arbor, Flint, Lansing, and Grand Rapids show the location of some of the highlights of these cities. Regional maps are also included to help you plan regional adventures. For more city and site information, check Chapter 2—City Listing, Chapter 15—Regional Adventures, and the Index.

State of Michigan

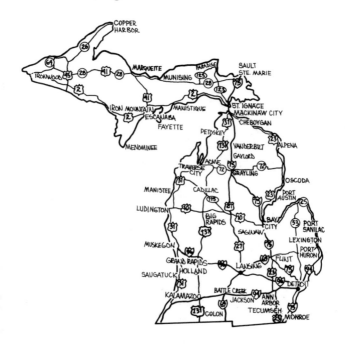

Five County / Southeastern Lower Michigan

Downtown Detroit

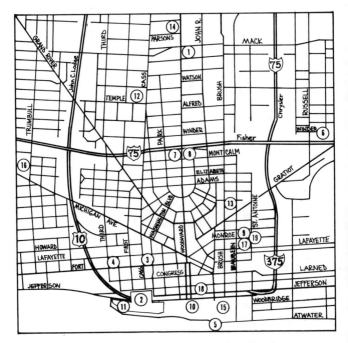

1. Bonstelle Theatre
2. Cobo Hall and Arena
3. Detroit Free Press
4. Detroit News
5. Detroit-Windsor Tunnel
6. Eastern Market
7. Fox Theatre
8. Gem Theatre
9. Greektown
10. Hart Plaza
11. Joe Louis Arena
12. Masonic Temple
13. Music Hall
14. Orchestra Hall
15. Renaissance Center
16. Tiger Stadium
17. Trapper's Alley
18. Trolley
19. Underground Railroad–
    Second Baptist Church

Cultural Center / New Center

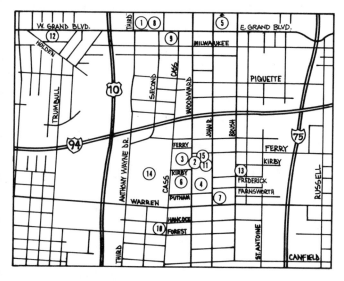

1. Attic Theatre
2. Children's Museum
3. Detroit Historical Museum
4. Detroit Institute of Arts
5. Detroit Police Horse Stables
6. Detroit Public Library
7. Detroit Science Center
8. Fisher Building
9. GM Building
10. Hilberry Theatre
11. International Institute
12. Motown Museum
13. Museum of African American History
14. Wayne State University
15. Your Heritage House

Southern Ontario

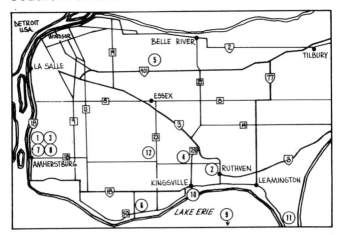

1. Amherstburg Boblo Dock
2. Colasanti's Gardens
3. Fort Malden National Historic Park
4. Jack Miner Bird Sanctuary
5. John Freeman Walls Historic Site
6. John R. Park Homestead
7. North American Black Historical Museum
8. Park House Museum
9. Pelee Island
10. Pelee Island Winery
11. Point Pelee
12. Southwestern Ontario Heritage Village

Windsor

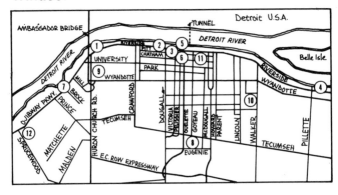

1. Ambassador Park
2. Art Gallery of Windsor
3. Chrysler Theater at Cleary International Centre
4. Coventry Gardens/Peace Fountain
5. Dieppe Gardens
6. Hiram Walker Historical Museum
7. MacKensie Hall
8. Queen Elizabeth Gardens
9. University of Windsor
10. Willistead Manor
11. Windsor City Market
12. Windsor Raceway

Ann Arbor

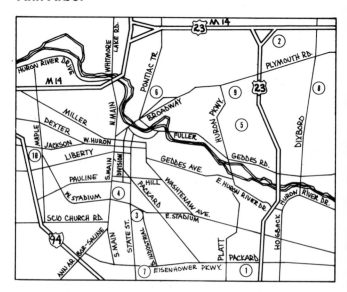

1. Cobblestone Farm
2. Ecology Center
3. Michigan Stadium
4. Phoenix Memorial Lab
5. Project Grow—Leslie Science Center
6. Scrap Box
7. U of M Matthei Botanical Gardens
8. U of M Music School—Stearns Collection of Musical Instruments
9. Veterans Park

Downtown Ann Arbor / U of M Campus

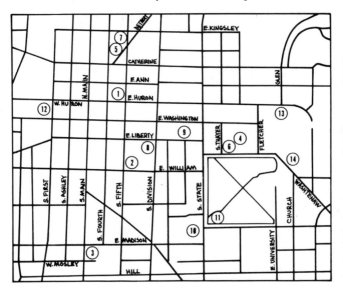

1. Ann Arbor Hands-On Museum
2. Ann Arbor Public Library
3. Ark
4. Burton Memorial Tower
5. Farmers' Market
6. Hill Auditorium
7. Kerrytown Plaza
8. Liberty Plaza
9. Michigan Theater
10. Michigan Union
11. Museum of Art
12. Performance Network
13. Power Center
14. U of M Exhibit Museum

Greater Flint Area

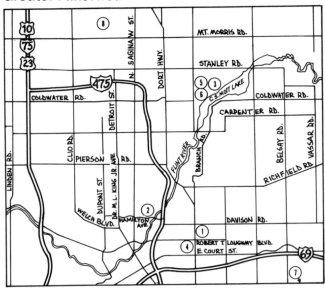

1. AC Spark Plug Tour
2. Buick City Tour
3. Crossroads Village / Huckleberry Railroad
4. Cultural Center
5. Mott Farm
6. Penny Whistle Place
7. Symanzik's Berry Farm
8. Wolcott Orchards

Downtown Flint

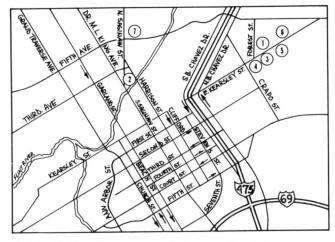

1. Alfred P. Sloan Museum
2. Children's Museum
3. Flint Institute of Arts
4. Library
5. Longway Planetarium
6. Whiting Auditorium—Youth Theater
7. Windmill Place

Greater Lansing Area

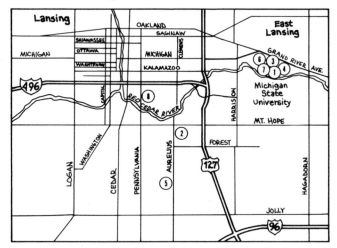

1. Abrams Planetarium
2. Carl E. Fenner Arboretum
3. Horticultural Gardens
4. Kresge Art Museum
5. Lorann Oils
6. Michigan Union
7. MSU Museum of Natural History
8. Potter Park Zoo

Downtown Lansing

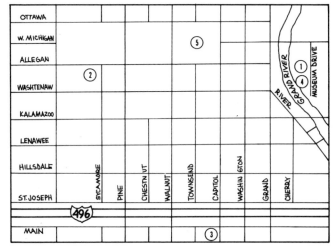

1. Impression 5 Museum
2. Michigan Historical Museum
3. Michigan Women's Historical Center and Hall of Fame
4. R.E. Olds Transportation Museum
5. State Capitol

Greater Grand Rapids

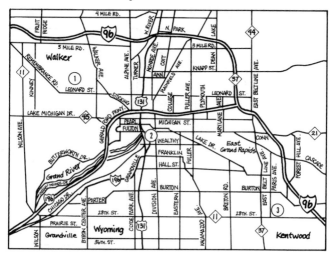

1. Blanford Nature Center
2. John Ball Park Zoo
3. Splash Family Water Park

Downtown Grand Rapids

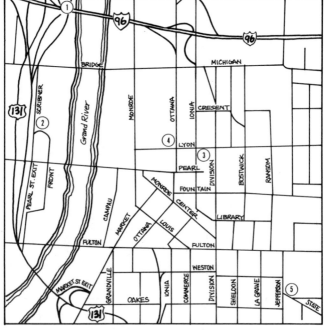

1. Fish Ladder
2. Gerald Ford Museum
3. Grand Rapids Art Museum
4. Calder Plaza
5. Grand Rapids Public Museum and Roger B. Chafee Planetarium

Michigan's Southwest

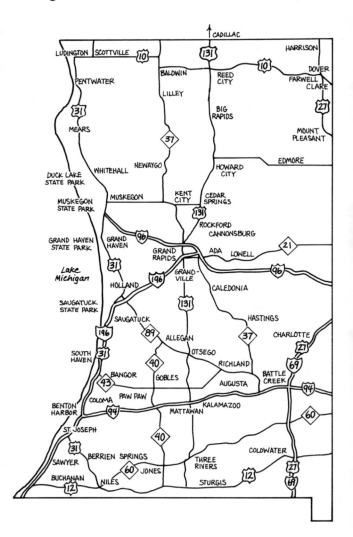

Northern Lower Peninsula

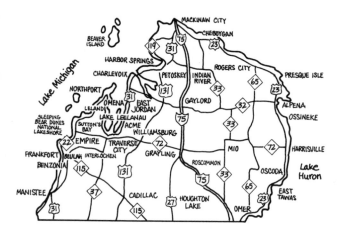

Upper Peninsula

4
MONTHLY
CALENDAR
OF SPECIAL EVENTS

We Michiganians love to celebrate our seasons, our ethnicity, our children, our products, our arts. Throughout the year, we hold hundreds of festivals and special events just perfect for family outings. Here is a monthly list of the area's best family-oriented annual events. If I missed your favorite festival, please send me the information and we'll try to include it in this book's next edition.

Be sure to check *The Detroit News'* Kid Stuff Calendar weekly for more up-to-the minute information. And keep a watchful eye on this calendar so you won't miss something special and have to wait an entire year for it to come around again.

January

Chilly Willy Winter Festival
Novi Parks and Recreation sponsors a day of activities including a snowman building contest, hayrides, and storytelling. 313-347-0400.

Christmas Tree Recycling
Drop off your Christmas tree during the first weekends in January at selected Oakland County Parks for use in park recycling projects. Call 313-858-0906 for locations.

Festival of Bands

Community bands from the Metro Detroit area join together for several sound-spectacular shows in Novi's Twelve Oaks Mall. 313-661-4604.

North American International Auto Show

Cobo Hall is transformed into a glitzy automobile heaven for nine days beginning the first weekend in January. The kids will enjoy the excitement, the shiny new cars, trucks and vans, and the fun promotions and giveaways. 313-643-0250.

Parkey's Winter Break

Join Parkey the Panda for breakfast or lunch several times during the year. He entertains young children with games, arts and crafts, and storytelling. The Parkey series includes Valentine's Day, St. Patrick's Day, Easter, Mother's Day, Halloween, and Thanksgiving. Sponsored by the Farmington Hills Recreation Department. 313-474-6115.

Plymouth Ice Sculpture Spectacular

Professional chefs and ice carvers from around the world work in frigid temperatures, wielding chisels and chain saws to create over 200 larger-than-life sculptures. Their ice art lines the streets of Plymouth's shopping district and fills Kresge Park. In order to see everything, dress warmly and put little ones in strollers. The Masonic Temple on Penniman, across from the park, sells hot chocolate and cookies. 313-453-1540 or 313-459-3264.

Sesame Street Live!

Fox Theatre hosts the 90-minute show of fast-paced song, dance, and vaudevillian routines performed by larger-than-life Sesame Street characters. Kids preschool to fourth grade will enjoy the heartwarming songs, colorful costumes, and silly shticks. 313-567-6000. For charging tickets by phone, Ticketmaster 313-645-6666.

Winterfest

Michigan's annual winter ice festival runs ten days and offers both indoor and outdoor activities, including ice sculptures, snow carving, dog sled racing demonstrations, carriage rides and KidsFest—complete with face painting, entertainment, arts and crafts, costumed characters, and kiddy rides. Michigan State Fairgrounds, 313-368-1000.

February

African American History Month

Many cultural institutions hold special children's events, workshops, and activities to highlight Black history. Of great interest: The Youtheatre's Saturday performances by nationally known African American theater troupes, 313-963-7680. African American Family Day at the Detroit Historical Museum, 313-833-1805. Films, performances, exhibits, and living history at the Museum of African American History, 313-833-9800.

Daddy-Daughter Valentine's Day Dances

During the first two weeks of February, more than two dozen local communities offer daddies and their daughters a 90-minute to two-hour deejay dance complete with punch and cookies, corsages or flowers, prizes, and a photo momento to take home. Sign up early—spots fill up fast.

A sampling: Allen Park, 313-928-0770. Bloomfield Hills, 313-433-0885. Clawson, 313-435-4500. Dearborn Heights, 313-277-7900. Farmington Hills, 313-473-9570. Fraser, 313-294-0450. Grosse Pointe, 313-885-4600. Hazel Park, 313-547-5535. Livonia, 313-261-2260. Madison Heights, 313-589-2294. Mt. Clemens/Chesterfield Township, 313-949-0400. Mt. Clemens/Harrison Township, 313-465-4555. Northville, 313-349-0203. Novi, 313-347-0400. Oak Park, 313-545-6400. Pontiac, 313-857-7688. Rochester, 313-651-6210. St. Clair Shores, 313-778-5811. Southfield, 313-354-9156. Troy, 313-524-3484. Warren, 313-268-8400. Waterford, 313-623-0900. West Bloomfield, 313-334-5660. Westland, 313-722-7620.

Paczki Day

In other cities, the day before Lent might be called Shrove Tuesday or Fat Tuesday, but in Hamtramck the last day to indulge in goodies is called Paczki Day, so named for paczkis (pronounced poonsh-keys), delicious fruit-filled pastries. Bring home a dozen. Hamtramck Chamber of Commerce, 313-875-7877.

Parkey's Valentine Breakfast

Parkey the Panda is back for a breakfast complete with story and craft. Farmington Parks and Recreation, 313-474-6115.

Rochester Hills Winter Festival

Snow sculpting, ice fishing, broomball games, and dogsled races. It's time for a little organized winter fun. 313-656-4673.

Valentine's Day

Check your local library for a Valentine's story hour or craft program. Also many community parks and recreation programs hold Valentine's Day dances. See Daddy-daughter listing.

March

Ann Arbor Pow Wow

One of the top Native American celebrations in North America takes place annually at Chrysler Arena in Ann Arbor and features songs, dances, and arts and crafts. 313-763-9044.

Day of Puppetry

The Detroit Puppeteers Guild presents a day of puppet-making workshops and fine puppet performances. 313-898-6341.

Detroit Kennel Club Dog Show

North America's largest, one-day, all-breed, benched dog show comes to Cobo Exhibition Center. A great opportunity to take the kids dog shopping. 313-224-1010.

Don't Miss the Easter Bunny

The Easter Bunny's March/April calendar (depending on when Easter falls) is packed with special bunny breakfasts, candy egg hunts, storytelling, and songs. Sure, he's at every mall, but you might want to sign the kids up for some of the area's very special Easter Bunny events.

A sampling: "Easter train," Macomb Mall, 313-293-7800. "Easter Bunny Breakfasts," Hudson's Restaurants, 313-443-6247. "Easter Bunny Brunch," Grosse Pointe War Memorial, 313-881-7511. "Easter Egg Hunt," Melvindale Parks and Recreation, 313-928-1201. "Mr. Bunny Egg Hunt," West Bloomfield Parks and Recreation, 313-334-5660. "Easter Spring Fling," Springfield Oaks, 313-625-8133. "Easter Egg Scramble," Sterling Heights, 313-977-6123, ext. 200. "Parkey's Easter Egg Hunt," Farmington Hills, 313-473-9570. "Eggstraordinary, Eggciting Eggs," Stony Creek Metropark, 313-781-4621. "Easter Egg Hunt," Southwest Detroit Parks and Recreation, 313-297-9337. "Great Marshmallow Drop," Elizabeth Park, Trenton, 313-261-1990. "Jacobson's

Easter Bunny Breakfasts": Dearborn—313-565-9500, Grosse Pointe—313-882-7000, Livonia—313-591-7696. The Easter Bunny's Mother usually visits the Youtheatre during its Easter-week performances, 313-963-7680.

Guernsey Farm Dairy
The dairy in Northville offers a free, once-a-year tour of its ice cream plant, plus a St. Paddy's Day party held every other year, 1-5 p.m., the Sunday before St. Pat's Day. 313-349-1466.

The Ice Capades
Ninety dazzling minutes full of showmanship, glitz, and talent. For little children, there are always several numbers with cartoon-costumed skaters. The Palace, 313-377-0100. For charging tickets by phone, Ticketmaster 313-645-6666.

Ice Shows—A March Sampling
The ice shows cometh in March and continue through May at area ice arenas. Here's a chance to see earnest local skaters strut their stuff in creative and colorful numbers. Your kids will adore seeing other children perform. Call for dates and times. Trenton's Kennedy Ice Arena, 313-676-7172. Birmingham Ice Arena, 313-645-0730. St. Clair Shores Civic Arena, 313-774-7530. Westland Sports Arena, 313-729-4560. Wyandotte's Yack Arena, 313-246-4515.

Maple's Sweet Story
Area nature centers, farms and metroparks offer maple sugar demonstrations and walks through sugar bush country, with hands-on tastes. Selected weekends, throughout March. Lloyd A. Stage Outdoor Education Center, 313-524-3567; Firestone Farm at Greenfield Village, 313-271-1620; U of M Dearborn Environmental Study Area, 313-593-5338; Kensington Farm Center, 313-685-1561; or Indian Springs Nature Center, 313-625-7280, or call toll-free, 1-800-47-PARKS.

Maple Syrup Festival
Step up close to the big maples and snitch a taste of the running sap, then walk over to the Sugar House and watch the sap being processed into maple syrup. Cranbrook Institute of Science offers children a look behind the grocery store shelves. Several weekends in March. 313-645-3200.

The Matzah Factory
See how matzah (unleavened bread used during the Jewish holiday of Passover) is made. Kids

wear baker's caps and are offered hands-on experience, plus a sample to take home. Jewish Community Center, West Bloomfield, 313-661-1000.

Purim Carnival

The ancient Jewish holiday is celebrated with a costume parade, food, carnival games, storytelling, and hamantaschen baking. Hamantaschen are traditional, sweet, fruit-filled pastries. Designed for kids preschool to early elementary. Jewish Community Center, West Bloomfield, 313-661-1000.

Royal Hanneford Circus

In addition to clowns, trapeze artists, and jugglers, this circus is famous for wonderful animal acts. See trained tigers, ponies, sea lions, dogs, and bears. The Palace, 313-377-0100.

St. Patrick's Day

One of Detroit's liveliest parades takes place the Sunday before St. Patrick's Day with lots of green hoopla and a stroll down Michigan Avenue in Corktown. Check newspaper listings for a full schedule of events, including Irish folksinging and ethnic dancing at local halls. Or call the Irish-American Club, 313-964-8700.

The Shrine Circus

Wild animals, cavorting clowns, prancing horses, daring trapeze artists—everything you always wanted in a circus and more. The kids can see from almost every seat in the State Fair Coliseum, 313-368-1000.

Spring Vacation Programs

A variety of community institutions, parks and recreation programs, and area libraries offer programs for children during spring break. A sampling: "Children's Easter Vacation Festival"—free movies, mime, puppets, magic, and stories at the Detroit Public Library, 313-833-4029. "Spring Banner Days"—free movies at the Southfield Public Library, 313-354-5342. "Spring Vacation Program"—daily swim, field trip, games, and crafts at the Farmington YMCA, 313-553-4020. "Spring Festevents"—free puppets, storytelling and theater at Birmingham's Baldwin Public Library, 313-647-1700.

April

Baby Animal Day
Upland Hills Farms brings the farm animals to the city, at the Birmingham Community House. 313-644-5832.

Celebration of Spring
A lumberjack festival, Arbor Day ceremony, and youth bike safety skills clinic. Cobblestone Farm and Buhr Park, Ann Arbor, 313-994-2928.

Detroit Public Schools Student Exhibition
Detroit school children share their dreams and visions in this joyous annual show (now more than a half a century old), which fills the Detroit Institute of Arts with puppets, drawings, sculpture, paintings, textiles, mixed media, and photography. Your kids will become inspired to run home and create. 313-833-7900.

Ice Shows—An April Sampling
Melvindale Ice Arena, 313-928-1200. Southfield Ice Arena, 313-354-9357. Dearborn's Adray Arena, 313-943-4098.

Kitefest
Join kite enthusiasts at Kalamazoo's River Oaks Park for a special weekend full of kite flying demonstrations, kite making workshops, and a celebration of the balmy winds of spring. The last weekend in April. 616-383-8778.

Law Day
The police and fire departments of Allen Park and Melvindale team up to demonstrate their wares and their capabilities. Kids are encouraged to touch and try. 313-928-0535.

Law Fair
Southfield's 46th District Court offers a day of legal merry making and information with McGruff, the crime-fighting dog; Officer Mac, the State Police remote control robot; demonstrations of lie-detectors, breathalizers, and police cars, plus balloons and coloring books. Held at the Tel-12 Mall, the last Sunday in April. 313-354-9377.

Sheepshearing Day
It's a Scottish Spring Festival at the Rochester Hills Museum complete with sheepshearing, old-fashioned craft demonstrations, bagpipes, highland dancing, and authentic food. 313-656-4663.

Vetavisit

Michigan State University's College of Veterinary Medicine holds an annual open house the third Saturday of April. Children are invited to look through microscopes, milk cows or goats, watch demonstrations of drug-sniffing dogs and sheep shearing, and meet llamas, horses and snakes. 517-355-6570.

May

Eastern Market Flower Day

Pile the kids in the little red wagon, stroll around Eastern Market, and buy your spring flowers at bargain prices. Be prepared for crowds. Usually mid-May and again in mid-June. 313-833-1560.

Heritage Festival

Rochester Municipal Park is the site of old-fashioned family fun, including a pioneer homestead, petting farm, craft booths, demonstrations, and pony rides. Usually the end of May. 313-651-9061.

Ice Shows—A May Sampling

Fraser Hockeyland, 313-294-2400. Berkley Ice Arena, 313-546-2460. Garden City Ice Arena, 313-261-3491.

It's All Happening at the Zoo

Belle Isle Zoo, Detroit Zoo Train, and Log Cabin Learning Center open for the season May 1. 313-398-0900.

Memorial Day Parades

Check your local city office for Memorial Day parade activities. These parades are very spirited, noisy, and full of local color.

Michigan Taste Fest

Celebrate Memorial Day weekend in Detroit's New Center Area with continuous children's entertainment, hands-on crafts and activities, samples of made-in-Michigan products and specialties of Michigan chefs, plus evening concerts by nationally known musicians. 313-872-0188.

Renaissance City Storyfest

A Wayne State University conference that offers evening storytelling concerts, perfect for family entertainment. 313-577-2150.

Spring Festival

Spring has sprung at the Kensington Farm and Nature Centers. There are lots of baby animals, sheep-shearing and wood-carving demonstrations, hayrides, and wildflower walks. 313-685-1561.

Tulip Time

Holland is ablaze with tulips, costumed dancers, musical shows, and parades, all celebrating the city's Dutch heritage. Usually the second week of May. Holland Chamber of Commerce, 616-396-4221.

Very Special Arts Festival

Over 100 artists and 150 performing artists celebrate the power of artistic creativity over physical and mental challenges. Two days of theater, dances, and music showcasing the talents of students with disabilities. Usually held the middle of May at a mall in Southeastern Michigan. 313-892-1750.

June

Belleville Strawberry Festival

Strawberry lovers, rejoice! Belleville, one of the Detroit area's biggest strawberry producers, celebrates the crop with a weekend of games, parades, and children's entertainment. 313-697-3137.

Carrousel of Nations

Windsor's many ethnic and cultural communities sponsor two weekends of multi-cultural experiences. Experience foods, sights, dances, and sounds of many cultures. 519-255-1127.

Children's Grove at the Frankenmuth Bavarian Festival

The Children's Grove includes a petting farm, kinder haus with hands-on craft activities, and theater tent with hourly puppet, clown, and musical show. Usually held mid-June. 517-652-8155.

Detroit Grand Prix

Belle Isle hosts the Indy cars, their drivers, and the fans. The island glitters in the sun and offers everyone a great view. Fans can take continuous bus, trolley, or boat shuttles to the island. The first weekend in June. 313-259-5400.

Heritage Day

The Troy Historical Museum sponsors a day of ethnic celebration and musical entertainment. Usually the fourth Sunday in June. 313-524-3570.

International Freedom Festival

Beginning mid-June through July 4, there are over 100 events celebrating the friendship between Canada and the United States, including parades, music, fireworks, boat races, and of particular note, two Children's Days. Windsor's Children's Day is held along the riverfront mid-June with a big wheel grand prix and a teddy bear picnic. Detroit's Children's Day is held in the University Cultural Center usually the last Wednesday in June. It's a "don't miss" potpourri of entertainment and hands-on activities sponsored by all Cultural Center institutions. 313-577-5088 (Detroit), 519-252-7264 (Windsor).

Juneteenth Celebration

Greenfield Village focuses on African American traditions, customs, and contributions during this weekend celebration of the Emancipation Proclamation. Usually the third weekend in June. 313-271-1620.

Log Cabin Day

Visit a Michigan log cabin and join in hands-on pioneer crafts and games during the last Sunday in June.

Michigan Challenge Balloonfest

There's something for every member of the family at Howell's annual three-day weekend event: more than 50 colorful hot-air balloons, skydivers, acrobatic stunt kites, antique cars, a medieval village and entertainment, arts and crafts, and a midway. Usually the last weekend in June. 517-546-3920.

Oak Park Funfest

Ten days of special activities celebrating Independence Day, including a parade, fireworks, and children's fun day. 313-545-6400.

Spirit of Detroit Thunderfest

The Detroit river is the course for the annual hydroplane races. School groups are also invited to tour the race pits as part of "New Kids on the Course." Watch the races from general admission and reserved seating available along the river, or free viewing from Belle Isle. Thursday-Sunday during the third or fourth weekend in June. To charge tickets by phone, Ticketmaster 313-645-6666. For information, 313-771-7333.

July

Ann Arbor Art Fair
Besides the displays by fine artists, there's enough food, street musicians (have you ever seen a grown man playing a piano in the middle of the street?), and stage entertainers to turn any child on to art. Be sure to take your budding artists over to Liberty Plaza on Liberty Street for the great Chalk Art-a-Thon. Usually held the third week in July. 313-994-5260.

Battle Creek International Balloon Championship
During the middle of this eight-day festival is children's day, when children meet Tony the Tiger, Ronald McDonald, and McGruff, and enjoy balloon launches, special entertainment, and games. 616-962-0592.

Children's Celebration
Flint's Cultural Center sets the stage for a day of hands-on activities and children's shows. Usually held mid-July. 313-762-1169.

Children's Days at the Ann Arbor Summer Festival
Free children's entertainment, dance, and gymnastic demonstrations precede the special headlining children's show. Usually several consecutive Sundays in early July. 313-747-2278.

Huron River Day
Learn about ecology and celebrate water sports at Ann Arbor's Gallup Park. The day's activities include canoe races, youth fishing derby, nature walk, children's games, crafts and entertainment, bicycle maintenance clinic, and windsurf sailing demonstrations. 313-994-2778.

July Fourth Festivities and Parades
Check you local city for parade and fireworks schedules. Area historic villages also offer special July Fourth activities. A sampling: Cobblestone Farm, Ann Arbor, 313-994-2928; Greenfield Village, Dearborn, 313-271-1620; Crossroads Village, Flint, 313-736-7100.

Palace Summerfest
For six glorious days, the Palace parking lot becomes transformed into a giant family fair with midway rides and games, NBA basketball action, outdoor concerts, fireworks and laser shows, and special entertainment—the Royal Hanneford Cir-

cus and Thrill Show were 1991 and 1992 headliners. 313-377-0100.

Port Huron's Blue Water Festival
Port Huron comes to life with family fun, including a carnival, midway, parade, and entertainment. 313-985-9623.

August

Abbott's Magic Get-Together
Magicians from all over the world meet in Colon, Michigan, to swap ideas, buy and sell magic paraphernalia, and practice their art. The public is invited to several shows during the four-day convention, held early August. 616-432-3235.

Detroit Mini Grand Prix
The New Center Area hosts a mini grand prix for the entire family. While 50 three-horsepower go-carts race in seven heats, Kids Korner offers children's activities: clowns, jugglers, balloon animals, free ice cream, storytelling, crafts, video games, and more. Usually a Saturday at the end of August. West Grand Boulevard and Second, Detroit, 313-875-MINI.

Michigan Festival
Say Yes! to Michigan and celebrate Michigan's homegrown culture, ethnic diversity, folk crafts, and performers. Ten days of continuous performances on ten different stages, held all over the Michigan State University Campus, in East Lansing. The Children's Stage and Creation Station feature children's entertainers and hands-on science and art projects. The Main Stage offers nationally known entertainers. Usually held mid-August. 517-351-6620.

Michigan State Fair
The Michigan farmer is still at the heart of this granddaddy of all Michigan fairs. Kids will love viewing the award-winning animals, collecting free made-in-Michigan samples in the coliseum, feeding the animals at the petting farm, and cheering for the little porkers in the Kowalski Pig Races. Every day offers a full variety of specialty acts (demolition derby, monster trucks, wrestling) and nationally known entertainers. I recommend taking advantage of all the fair freebies; midway rides are very expensive. Held the last weekend in August through the first weekend in September. 313-368-1000.

Oakland County 4-H Fair
Springfield Oaks in Davisburg hosts livestock exhibits, demolition derby, pro-wrestling, a truck pull, and carnival rides. Usually opens the fifth Monday, prior to Labor Day. 313-634-8830.

Renaissance Festival
The sixteenth century comes to vivid life with authentically costumed roving players, jugglers and jousters, wenches and knaves, a village marketplace, plus Renaissance-flavored games and rides. The kids will enjoy the continuous merriment and ribald entertainment. Held weekends in the Holly area from mid-August through the end of September. "Childhood's Quest," a weekend with special children's activities, is usually held the first weekend. 313-645-9640.

Royal Oak Grand National
Kids thrill to the sights and sounds of over 30 remote control, quarter-scale cars vrooming around a 150-lap race course. Music, mimes, clowns, food, and face painting turn downtown Royal Oak into a large street fair. Usually held on a Saturday late in August. 313-547-4000.

War of 1812 Battle Re-enactments
The War of 1812 comes to life with two days of battle re-enactments, complete with soldiers, Indians, and early Michigan settlers. Usually held the third weekend in August. Elizabeth Park, Trenton. 313-674-7300.

Ypsilanti Heritage Festival
Parades, concerts, living history encampment, old-fashioned circus, and antique car shows highlight Ypsilanti's historical past. Usually held at the end of August. 313-482-4920.

September

Art in the Park
While Mom and Dad browse through the art fair, children can create at the art station and have their faces painted. Usually held the second weekend in September. Shaine Park, Birmingham. 313-645-1173.

Autumn Fest
Watch apple cider and honey being made, jump into a haystack, and play old-fashioned harvest games at Cranbrook Institute of Science, Bloomfield Hills. Several consecutive weekends at the end of September. 313-645-3220.

Autumnfest

The city of Southfield celebrates its pioneer history with a day full of butter churning, rug weaving, farm animals, dancing, singing, and touring the old Mary Thompson home, built in 1831. Usually the second Sunday of the month. 313-354-9603.

Autumn Harvest Festival

It's autumn at Greenfield Village in Dearborn. Celebrate the changing season with harvest activities, cider making, and entertainment. Held the last weekend in September. 313-271-1620

Children's Fair at the Detroit Festival of Arts

Join Detroit's biggest street party and celebrate the arts. More than 70 free activities for children, including face painting, puppet making, chalk drawing, musical performances, and storytelling, plus a chance to act as TV anchors in Channel 2's model television studio. Held on the Wayne State University Campus, mid-September. 313-577-5088.

Depot Days

South Lyon's McHattie Park complex, which includes Witch's Hat Depot Museum, Washburn one-room schoolhouse, and a red caboose, set the stage for a weekend of old-fashioned, small town activities, including a celebrated frog jumping contest. Held the first weekend after Labor Day. 313-437-1735.

Fall Festival

Ann Arbor's Cobblestone Farm sponors a traditional nineteenth-century harvest festival featuring cooking, crafts, hayrides, and a corn husking bee. 313-994-2928.

Fall Festival

Kensington Metropark celebrates the season with family activities: hay rides, puppet shows, woodcraft demonstrations, nature crafts, clowns, candle dipping, and apple cider making. Usually a mid-September weekend. 313-685-1561.

Heritage Harvest Day

Seven Ponds Nature Center celebrates Autumn with colonial crafts, sheep-to-shawl and pioneer skill demonstrations, antique steam engines, old-time tools and equipment, children's games, and petting farm. Usually held in early September. 313-796-3200.

Miller Lite Montreux/Detroit Jazz Festival

Just for kids—listen as Michigan high school and college bands jazz it up and get into the action. Held the first week in September. 313-259-5400.

Victorian Festival

Downtown Northville and Mill Race Village host a variety of turn-of-the-century activities including horse drawn carriage rides, trolley rides, family contests and games, fortune telling, strolling musicians, mimes and entertainment. Usually held the second weekend in September. 313-349-7640.

Wiard's Orchards Country Fair

It's a country fair every September and October weekend, at Wiard's Orchards in Ypsilanti. You can pick apples and pumpkins, take a pony or miniature train ride, play games, watch craft demonstrations, listen to country music, and eat harvest foods. 313-482-7744.

October

Children's Halloween Ball

For a donation to the Children's Leukemia Foundation of Michigan, your little urchin gets a pizza dinner, beverage, goody bag, and entertainment. Community House in Birmingham. 313-353-8222.

Fall Fun Days at Symanzik's Berry Farm

Walk through a corn stock forest into a pumpkin patch bathed in sunlight. Children can pick their own pumpkins and gourds, play in a mock barn, visit farm animals, and take a ride on "space trollies." Weekends during October. 313-636-7714, 313-636-2775.

Halloween Parties

During the last two weeks of October, little ghosts and goblins are invited to costume parties and haunting nature walks at area institutions. A Sampling: "Zoo Boo," at the Detroit Zoo, 313-398-0900. Belle Isle Zoo's "Halloween Zoobilee," 313-398-0900. Rochester's Dinosaur Hill "Halloween Hoot," a walk through a haunted forest, 313-656-0999. Independence Oaks' "Nature Fears and Halloween Fables," a story walk through the woods, 313-625-6473. "Halloween Haunt" at Cranbrook Institute of Science, 313-645-3200. "Bloomer Haunted Forest" in West Bloomfield, 313-334-5660. "Spooky Saturday" at Flint's Sloan Museum, 313-760-1169. "Nain Rouge" at Detroit's Historical Museum, 313-833-1805. "Halloween of the Past," at the Wolcott Mill Metropark, 313-749-5997. "Huckleberry Ghost Train," at Flint's Crossroads Village, 1-800-648-7275. Halloween stories, African dance performances, and refreshments at the Museum of African American History, 313-833-9800. Trick-or-treating and a Halloween play at the Edsel and Eleanor Ford House in Grosse Pointe Shores, 313-884-4222. "Haunted Hollow," Troy Parks and Recreation nature walk, 313-524-3484. "Haunted Forest," Clintonwood Park, Clarkston, 313-625-8223. "Maybury Madness," Maybury State Park forest walk, Northville, 313-349-0203.

Harvest Home Festival

The Troy Historical Museum sponsors nineteenth-century fall harvest activities for the entire family. Bob for apples, design your own scarecrow, participate in a hay bale toss or corn husk and shelling contest. Usually early October. 313-524-3570.

Harvest Jubilee

All aboard! Enjoy a fall color tour on the Huckleberry Railroad, near Flint. Then walk around historic Crossroads Village and enjoy country bands, cider making, kite flying exhibitions, and craft demonstrations. Usually mid-October. 313-736-7100.

Haunted Houses

For some families, Halloween isn't Halloween without blood curdling screams and gruesome tableaux. Many area haunted houses are run by community groups and your entrance fee helps raise money for worthwhile programs. But please beware—most haunted houses are not suitable for very young children or the faint-hearted.

Here is a sampling of rooms with a boo: Warren Goodfellows Haunted Gallery, 313-524-4964. House of Nightmares, Warren, 313-588-0513. Blake's Big Apple Orchard Haunted Barn, Armada, 313-784-9710. Suicide Saloon, Wyandotte, 313-284-3861. Langenderfer Farm, 313-856-4283. Haunted House, Livonia Mall, 313-476-1166. Haunted Hayride, Big Red Apple Orchard, Romeo, 313-726-0100. The following area Jaycees also offer haunted houses: Allen Park, 313-383-3974. Dearborn Heights/Garden City, 313-274-6036. Farmington, 313-441-5669. Flushing, 313-659-5409. Livonia, 313-525-3657. Madison Heights (Mutilation Mansion), 313-398-1948.

Monroe, 313-457-6650. Milford, 313-624-4413. Novi, 313-348-6684. Oxford, 313-628-6346. Pontiac, 313-681-9671. Plymouth/Canton, 313-455-6620. Redford, 313-538-9265. Riverview, 313-283-2639. Rochester, 313-375-5681. Salem, 313-348-9736. Taylor, 313-291-2109. Union Lake, 313-363-0866. Warren, 313-524-4964. Waterford, 313-332-9582. Westland, 313-729-4560. Woodhaven, 313-295-0167. Wyandotte, 313-388-8318.

Old World Market
Southfield Civic Center Pavilion houses Detroit's largest ethnic festival, full of food, music, and crafts of over 25 nationalities. Usually mid-October. 313-871-8600.

Pioneer Days
The Waterloo Farm in Stockbridge comes to life with demonstrations of nineteenth-century fall harvest crafts, food, and music. Usually the first Sunday in October. 517-596-2254.

Ringling Brothers and Barnum & Bailey Circus
The circus comes to Joe Louis Arena with ferocious tigers, majestic elephants, silly clowns, and daring trapeze artists. Did you expect anything less? Usually early October. 313-567-6000 or for charging tickets by phone, Ticketmaster 313-645-6666.

Southern Michigan Railroad Fall Color Tours
The fall color tour leaves Tecumseh and Clinton each weekend in October for a one-hour-and-twenty-minute ride. 517-456-7677.

Storytelling Festival
The Detroit Story League and Dearborn's Henry Ford Community College sponsor a one-day storytelling festival that includes storytelling workshops for adults and matinee and evening family storytelling concerts. Usually the second Saturday in October. 313-478-6339.

Upland Hills Pumpkin Festival
Upland Hills Farms in Oxford turns your pumpkin picking into a Halloween experience. On hand are the Great Pumpkin, Hildegard the Witch, and Farmer Webster, plus hay and pony rides, a petting farm, country fiddler, play area, haunted house, and harvest foods. Weekends during October. 313-628-1611.

Youtheatre
The Youtheatre kicks off its season at the beginning of October offering performances of puppetry, mime, music, drama, and children's entertainers. Every Saturday through May, 313-963-7680.

November

Annual Dance Concert Series
Wayne State University Dance Company presents an annual dance concert for children. School groups are welcome during that week; the public is invited to weekend performances. Usually held mid-November. 313-577-2150.

Detroit A Glow/Community Sing-a-long
Crowds gather after work on the Monday before Thanksgiving to watch as the Hart Plaza Christmas tree lights are turned on. A community sing-along is held in Cobo Arena following the lighting ceremony. 313-961-1403

Detroit Thanksgiving Festival
Floating bumblebees, the seven dwarfs, dinosaurs, and Santa himself. Detroit's answer to the Macy's Parade takes place along Woodward Avenue on Thanksgiving Day morning. Dress warmly and arrive early for a good view. Reserved bleacher seats are available for a fee. The parade kicks off a weekend Thanksgiving celebration, including the Little Gobbler's Race (the morning of the parade), Santa's Studio Tour (the two weekends following the parade), where you'll take a behind-the-scenes peek at parade construction and see up close the giant inflatables and papier-mache head collection, and A Parade of Rides and Games, an indoor carnival held at Cobo Center, beginning Thanksgiving Day and running through early December. 313-923-7400.

Festival of Trees
Cobo Hall is transformed by 100 profesionally decorated trees, a gingerbread village, and an aisle of wreaths. Children can visit with Santa in Santaland. Begins just before Thanksgiving and runs through Thanksgiving weekend. 313-224-1010.

Michigan Opera Theatre Family Day
A special day of family fun, treats, and activities corresponding to the opera theater's performance, which is always suitable for children. 313-874-7464.

Native American Activity Day
Families experience a real-life, hands-on look at the customs and lifestyles of Native Americans while making headbands, clay pots and fry bread, watching demonstrations, and listening to Indian legends. Usually a weekend in mid-November. Cranbrook Institute of Science, 313-645-3200.

A Renaissance Christmas
The Renaissance Center offers a Santa parade, petting farm, children's only shop, family movies, stories, and crafts, plus musicians, magic, strolling players, puppets and jugglers, all Renaissance-style. The Saturday of Thanksgiving weekend. 313-568-5600.

Walt Disney's Magic Kingdom on Ice
Mickey Mouse and his friends fill the ice at Joe Louis Arena with color and movement as they act out a favorite Disney story. Usually early November, but in recent years has come to town in March. 313-567-6000. Ticketmaster 313-645-6666.

December

Detroit's holiday season officially opens with Santa's grand arrival during the Thanksgiving Parade. From November 24 through December 31, the city is a child's paradise, decorated in tinsel and lights, full of jolly St. Nicks at every mall. Families have their pick of puppets, plays, concerts, caroling, parades, festivals, workshops, and breakfasts with Santa. Here is a sampling of the city's very special holiday events. Keep an eye on your newspaper calendars for specific times and dates.

Puppets, Plays, Shows, and Concerts

Children's Classics
The following theaters and troupes have fine productions of children's classics during December: Youtheatre, Detroit, 313-963-7680. Marquis Theatre, Northville, 349-8110. Greenfield Village Theatre Company, Dearborn, 313-271-1620. Macomb Center for the Performing Arts, Mount Clemens, 313-286-2222. Flint Youtheatre, Flint, 313-760-1018. Bonstelle Theatre, Detroit, 313-577-2960 (every other year they perform "A Christmas Carol"). Grosse Pointe Children's Theatre, Grosse Pointe, 313-881-7511.

A Christmas Carol

Don't forget to treat the kids to their annual dose of Scrooge and Bob Cratchit. Two theaters annually perform the classic tale: Macomb Center for the Performing Arts, Mount Clemens, 313-286-2222. Meadow Brook Theater, Rochester, 313-377-3300.

Harlem Globetrotters

With their famous theme song "Sweet Georgia Brown" playing in the background, the Globetrotters skip around the Joe Louis Arena and The Palace, showing off fancy footwork and basketball tricks. Kids love the teasing banter and the surprises. If you sit up close, you might get a free treat . . . or quite wet. Usually early December. 313-567-6000 (Joe Louis), 313-377-0100 (The Palace).

Holiday Planetarium and Lasera Shows

Cranbrook Institute of Science offers the holiday lasera show, "Ornaments," and two holiday planetarium shows, "The Christmas Star" and "Wonderful Rocket," 313-645-3200. The Children's Museum in Detroit offers two holiday planetarium shows, 313-494-1210. University of Michigan Exhibit Museum Planetarium, offers two holiday planetarium shows, 313-764-0478. Holiday planetarium shows are also offered at Flint's Longway Planetarium, 313-760-1181, and MSU's Abrams Planetarium, 517-355-4672.

Nutcracker Suite

There will be many performances of the Nutcracker this month. Each triumphs the season with vibrant and magical costumes, scenery, music, and dance. The Detroit Symphony Orchestra with Marygrove Dancers at the Fox Theatre, Detroit, 313-833-3700. The Birmingham-Bloomfield Symphony with the Michigan Ballet Theater at West Bloomfield High School, West Bloomfield, 313-643-7288.· The Ann Arbor Chamber Music Orchestra and the Ann Arbor Civic Ballet at Michigan Theater, Ann Arbor, 313-668-8397.

Old-Fashioned Villages and Out-of-the-Ordinary Visits with Santa

Brunch with Santa

After a child-pleasing brunch, Santa arrives by helicopter and visits with the children. The day ends with gifts and caroling. Grosse Pointe War Memorial, Grosse Pointe Farms. Several Saturdays in December. Call for reservations. 313-881-7511.

A Child's World at Christmas
Dearborn's Henry Ford Museum relives Christmas traditions from past generations. There's a towering tree decorated with cookies, candy, and small toys; an animated Lionel train layout; and holiday puppet show. Santa presides over all the merriment. Early December through early January. 313-271-1620.

Christmas at Crossroads ·
Flint's Victorian village is decked out in holiday cheer, with special Christmas shows, traditional crafts, and rides in horse-drawn wagons, sleighs, or on the Huckleberry Railroad. From Thanksgiving weekend through the end of December. 313-736-7100.

Christmas at the Detroit Historical Museum
Don't miss the annual old-fashioned holiday fun: the decorated Old Detroit Streets, the miniature Lionel train chugging around an antique village, and the exhibit of antique children's toys. 313-833-1805.

Christmas Carnival
Cobo Hall becomes a large indoor playground, decorated for the holidays with animated displays. Wait in line to see Santa. Daily, the first two weeks of December. 313-224-1184.

Christmas Past In Greenfield Village
The village is decked out in holiday finery. Costumed staff demonstrate old-fashioned crafts, food preparation, and decorating. Plus holiday music, sleigh rides, shopping, and an 1850s holiday meal in the Eagle Tavern. Early December through early January. 313-271-1620.

Country Christmas
Ann Arbor's Cobblestone Farm, a ninteenth-century historic farmstead, offers traditional craft and holiday baking demonstrations, caroling, and children's games. Usually held the first Sunday in December. 313-994-2928.

Fantasyland
Visit with Santa and enjoy the many nativity scenes and elaborate, electrical winter and holiday scenes. Lincoln Park. Daily through Christmas Eve. 313-386-1817.

Hanging of the Greens

Create holiday ornaments, listen to holiday music, and stroll through the decorated historic village at the Troy Historical Museum. First Sunday in December. 313-524-3570.

Holiday in Lights

The Detroit Visitor Information Center offers maps for a self-guided driving tour of Detroit and Windsor's holiday decorations. 313-567-1170.

Holiday Merrymaking

Mid-December, the Edsel and Eleanor Ford House in Grosse Pointe Shores presents an evening of family holiday entertainment, including a Christmas sing-along, punch, and cookies. 313-884-4222.

Holly Day Festival

Historic Franklin village revives the spirit of a small town Christmas with carriage rides, home tours, craft and food demonstrations, and carolers. Usually the first Saturday in December. 313-855-1576.

Holly's Olde-Fashioned Christmas Festival

Quaint shops, seasonal decorations, entertainment, and strolling characters from *A Christmas Carol* create a festive mood in Holly's Battle Alley. Weekends throughout December. 313-634-1900.

Junction Valley Railroad

Ride a miniature train down a hill twinkling with over 50,000 Christmas lights, visit with Santa, and make an ornament. Train rides are offered the first three weekends in December. Bridgeport. 517-777-3480.

Noel Night

The University Cultural Center is aglow with lights, music, choirs, plus activities and entertainment for children inside and outside all the institutions. Early December. 313-577-5088.

Santa Express Train

Roseville's Macomb Mall offers youngsters the chance to ride a miniature Christmas train around a fantasy winter scene full of dancing bears and elves. Daily throughout December. 313-293-7800.

Santa's at the Detroit People Mover

Santa holds court from noon to 4 p.m. the second and third Sundays in December at the Times Square Station. Free gifts, refreshments, and family entertainment. 313-962-RAIL.

Santa Train

Meet and greet Santa during a 90-minute train ride the first three weekends in December, Adrian-Blissfield Railroad, 517-265-3626.

Santa's Workshop

Take a trail through the snowy woods to Santa's workshop, meet with him, enjoy a bowl of oyster stew, and receive a small present. Henry Ford Estate-Fairlane, Dearborn. Early December. Call for reservations: 313-593-5590.

Snacks with Santa

Kensington Metropark Farm Center sets the pastoral stage for a chat with Santa, sleigh ride, and snack. Usually held the first weekend in December. 1-800-47-PARKS.

Storybook Display at Northland Hudson's

Each year Hudson's recreates a favorite children's story with a series of animated, audio-visual tableaux which comes to life with exquisitely costumed, moving storybook characters. "Peter Pan" was the 1991 display. Families can enjoy the adjacent gift shop and a storybook theme lunch at Hudson's restaurant. 1-800-282-2450.

Storytime with Santa and the Animals

Enjoy a puppet show, chat with Santa, make a bird feeder, and take a trail walk. Dinosaur Hill Nature Preserve, Rochester. Second Sunday in December. Call for reservations. 313-656-0999.

A Wondrous Christmas at Meadow Brook Hall

Knole Cottage, a six-room children's playhouse on the grounds of Meadow Brook Hall, becomes Santa's home for 12 days after Thanksgiving. Older children will appreciate the decorations and floral displays in Meadow Brook Hall, the 120-room mansion. 313-370-3140.

Other December Happenings

Chanukah Celebrations

Celebrate the Jewish Festival of Lights with special puppet shows or children's theater at the Jewish Community Center, in West Bloomfield, 313-661-1000 or Oak Park, 313-967-4030.

Excellent Electrical Event

Cranbrook Institute of Science offers families a week of electrical demonstrations, science shows, family activities, laser and planetarium shows. Held during winter vacation. 313-645-3200.

First Night

An annual, non-alcoholic, wholesome family New Year's celebration with continuous entertainment, including puppets, music, dance, theater, mime, storytelling, juggling, craft workshops, teen dance, and—as a grand finale—a midnight laser show and sing-along. Held from 4 p.m. to 1 a.m. at selected sites in downtown Birmingham. 313-540-6688.

Kwanzaa Celebrations

During the seven days of Kwanzaa, celebrate African American values, customs, and heritage with family activities, storytelling, concerts, and workshops at the Museum of African American History, 313-833-9800; Children's Museum, 313-494-1210, and Nsoroma Institute, 313-868-3150.

Vacation Day Specials

For families looking for special vacation activities, Detroit's Children's Museum offers a week's worth of daily planetarium shows and workshops. 313-494-1210.

5
MUSEUMS

There's nothing like a museum to awaken children's creativity and curiosity about the world. Yet, even a museum full of dinosaur bones, space suits, African masks, or Van Goghs can be a formidable place for a young child. Try to make the museum outing match your child's temperament and interests. Never try to see everything. Just spend a brief time (no more than two hours at a time) visiting several exhibits. Take a break to have a snack—kids will remember giant cookies, space ice cream, or peppermint sticks—and be sure to visit the gift shop. Most area museums have a wide variety of children's toys, books, and trinkets, many for under $3. Leave before everyone is exhausted, let your children take home a special gift, and they'll be eager to return.

Abbreviations: SP—site offers school programs; T—site offers group tours; H—wheelchair accessible.

SP T H	Ethnic

African Heritage Cultural Center
21511 West McNichols, Detroit
313-533-3828

Location: In the old Redford Public Library, on the corner of McNichols and Burgess
Hours: 9 a.m-3 p.m. Monday-Friday, Detroit Public School tours only. 4-8 p.m. Monday-Friday, open to the public. Call ahead to schedule tours.

Admission: Free
Ages: 4 and up
Plan: Under one hour
Parking: Free in lots to the west and south of building
Lunch: Cafeteria is available to school groups
Facilities: Bathrooms

Created from the 1990 State Fair exhibit, "African Origins," the African Heritage Cultural Center traces man's beginning in Africa and his spread throughout the ancient world. Exhibits range from a model of the 3-million-year-old Australopithecine, Lucy, to a scale model of a temple in the city of Timbuktu.

SP T H   Natural History

Alfred P. Sloan Museum
1221 East Kearsley Street, Flint
313-760-1169

Location: Flint's Cultural Center, off of I-475 and I-69 in downtown Flint
Hours: 10 a.m.-5 p.m. Tuesday-Friday. Noon- 5 p.m., Saturday and Sunday. Open 10 a.m.- 5 p.m., Monday during July and August. Closed major holidays.
Admission: $3 adults, $2.50 seniors, $2 children 5 to 12, under 5 free. Group rates and family memberships available.
Ages: 3 and up
Plan: Half day visit
Parking: Free on site
Lunch: Picnic area on front lawn. Windmill Place, an indoor festival marketplace, is located nearby and offers a wide variety of food booths. Or try Halo Burger, Flint's fast-food burger.
Facilities: Bathrooms, drinking fountain. The museum store has a large collection of dinosaur gifts.

The Sloan is primarily known for its large collection of antique and experimental cars tracing the city's love affair with the automobile. The museum is also full of engaging exhibits covering the spectrum of natural history. Peek into a large, well-furnished dollhouse, meet Sheriff Tuffy Tooth, play hands-on games in a Health Education gallery, and step back into Genessee County history in the recreated fur trader's cabin, lumber camp, and pioneer log cabin. Small children will marvel at the mastodon skeleton; older children will be interested in the Pierson's Children's Gallery, which features finely crafted dolls resembling famous people in world history.

| SP T H | Hands-On Science |

Ann Arbor Hands-On Museum
219 East Huron Street, Ann Arbor
313-995-5439

Location: Downtown Ann Arbor, across from City Hall, at the corner of Fifth and Huron Streets.
Hours: 10 a.m.-5:30 p.m., Tuesday-Friday. 10 a.m.-5 p.m., Saturday. 1-5 p.m., Sunday. Groups can make special arrangements for morning visits. Children's classes are held on Saturday mornings.
Admission: $10 family, $3.50 adults, $2.50 children and seniors, and under 3 free. Family memberships available.
Ages: All ages
Plan: Half day visit. Once the kids get busy, they won't want to leave.
Parking: Structures on adjacent streets, or use metered street parking
Lunch: There are many restaurants on the U of M campus. For fast food close by: Burger King on Liberty Street, McDonald's on Maynard.
Facilities: Bathrooms, elevator, and imaginatively stocked gift shop

Become enveloped in a bubble; make waves; fly a mini hot air balloon; command a robotic arm; play tic-tac-toe with soft foam balls; create a rainbow; climb into a structure of reflecting mirrors. The Ann Arbor Hands-On Museum is one of the area's most ambitious and successful "please-touch" museums. Four floors of exhibits offer would-be scientists a variety of sensory experiences and just plain fun.

On your first visit, it takes a few minutes to get accustomed to the activity. If you're visiting with preschoolers, start on the second floor with the bubbles and Discovery Room. Older elementary children enjoy the third floor's darkened optics and light gallery and the fourth floor's computers and games.

SP T   Ethnic

Arab Folk Heritage Museum
Arab Community Center
2651 Saulino Court, Dearborn
313-842-7010

Location: Off Vernor and Dix Roads
Hours: 9 a.m.-5 p.m., Monday-Friday
Admission: Free. $1/child for tours.
Ages: All ages
Plan: Under one hour
Parking: Use lot in front of the center
Lunch: Many ethnic eateries nearby
Facilities: Bathrooms, library, lounge

Winding through the hallways of the community center and in a large exhibit room are wall-mounted display cases of Arab heirlooms and treasures as well as artifacts demonstrating Arab culture, history, religion and lifestyle. Included are Saudi Arabian rugs, pots and baskets, and scale models of Middle Eastern architecture. The center also houses a lending library with audio-visual aids available for teachers and will arrange school group visits to a local mosque and ethnic restaurant.

SP T H   Art

Art Gallery of Windsor
445 Riverside Drive, Windsor
Ontario, Canada
519-258-7111

Location: Riverside Drive and Bruce Street
Hours: 11 a.m.-5 p.m., Tuesday, Wednesday, Saturday. 11 a.m.-9 p.m., Thursday and Friday. 11:30 a.m.-5 p.m., Sunday. Closed Monday.
Admission: Free
Ages: 6 and up
Plan: Short visit
Parking: Use lot on the corner of Bruce and Pitt Streets
Lunch: Third floor Gallery Cafe restaurant is a cafeteria with a great view of the Detroit River and skyline
Facilities: Bathrooms. Gift shop offers children's items.

The Art Gallery of Windsor is a spacious, attractive building whose collection represents two centuries of Canadian art. The gallery is small enough that children are able to walk through without becoming tired and they will find lots of visually exciting objects—especially the outdoor and Inuit sculpture. A children's gallery on the first floor also offers changing exhibits. Hands-on workshops, films, and multi-cultural events are offered throughout the year.

SP H   Culture & Arts

Children's Museum

67 East Kirby, Detroit
313-494-1210

Location: In the Cultural Center, just north of the Detroit Institute of Arts. A prancing silver horse sculpture made of chrome car bumpers sits on the front lawn.
Hours: 1-4 p.m., Monday-Friday. 9 a.m.-4 p.m., Saturday. Workshops 10 a.m. and 2 p.m. every Saturday during the school year and 2 p.m., Monday-Friday during the summer. Planetarium shows, 11 a.m and 1 p.m., Saturdays; afternoons only during the summer.
Admission: Free for museum. $1 for workshops
Ages: Geared to elementary school age children
Plan: Half day, including workshop and planetarium show
Parking: Use metered parking along Kirby or park in the Science Center lot on John R ($3) and walk a block to the museum
Lunch: The DIA Kresge Court Cafe is across the street
Facilities: Bathrooms, drinking fountain. Gift shop with lots of handmade and educational toys and gifts.

The Children's Museum is one of Detroit's best kept secrets. Its Saturday morning and summer afternoon workshops are consistently well-organized, creative explorations of the arts, taught by Detroit Public School teachers. Throughout the house are displays of stuffed and live animals, musical instruments, puppets, old-fashioned toys, boats and ethnic crafts. Be sure to notice the large, elaborately furnished Jeremiah Hudson dollhouse.

The Planetarium shows, held in a small, intimate room, and offered with a sense of humor and wonder, are wonderful first-time stargazing experiences for young children.

SP T H   Hands-On Creative Play

Children's Museum
432 North Saginaw Street, Flint
313-238-6900

Location: On basement level of the Northbank Center building, downtown Flint, North Saginaw and Second Avenue
Hours: 10 a.m.-5 p.m., Monday-Saturday. Noon-5 p.m., Sunday. Closed Sunday during the summer. Special workshops held on Saturdays throughout the year.
Admission: $11 family, $3 adult, $2.50 children, 2 and under free. Group rates and family memberships available.
Ages: 2 to 13 years
Plan: Half day
Parking: Free parking on Second Avenue
Lunch: Juice machine. Picnic areas on south side of building. Windmill Place, an indoor food emporium, is several blocks away.
Facilities: Bathroom, drinking fountains, elevator. Small gift shop with lots of inexpensive items.

With carefully planned true-to-life displays, Flint's Children's Museum invites children to role-play various occupations and hobbies, providing them with the props and costumes for pretending. Children become firefighters, dentists, doctors, judges, clowns, and musicians. There's a bank vault, a jail, and a child-sized TV studio, where a child can become a weather forecaster or talk-show host. There's a Cinderella Coach and a Red Baron airplane, plus an atrium full of bones, stones, and insects. Children also like to play with "Stuffee," a five-foot-tall stuffed character, who comes complete with removeable lungs, heart, appendix, stomach and other organs. Your kids won't want to leave.

SP T H   Art

Cranbrook Academy of Art Museum
500 Lone Pine Road, Bloomfield Hills
313-645-3312, 313-645-3323
(group tour information)

Location: Use the entrance to the Cranbrook Educational Community, the farthest east off Lone Pine Road between Lahser and Cranbrook Roads

Hours: 1-5 p.m., Wednesday-Sunday. Tours for school groups are available.

Admission: $3 adults, $2 children and seniors. Under 7 free. Family membership available.

Ages: 5 and up. The guards are very wary of young children. Please be sure to hold onto your children since many of the exhibits are three-dimensional and easy to bump into.

Plan: Under one hour

Parking: Park along the semi-circle in front or in the lot on the east side of the museum

Lunch: The Cranbrook Institute of Science, just down the road, has several vending machines and a lunch room. Picnicking on Cranbrook grounds is strictly forbidden.

Facilities: Bathrooms on lower level. Gift shop has a small selection of children's art books and beautifully illustrated picture books.

If you think this museum is off limits to children, you are missing one of the finest visual art experiences the city has to offer your children. The museum is connected to the Cranbrook Art Academy and is a haven for the avant-garde and contemporary. Most of the exhibits show the unusual and witty. Kids love this kind of art. We once saw a drawing of a nose and a colorful doghouse sculpture, and my kids' sense of art has never been the same. Try to visit during the spring Student Show.

SP T H   Hands-On Science

Cranbrook Institute of Science

500 Lone Pine Road, Bloomfield Hills
313-645-3200

Location: Use the entrance to the Cranbrook Educational Community, the farthest east off Lone Pine Road between Lahser and Cranbrook Roads. You'll know you're there when you see the stegosaurus.

Hours: 10 a.m.-5 p.m., Monday-Thursday. 10 a.m.-10 p.m., Friday and Saturday. 1-5 p.m. Sunday. Closed on major holidays. Lasera shows: 7:30, 8:30, 9:30, 10:30 p.m. Friday. 2:15, 3:45, 8:30, 9:30, 10:30, 11:30 p.m., Saturday. 2:15, 3:45 p.m. Sunday. Planetarium Shows: 12:30, 1:30, 3,

7:30 p.m. Saturday. 1:30, 3 p.m., Sunday. Discovery Room/Nature Place: 1-5 p.m., Saturday and Sunday.

Admission: $4 adults, $3 children ages 3-17 and seniors, under 3 free. Admission rates increase for special exhibits or during summer hours. Family membership and group rates available. Planetarium: $1 additional, members free. Lasera: $1.50 additional for daytime shows. $2.00 after 6 p.m.

Ages: All ages for the museum. 5 and up for most lasera and planetarium shows.

Plan: Half day visit

Parking: Lot adjacent to and in front of building

Lunch: A lunch room with vending machines

Facilities: Bathrooms, drinking fountain on lower level. Two gift shops offer a wonderful selection of science toys. The Dino Shop specializes in dinosaur gifts; the lobby shop has everything else.

Cranbrook Institute of Science is the all-purpose science museum for children of all ages. Hands-on exhibits, a Discovery Room full of touch-me displays, lasera and planetarium shows, science demonstrations, and seasonal family events encourage science creativity and exploration.

Family membership is well worth its price. The membership allows you free entrance into the Detroit Science Center and Lansing's Impression 5 Museum as well as the Institute's spring Maple Syrup Festival and Autumn Fest, perfectly choreographed sensory events celebrating the seasons. For a fee, your children can also take classes at the Institute throughout the year.

SP T H   History

Dearborn Historical Museum: McFadden Ross House and Exhibit Annex

915 South Brady, Dearborn
313-565-3000

For full information, see Historic Sites

`SP T`   Fire-Fighting Equipment

Detroit Fire Department Historical Museum

2737 Gratiot Avenue, Detroit
313-596-2956

Location: One mile north of Fisher Freeway (I-75) on Gratiot. The museum is off the beaten track; be sure to call for exact directions.
Hours: Tours are offered 9 a.m.-3 p.m., Monday-Friday, by reservation only
Admission: Nominal fee
Ages: All ages
Plan: 1-1½ hour tour
Parking: On street, adjacent to building
Lunch: Hop back on the expressway and drive to Eastern Market or your favorite neighborhood restaurant
Facilities: Bathrooms upstairs

The red brick building with the large yellow doors, Detroit's oldest standing Engine House, is full of beautifully restored fire rigs, fire-fighting clothing, and artifacts. It offers children a glimpse into the exciting and dangerous history of Detroit fire fighting.

Kids are allowed to play fire chief. They try on the clothes, sit up on the rigs, and ring the bells. Upstairs, there's an authentic brass firepole. Kids peek down 30 feet to the first floor and imagine hurried firefighters whooshing down the pole. Children will also watch a fire safety video presentation. School and civic groups are encouraged to reserve tour dates.

`SP T H`   History

Detroit Historical Museum

5401 Woodward Avenue, Detroit
313-833-1805

Location: In Cultural Center, across from the Detroit Institute of Arts, on Woodward Avenue
Hours: 9:30 a.m.-4 p.m., Wednesday-Friday. 10 a.m.-5 p.m., Saturday and Sunday. Closed major holidays. Craft workshops, selected Saturdays.
Admission: Free, donations accepted
Ages: All ages
Plan: Short visit

Parking: Use street meters or free lot on west side of building
Lunch: Go across the street to the Detroit Institute of Art's Kresge Court Cafe
Facilities: Bathrooms on lower level. Beautifully appointed gift shop with many old-fashioned replicas and hand-made toys.

If you grew up in Detroit, you will hardly recognize the newly refurbished historical museum. Exhibits are fresh, creative, and well-lit. The old favorites are still as wonderful as ever. Introduce your children to the basement level's "Streets of Old Detroit," the hauntingly authentic cobblestone streets full of old shop windows and talking mannequins. Adjacent to the "Streets" is the new Antique Toy Museum Gallery boasting an elaborate Lionel train village and a variety of antique toys.

On the third floor, there's a new costume gallery and furnished doll houses. Older children will also enjoy the main floor exhibit of artifacts and curious objects that tell Detroit's history.

SP T H   Art

Detroit Institute of Arts (DIA)

5200 Woodward Avenue, Detroit
313-833-7900
313-833-7981 (student tour information)

Location: In the heart of the Cultural Center, on the east side of Woodward Avenue, just south of Kirby
Hours: 11 a.m.-4 p.m., Wednesday-Sunday. Closed Monday, Tuesday, and major holidays.
Admission: Suggested fee: $4 adults, $1 children, Founders members free
Ages: All ages
Plan: Half day visit
Parking: Use the Detroit Science Center lot east of the DIA on John R, $3 for all day parking. Available meter parking on street is difficult to find.
Lunch: The Kresge Court Cafe is a pleasant cafeteria offering a wide selection of hot and cold meals, plus snacks. Be sure to show your kids the faces and gargoyles in stone along the walls of the dining room. You could bring your lunch and augment it with a snack or drink. The dining room has open access; it isn't necessary to go through the food line. Hours: 11 a.m.-4 p.m., Wednesday-Saturday. 1-4 p.m., Sunday.

Facilities: Bathrooms and drinking fountain near the cafe. The gift shop, located at the Farnsworth entrance, has a children's section full of beautifully illustrated picture books, books about artists, t-shirts, and art supplies.

The DIA has wonderful secrets and visual delights for children of all ages. However, due to budget cuts, the galleries are open on a rotating basis. North side galleries, including mummies, African, Native American, Modern and American art—what children love best—are open 11 a.m.-1:30 p.m. South side galleries, including European art, are open 1:30-4 p.m. Be sure to begin your visit walking through the rainbow hallway to the Kresge Court Cafe and up the hidden, winding wrought iron staircase to the Great Hall's showcases of knights' armor and swords. The Rivera Court, with the famous Diego Rivera murals, is straight ahead. The kids will enjoy playing two computer games: "The Thinker" is located on the main level on the edge of the red-carpeted area near the restrooms and phones; "Colorware" is located on the second floor in a modern gallery.

SP T H   Hands-On Science

Detroit Science Center

5020 John R, Detroit
313-577-8400

Location: One block east of Woodward on the corner of Warren and John R, behind the DIA
Hours: 9 a.m.-2 p.m., Monday-Friday. 10 a.m.-6 p.m., Saturday and Sunday. Closed major holidays. Omnimax Theatre shows Omnimax movies throughout the day. (Preschoolers might be uncomfortable with the Omnimax movie's motion and speed.)
Admission: $6.50 adults and children 12 and up, $4.50 children under 12 and seniors, under 4 free. Family membership gives you free admission to Cranbrook Institute of Science and Lansing's Impression 5 Museum except for special events.
Ages: All ages
Plan: Half day visit
Parking: Lot adjacent to entrance, off John R, $3 all day parking
Lunch: Vending machines

Facilities: Bathrooms and drinking fountain on basement level. Gift shop near entrance has great science and space items.

At the Detroit Science Center, children can peek into a space capsule, ride a rainbow escalator, meet Ozzie the Robot, create giant bubbles, try a computer voice synthesizer, look in fun-house mirrors, ride a stationary bike, and become immersed in an Omnimax movie experience.

There are over 50 hands-on exhibits inviting children to touch, explore, and learn about computers, the human body, machines, physics and communications.

SP T   History

Dexter Area Museum
3443 Inverness, Dexter
313-426-2519

Location: At Inverness and Fourth Street
Hours: 1-3 pm., Friday and Saturday, May 1-Christmas. Tours by appointment, only.
Admission: Free. Family membership available.
Ages: 5 and up
Plan: Under one hour
Parking: Free on site
Lunch: Many restaurants are located in Ann Arbor, 20 minutes east off I-94
Facilities: Bathrooms. Gift shop offers toys, craft, and hobby books.

This 1883 church built by early German settlers showcases local history items. Children will enjoy the early dentist's office, printing equipment, antique toys and dolls, telephone switch board, and old household appliances.

SP T H   Ethnic, Hands-on Creative Play

Discovery Room
Jewish Community Center
6600 West Maple Road, West Bloomfield
313-661-1000, ext. 346 or 252

Location: On the Jewish Community Center's second floor
Hours: 4-7:30 p.m. Monday and Wednesday. 9:30-11:30 a.m. Tuesday. 5-8 p.m. Thursday. 9:30 a.m.-3 p.m. Sunday. Closed Friday and Saturday.

Admission: Free
Ages: 3 to 7 years
Plan: Short visit
Parking: Free parking in two lots adjacent to Center
Lunch: Kosher cafeteria on the Center's main floor
Facilities: Bathrooms, drinking fountains, elevator. Small gift counter on main floor with Jewish holiday items, candy, and gum.

Discovery Room is a well-planned and creatively executed hands-on Jewish museum, designed to let young children explore, create, and role-play while learning about the Detroit Jewish community, Israel, the Bible, and Jewish holidays. There are many self-contained thematic environments, each with a variety of sensory activities, educational toys, and take-home resource materials for parents. While lively music plays overhead, children can shop in "Greenberg's Grocery"; scribble out a story at "The Jewish News"; play wedding with Ken and Barbie dolls in a miniature synagogue; take a trip aboard an El Al jet, and build the Old City of Jerusalem with blocks. Attention all Jewish grandparents: This is a perfect grandparent-grandchild outing.

SP T H   Marine History

Dossin Great Lakes Museum

100 Strand
Belle Isle Park, Detroit
313-267-6440

Location: Cross the Belle Isle Bridge and go southeast to Strand Road on the south shore of Belle Isle
Hours: 10 a.m.-4 p.m., Wednesday-Sunday. Closed major holidays.
Admission: Free. Suggested donation $1 adults, 50 cents children 12 to 17.
Ages: All ages
Plan: Short visit
Parking: Free on site
Lunch: Belle Isle is full of picnic tables. During the summer, there are food concessions near the zoo and playground.
Facilities: Bathrooms, drinking fountain. Gift shop has nautical items.

You won't get seasick at the Dossin Museum, but you will come away with a better understanding of ships, their innards, and perils at sea. There's a large collection of scale-model Great Lakes ships, a spectacular carved oak Gothic Room, once a smoking lounge on a 1912 steamer, and a room full of shipwreck exhibits spanning two centuries of shipping tragedies. Kids can view Detroit and Windsor through the periscope that goes up through the roof, practice navigating in an authentic freighter pilothouse that extends over the Detroit River, and pose next to the War of 1812 cannon on the museum lawn.

SP T H   Hands-On Gallery

Ella Sharp Museum
3225 Fourth Street, Jackson
517-787-2320

For full information, see Historic Sites

SP T H   Art

Flint Institute of Arts
1120 East Kearsley Street, Flint
517-234-1695

Location: Flint's Cultural Center, off of I-475 and I-69 in downtown Flint
Hours: 10 a.m.-5 p.m., Tuesday-Saturday. 1-5 p.m., Sunday. Also 7-9 p.m., Friday, October-May.
Admission: Free
Ages: All ages
Plan: Short visit
Parking: Use lot adjacent to Sloan Museum
Lunch: Drive to nearby Windmill Place
Facilities: Bathrooms, drinking fountain, gift shop

Flint's art museum offers children a sampling of art from every period of history. Children will enjoy the collection of paperweights displayed in lighted tables, the modern sculpture gallery, and the exterior court sculpture that moves with the wind.

SP T H History, Ethnic

Presently closed due to budget cuts; hopes to re-open soon. Call to schedule group tours.

Great Lakes Indian Museum

Fort Wayne
6325 West Jefferson, Detroit
313-297-9360

Photos of courageous-looking Indian chiefs, intricately carved wooden peace pipes, colorful clothing, and historic weapons tell the story of the Great Lakes Indians. An Indian burial mound dating to 750 A.D., the last surviving burial mound in the Detroit area, is adjacent to the museum.

SP T H History

Greenmead Museum and Historical Village

38125 Eight Mile Road, Livonia
313-477-7375

For full information, see Historic Sites

SP T H Transportation and History

Henry Ford Museum

20900 Oakwood Boulevard, Dearborn
313-271-1620

Location: Michigan Avenue and Southfield Freeway
Hours: 9 a.m.-5 p.m., daily. Closed Thanksgiving Day and Christmas Day.
Admission: $11.50 adults, $10.50 seniors, $5.75 children 5 to 12, under 5 free. Group rates, family membership, annual pass, and two-day pass available.
Ages: All ages
Plan: Half day or full day. With small children, it's impossible to comfortably visit both the museum and adjacent Greenfield Village in one day.
Parking: Use free lots adjacent to the museum and village
Lunch: American Cafe or Corner Cupboard

Facilities: Bathrooms and drinking fountains in several locations. The Greenfield Village Theatre Company, located in the museum, often performs children's theater during December. The two gift shops near the museum entrance are well stocked with old fashioned coloring books, model cars and trains, books, candies, and toys.

Henry Ford Museum is the repository of automobile and aviation history, American furnishings, social history, and other collections begun by its founder, Henry Ford. Its 12 acres of memorabilia and artifacts are undergoing extensive re-design and have been successfully re-packaged into wonderful, state-of-the-art, user-friendly, interactive exhibits.

Try to visit the highlights. Children will enjoy the new permanent exhibits, "The Automobile in American Life," and "Made in America," plus the Abraham Lincoln assasination artifacts—his shawl, theater program, and rocking chair. The entire family will enjoy playing on "The Innovation Station," a Willy Wonka-like gizmo powered entirely by human energy, creative thought, and co-operation. Pick up your play time tickets at the entrance for one of the daily 20-minute games.

One recommended strategy for enjoying the museum and village—become a family member or buy a seasonal pass. Then you will feel comfortable making many short visits throughout the year.

SP T H-main floor   History

Hiram Walker Historical Museum

254 Pitt Street West,
Windsor, Ontario, Canada
519-253-1812

Location: Pitt Street West and Ferry Street
Hours: 10 a.m.-5 p.m., Tuesday-Saturday. 2-5 p.m., Sunday. Closed Monday.
Admission: Free
Ages: 6 and up
Plan: Less than an hour
Parking: Use metered lot
Lunch: Restaurants and riverside picnic areas nearby
Facilities: Bathrooms

There are Indian artifacts, pioneer objects, firearms, furniture, and tools on display in this very small museum, once the home of Francoise Baby. Kids enjoy calling the house the "BAH-bee" house and playing with hands-on activities in the lower level.

SP T H   History

Holocaust Memorial Museum

6602 West Maple Road, West Bloomfield
313-661-0840

Location: On the Jewish Community Center Campus, west of Drake Road. Connected to the Jewish Community Center.
Hours: 10 a.m.-3:30 p.m., Sunday-Thursday. 1 p.m., Sunday free public tour. School group tours are encouraged; educational materials are available for pre-visit preparation.
Admission: Free
Ages: Not recommended for children under sixth grade
Plan: Short visit
Parking: Two lots adjacent to building
Lunch: Cafeteria on main floor of Jewish Community Center
Facilities: Bathrooms. Archives and library.

Children need preparation before visiting the Holocaust Memorial Museum. The museum's explicit displays, videos, and photos offer an insightful and emotional look at the destruction of European Jewry during the Holocaust. Guided group tours are highly recommended.

SP T H   Hands-On Science

Impression 5 Museum

200 Museum Drive, Lansing
517-485-8116
517-485-8115 (recorded information)

Location: Between Grand and Cedar Avenues, three blocks east of the Capitol
Hours: 10 a.m.-5 p.m., Monday-Saturday. Noon-5 p.m., Sunday. Closed on July 4 and Labor Day.
Admission: $3.50 adults, $2.50 children 4 to 12, $2 seniors, 3 and under free. Group rates and family memberships available.
Ages: All ages
Plan: Half day. The kids won't want to leave.

Parking: Lot behind building
Lunch: A cafe on the first level closes one hour before museum closing
Facilities: Bathrooms, drinking fountain, coat check. Gift shop with extensive selection of science items.

Children and adults skip from exhibit to exhibit, playing, touching, building, and experimenting in this giant science playground. There's something for every age. Break into a jazzy tune on a giant cello in the Music Room; explore Botany; climb in darkness through the Touch Tunnel; play with shadows and rainbows in the Light Room; create undulating bubbles at the Bubble Table. Learn scientific principles while having fun. Daily scheduled demonstrations in the Chemistry lab.

SP T H   Ethnic

International Institute

111 Kirby, Detroit
313-871-8600

Location: Just east of the Children's Museum, north of the DIA
Hours: 9 a.m.-5 p.m., Monday-Saturday. Call to arrange school or group tours.
Admission: Free. Nominal fee for school tours.
Ages: Elementary school children and up
Plan: Under one hour
Parking: Meters across the street or use Science Center Parking Lot on John R
Lunch: Melting Pot Cafe, featuring ethnic food, 11 a.m.-2 p.m., Monday-Friday during the school year.
Facilities: Bathrooms. The "Tiny Shop" offers international toys and greeting cards in many languages, plus UNICEF gift shop with cards and books.

The "Hall of Nations" exhibit showcases objects, clothing, and musical instruments from countries around the world. Since school programs are held in this room, call ahead to be sure the exhibit room will be free during your visit.

`SP T H`   Art

Kresge Art Museum

Michigan State University, East Lansing
517-355-7631

Location: On Auditorium Road, MSU campus
Hours: 11 a.m.-4 p.m., Monday-Friday. 1-4 p.m., Saturday and Sunday, mid-May-July 31. 9:30 a.m.-4:30 p.m. Monday, Tuesday, Wednesday, Friday. Noon-8 p.m. Thursday. 1-4 p.m. Saturday and Sunday. Labor Day-mid-May. Closed August and between Christmas and New Year's Day.
Admission: Free. Family memberships available.
Ages: All ages
Plan: Short visit
Parking: Meters in front of building. 50 cent parking tokens are available at the front desk.
Lunch: Burger King and vending machines are located in the Michigan Union, corner of Abbott and Grand River. Many other restaurants are located on Grand River, across from campus.
Facilities: Bathrooms. Small gift cart with inexpensive items.

Small museums of art are always fun for children; they can digest the art experience. The Kresge Art Museum offers changing exhibits of art spanning art history, from prehistoric to contemporary, in an uncluttered, relaxing environment.

`SP T H`   Michigan History

Michigan Historical Museum

717 West Allegan, Lansing
517-373-3559, 517-373-2353 (tours)

Location: Several blocks west of the Capitol, on Allegan between Butler and Sycamore Streets
Hours: 9 a.m.-4:30 p.m., Monday-Friday. 10 a.m.-4 p.m., Saturday. 1-5 p.m., Sunday. Call to arrange group or school tours. Special activities include craft demonstrations and family workshops.
Admission: Free
Ages: All ages
Plan: Half day
Parking: Large parking lot adjacent to the museum charges 25 cents per hour

Lunch: Vending machines
Facilities: Bathrooms. Gift shop with Michigan souvenirs, history books, Made-in-Michigan products.

This brand new, 315,000-square-foot facility offers both children and adults a multi-sensory vision of Michigan's past, from prehistoric times to the nineteenth century, told through the eyes of Michigan's people. Hands-on audio-visual exhibits present Michigan's Indians, Michigan's role in the anti-slavery movement, pioneer life, coal mining days, the lumber era, and a new exhibit about growing up in Michigan. Kids will enjoy walking into a mine shaft and entering the facade of a lumber baron's home.

SP T H   Space

Michigan Space Center
2111 Emmons Road, Jackson
517-787-4425

Location: Jackson Community College campus
Hours: January-April: 10 a.m.-5 p.m., Tuesday-Saturday. Noon-5 p.m., Sunday. May-Labor Day: 10 a.m.-5 p.m., Monday-Saturday. Noon-5 p.m., Sunday. Call for hours, Labor Day-Christmas.
Admission: $10 family rate, $3.50 adults, $2.50 students and seniors, 5 and under free. Group rates available.
Ages: All ages
Plan: Short visit
Parking: Lot adjacent to museum
Lunch: Vending machines with pop, treats, and sandwiches, tables in lobby. Picnic tables on grounds.
Facilities: Outdoor play area, bathrooms, drinking fountain. Gift shop with a variety of low-cost items. Be sure to try the astronaut ice cream (for maximum enjoyment, let the freeze-dried bits melt in your mouth, don't chew them).

The Michigan Space Center brings space travel down to earth. Hands-on experiences, true-to-life diplays, and used National Aeronautics and Space Administration artifacts help kids understand life in space from the astronaut's point of view. The museum even attempts to answer those nitty-gritty questions kids always ask, such as: How do astronauts go to the bathoom? Take a shower? Eat? There are space suits worn by the first astronauts, a space shuttle shower, space food, and moon rocks. Be sure to check with the gift shop for the movie schedule.

| H | Sports History |

Michigan Sports Hall of Fame

Cobo Hall, One Washington Boulevard
Detroit
313-224-1010

Location: Washington Boulevard at Jefferson. Gallery is hanging on the walls, second floor, Cobo Hall.
Hours: 24 hours daily
Admission: Free
Ages: All ages
Plan: Less than an hour
Parking: Use Cobo Arena garage
Lunch: Several restaurants within Cobo Hall
Facilities: Bathrooms, drinking fountain on each floor of Cobo Hall

Children with a love of sports will enjoy a stroll through these hallways, where Michigan sports heroes have been immortalized.

| SP T H | Michigan & Natural History |

Michigan State University (MSU) Museum

101 West Circle Drive
Michigan State University Campus
East Lansing
517-355-2370

Location: West Circle Drive, on the MSU campus
Hours: 9 a.m.-5 p.m., Monday, Tuesday, Wednesday, Friday. 9 a.m.-9 p.m., Thursday. 1-5 p.m., Saturday and Sunday. 9 a.m.-1 p.m., home football Saturdays. Group tours available.
Admission: Free, suggested $2 adult donation.
Ages: All ages
Plan: Short visit
Parking: Metered parking in front. 50 cent meter tokens can be purchased in museum office.
Lunch: Burger King and vending machines are located in the Michigan Union, corner of Abbott and Grand River. Many other restaurants are lo-

cated on Grand River Avenue, across from campus.

Facilities: Bathrooms. General store-gift shop with a variety of inexpensive gifts.

The MSU museum is small enough for kids to comfortably see almost every display. There are dramatic dioramas of cave people, an old fashioned city street, a full-sized, hungry-looking bear, stuffed animals, dinosaur bones, and a lower level full of evocative African and Indonesian masks.

In the Family Room, a relaxing corner of the lower level set aside for hands-on exploration and quiet activity, kids can read, play a computer game, or draw.

SP T H   Women's History

Michigan Women's Historical Center and Hall of Fame

213 West Main Street, Lansing
517-484-1880

Location: Off I-96, Main Street exit, six blocks south of the State Capitol building, adjacent to Cooley Gardens
Hours: Noon-5 p.m., Wednesday-Friday. 2-4 p.m., Sunday.
Admission: $2.50 adults, $1 students 5 to 18. Group rates available.
Ages: Third grade to adult
Plan: Short visit
Parking: Free parking at Cooley Garden entrance off Capitol Avenue
Lunch: Picnic area in Cooley Garden
Facilities: Bathrooms. Gift shop selling books, notecards, posters, and American women paper doll cutouts.

From abolitionist Sojourner Truth to former First Lady Betty Ford, the Women's Center offers a picture of the lives, achievements, and history of Michigan women. Children old enough to appeciate historical exhibits will enjoy learning about famous Michigan women. The center also features original artwork by Michigan women.

SP T H   History

Monroe County Historical Museum

126 South Monroe Street, Monroe
313-243-7137

Location: South Monroe Street (M-125) and Second Street
Hours: 10 a.m.-5 p.m., Monday-Sunday, May 1-Labor Day. 10 a.m.-5 p.m., Tuesday-Sunday, Labor Day-April 30.
Admission: Free, donations accepted
Ages: All ages
Plan: Under one hour
Parking: Free on site
Lunch: Restaurants available in town
Facilities: Bathrooms. Gift shop with early history, Woodland Indian, and General Custer items.

Woodland Indian displays, military items, and General George Custer memorabilia.

SP T H   Music, Ethnic

Motown Museum

2648 West Grand Boulevard, Detroit
313-867-0991

Location: Off Lodge Freeway, West Grand Boulevard exit, west one block
Hours: 10 a.m.-5 p.m., Monday-Saturday. 2-5 p.m. Sunday.
Admission: $3 adults, $2 children
Ages: 6 and up
Plan: Short visit
Parking: Free parking on street
Lunch: Eat in the nearby New Center Area's Fisher Building, GM Building, or New Center One
Facilities: Bathrooms, gift shop

Enter the modest white stucco house with its "Hitsville, USA" sign and be transported back to the 1960s. Motown hits play softly in the background and bring to life the displays of Motown memorabilia: gold and platinum records, sequin-covered costumes worn by the stars, colorful album covers, and priceless photos. In addition, see up-close Michael Jackson's white sequined glove. Enter Studio A and see where the Motown sound was created. This is Detroit's answer to Nashville, Tennessee.

SP T H   African American History

Museum of African American History

301 Frederick Douglass, Detroit
313-833-9800

Location: In the Cultural Center, two blocks east of the DIA. Turn onto Frederick Douglass off Mack.
Hours: 9:30 a.m.-5 p.m., Wednesday-Saturday. 1-5 p.m., Sunday. Closed Monday and Tuesday.
Admission: Free, donations welcome
Ages: All ages
Plan: Short visit
Parking: Free parking lot in front of museum
Lunch: Drive over to the DIA Kresge Court Cafe
Facilities: Bathrooms, drinking fountain in lobby. Gift shop with many African American heritage gifts: greeting cards, commemorative stamps, coloring books, and books.

Enter through intricately carved wooden portals and become immersed in tracing a people from their homeland in Africa through voyage to America, slavery, and heroic actions during the Abolitionist period. Photographs, maps, paintings, artifacts, sculptures, and audio phones tell the compelling story. Children of all ages will come away with important lessons in courage and humanity.

SP T H   Art

Museum of Art

525 State Street, Ann Arbor
313-764-0395

Location: In the heart of The University of Michigan's Central Campus, across from the Michigan Union
Hours: 11 a.m.-5 p.m., Tuesday-Saturday. 1-5 p.m., Sunday
Admission: Free
Ages: Older children, or young children who enjoy art
Plan: Less than an hour
Parking: Use metered parking on the street
Lunch: Many restaurants nearby

Facilities: Bathrooms, drinking fountain, gift shop with a variety of art-inspired items

The Museum of Art is a small building with just enough art for a quick visit and introduction to art. The museum gift shop sells an inexpensive treasure-hunt coloring book that offers families a self-guided tour of the art collection.

SP T H   Michigan & Natural History

Museum of Art and History

1115 Sixth Street, Port Huron
313-982-0891

Location: ½ mile off US-25, corner of Wall and Sixth Streets
Hours: 1-4:30 p.m., Wednesday-Sunday
Admission: Donations
Ages: All ages
Plan: Short visit
Parking: Adjacent to museum on street
Lunch: Drive into town
Facilities: Bathrooms, gift shop

Three hundred years of local history are displayed in a restored, three-story home. Of interest to children are Indian artifacts, a pioneer log home, and artifacts from Thomas Edison's boyhood home.

SP T H   African American History

Presently closed due to budget cuts; hopes to reopen soon. Call to schedule group tours.

National Museum of Tuskegee Airmen

Historic Fort Wayne
6325 West Jefferson, Detroit
313-297-9360

Photographs, uniforms, and memorabilia tell the story of the Tuskegee Airmen, the country's first Black Army Air Force Battalion.

SP T H   History

Navarre-Anderson Trading Post and Country Store Museum

North Custer Road at Raisinville Road
Monroe
313-243-7137

For full information, see Historic Sites

SP T H   African American History

North American Black Historical Museum

277 King Street
Amherstburg, Ontario, Canada
519-736-5433

Location: From the tunnel, take Riverside Drive (Highway 18) into Amherstburg
Hours: 10 a.m.-5 p.m., Wednesday-Friday. 1-5 p.m. Saturday and Sunday.
Admission: $2 adults, $1 students and seniors.
Ages: All ages
Plan: Short visit
Parking: Adjacent to museum
Lunch: Eat in Amherstburg or nearby city of Sandwich
Facilities: Bathrooms, gift shop

The Windsor area meant freedom for runaway slaves on the Underground Railroad as they moved through Detroit. The North American Black Historical Museum preserves the heritage of Essex County's Black community, which had its beginnings during this turbulent era. The museum, 1855 log house, and Nazarene A.M.E. Church depict Black origins from Africa through slavery, followed by freedom and development.

SP T H   History

Park House Museum

214 Dalhousie Street
Amherstburg, Ontario, Canada
519-736-2511

For full information, see Historic Sites

SP T H   History

Pine Grove Historical Museum
405 Oakland, Pontiac
313-338-6732

For full information, see Historic Sites

SP T H   History

Plymouth Historical Museum
155 South Main Street, Plymouth
313-455-8940

Location: Main and Church Streets, two blocks north of downtown Plymouth
Hours: 1-4 p.m., Wednesday, Thursday, Saturday. 2-5 p.m. Sunday. Open any time by appointment for groups of 20 or more.
Admission: $4 family, $1.50 adults, 50 cents children 5-17, under 5 free. Family membership available.
Ages: 5 and up
Plan: Short visit
Parking: Use lot on south side of building
Lunch: Drive back to downtown Plymouth
Facilities: Bathrooms. Gift shop with many folk toys, Indian items, and handcrafted dolls.

This is an engaging historical museum set up with kids in mind. On "Main Street Plymouth," kids can peek into storefronts representing trades and professions of the early 1900s. Downstairs is a hands-on area that helps children understand the olden days through make-believe. They can try on clothes from grandma's trunk, play with old-fashioned foods from a general store bin, and use McGuffey's Primers and slates to play school.

SP T H   Transportation History

R.E. Olds Transportation Museum
240 Museum Drive, Lansing
571-372-0422

Location: Off Michigan Avenue, two blocks east of the Capitol

Hours: 10 a.m.-5 p.m., Monday-Saturday. Noon-5 p.m. Sunday.
Admission: $7.50 family, $2.50 adults, $1.50 seniors and children, under 5 free. Group rates and family membership available.
Ages: 5 and up
Plan: Under one hour
Parking: Free lot on site
Lunch: Cafe across the parking lot in Lansing's Impression 5 Museum
Facilities: Bathrooms. Gift shop with model car kits, car posters, pictures.

R.E. Olds Transportation Museum, with its extensive collection of antique cars, posters, pictures, advertisements, and old motoring clothing, is a must for children with a passion for cars. Special event: Riverfest on Labor Day weekend showcases antique cars.

SP T H   History

River Raisin Battlefield Visitor's Center
1403 East Elm Street, Monroe
313-243-7136

Location: 1/4-mile west of I-75, on Elm and Detroit Avenue
Hours: 10 a.m.-6 p.m. daily
Admission: Free
Ages: All ages
Plan: Under one hour
Parking: Free on site
Lunch: Restaurants available in town
Facilities: Bathrooms

"Remember the Raisin!" Monroe's fiery role in the War of 1812 comes to life in this museum. A fiber optic map of the battle is projected onto a wall and details the movement and fighting of the British. American, and Native American forces.

SP T   History

Rochester Hills Museum at Van Hoosen Farm
1005 Van Hoosen Road, Rochester
313-656-4663

For full information, see Historic Sites

T   Military History

Selfridge Military Air Museum

Selfridge Air Base, Mount Clemens
313-466-5035

Location: Take I-94 east to exit 240 (Hall Road),
then two miles east on Hall Road to the Air Base
Hours: 1-5 p.m., Sunday, April 1-November 1
Admission: Donations
Ages: 5 and up
Plan: Under one hour
Parking: Free, on site
Lunch: Picnic tables
Facilities: Bathrooms. Small gift counter with
model airplanes and aviation toys.

Most children will be able to see the Air Force
and National Guard exhibits in the low-slung
building in several minutes, but they will want to
spend a lot of time outdoors playing in the field of
once-heroic, now-grounded Navy and Air Force
planes. Sunday airplane maneuvers will also
keep the kids entertained. They will hear and see
the planes zooming across the sky.

SP T H   Music

Stearns Collection of Musical Instruments

1100 Baits Drive, Ann Arbor
313-763-4389

Location: School of Music Galleries, University
of Michigan North Campus
Hours: During the school year: 10 a.m.-5 p.m.,
Thursday and Friday. 1-8 p.m. Saturday and Sun-
day. May-August: 10 a.m.-5 p.m., Thursday, Fri-
day, and Saturday. Guided tours are available by
appointment at these and other times.
Admission: Free. Tours are $1 per person.
Ages: 5 and older
Plan: Under one hour
Parking: Metered lot in back of building
Lunch: Snack bar open daily. For lots of restau-
rants, drive onto the main UofM campus.
Facilities: Bathrooms

For children fascinated by music and instruments, here's an opportunity to see unusual instruments both old and new. Among the many

fascinating examples, kids are sure to notice the Damaru, a Tibetan drum made from a human skull, African thumb pianos, and the very modern Moog synthesizer.

SP T   History

Troy Museum and Historic Village Green

60 West Wattles, Troy
313-524-3570

For full information, see Historic Sites

SP T H   Natural History

University of Michigan Exhibit Museum

1109 Geddes Avenue, Ann Arbor
313-763-6085
313-764-0478 (group tours)

Location: Geddes Avenue near Washtenaw Avenue, on the UofM Central Campus
Hours: 9 a.m.-5 p.m., Tuesday-Saturday. 1-5 p.m., Sunday. Planetarium shows: 10:30 and 11:30 a.m., 2, 3, and 4 p.m., Saturday. 2, 3, and 4 p.m. Sunday. Closed Monday.
Admission: Museum, free. Planetarium show, $2 on Saturday mornings, $2.50 all other shows.
Ages: All ages. Planetarium shows: 5 and older except for Saturday morning shows.
Plan: Half day including planetarium show
Parking: Use the public structure on Fletcher Street
Lunch: Walk into campus
Facilities: Bathrooms and drinking fountain. Gift shop with variety of inexpensive dinosaur and science items.

The University of Michigan Exhibit Museum is the best Michigan has to offer the dinophile in your family. Its second floor is full of dinosaur fossils. There is a fully mounted allosaurus skeleton and a duck-billed anatosaurus skeleton, the giant leg of a brontosaurus, and the extinct elephant bird's tremendous egg. Kids walk through and can't believe their eyes. For a bird's eye view, walk up to the third floor and peek over the balcony onto the backs of the prehistoric monsters. The museum's extensive stuffed wildlife collection will also delight younger children.

SP T   History

Waterloo Area Farm Museum

9998 Waterloo-Munith Road, Stockbridge
517-851-7636, 313-769-2219

For full information, see Historic Sites

SP T H   History

Witch's Hat Depot Museum

300 Dorothy Street, South Lyon
313-437-1735

Location: Just south of downtown South Lyon, in McHattie Park
Hours: 1-5 p.m., Thursday and Sunday. Call to arrange school and group tours.
Admission: Free
Ages: Elementary school children and up
Plan: Under one hour
Parking: Free paking in lot adjacent to museum
Lunch: Family-owned retaurants and fast-food franchises are located in town, on Lafayette and Lake Streets.
Facilities: Bathrooms, gift counter

At the Witch's Hat Depot Museum, history has been carefully coddled and cataloged. The two tidy rooms of the restored 1909 railroad depot are brimming with artifacts of everyday life from the 1860s to the 1940s, including a potpourri of children's clothing, dolls and toys, farm and kitchen implements, Civil War and World War I uniforms, and photographs.

Named "Witch's Hat" for its unique roof resembling a witch's cone-shaped hat, the museum is part of McHattie Park's historic complex which also includes the Washburn one-room schoolhouse and an authentic red caboose. Children can climb up onto the caboose and play engineer and sit at small wooden desks in the restored schoolhouse and practice their lessons on slates. Depot Days, scheduled on the first September weekend after Labor Day, features old-fashioned, small town activities, entertainment, and children's games.

SP T   Military History

Yankee Air Force Museum

Willow Run Airport, Ypsilanti
313-483-4030

Location: Willow Run Airport, Hangar 2041, east side of field
Hours: 10 a.m.-4 p.m., Tuesday-Saturday. Noon-5 p.m., Sunday.
Admission: $4 adults, $3 seniors, $2 children 5-12. Under 5 are free. Group rates available.
Ages: 6 and up
Plan: Under one hour
Parking: Free, on site
Lunch: Drive into Ypsilanti or Belleville
Facilities: Bathrooms. Gift shop with aviation pins, patches, books, models and posters.

For children with a passion for airplanes, a visit to the Yankee Air Force Museum is a must. Housed in a tremendous hangar are colorful examples of World War II and Korean War era airplanes. Aviation history exhibits are on the second level. Feel free to engage the volunteers in discussion; they will gladly give you an informal tour of the aircraft.

SP T H   Ethnic, Art

Your Heritage House

110 East Ferry, Detroit
313-871-1667

Location: One block north of DIA, corner of Ferry and John R
Hours: Call to schedule an appointment or tour
Admission: Fee for classes
Ages: Preschool and up
Plan: Under one hour
Parking: Metered parking along John R
Lunch: Go to the DIA Kresge Court Cafe
Facilities: Bathrooms

Your Heritage House offers children programs in fine arts instruction throughout the year. The beautifully restored pre-World War I home also offers a wide selection of Black heritage materials including folk tales, field recordings, and African and rural South handcrafts and household implements. Children are allowed to play with the doll, puppet, and musical instrument collection. There are also changing fine arts exhibits. If you know you'll be in the Cultural Center, call to make an appointment.

SP T   History

Ypsilanti Historical Society and Museum

8220 North Huron Street, Ypsilanti
313-482-4990

Location: Off I-94, exit 183, follow Huron Street to Cross Street. On the east side of Huron Street.
Hours: 2-4 p.m., Thursday, Saturday, and Sunday
Admission: Free
Ages: 6 and up
Plan: Under one hour
Parking: Metered parking on street. City lots nearby
Lunch: Depot Town offers several restaurants
Facilities: Bathrooms, drinking fountain. Gift shop has old-fashioned toys.

The restored Victorian home offers authentic furnishings, period clothing, home and farm tools and implements, plus changing exhibits from the 1800s. Children who are interested in history and old enough to understand "look but don't touch," will especially enjoy the winding staircase, Scottish Drum and Bugle Corps uniform, dollhouse, and old toys.

6
HISTORIC SITES

Listed in this chapter are a diverse assortment of nineteenth-century restored homes, villages and farmsteads, forts, auto baron mansions, lighthouses, and landmarks. Michigan's historic sites often reveal its communal pioneer history and the important role it played in the automobile industry. Many sites have a commitment to living history, offering demonstrations and costumed guides that are quite appealing to children five and older. While the auto baron homes tours are not geared specifically to children, each home has aspects that children will find interesting. After accompanying me on many homes tours, my children are quite adept at staying near the guide and asking questions. They now see history as an accumulation of many personal stories.

Abbreviations: SP—site offers school programs; T—site offers group tours; H—wheelchair accessible.

U.S.-Canada Bridge

Ambassador Bridge
Juncture of I-75 and I-96, Detroit
313-226-3157

For children, a drive across this bridge is high adventure. Peeking out the window, they can see both the Detroit and Windsor skylines, as well as the Detroit River and its barge traffic. When we visit Windsor, we always try to use both the bridge and tunnel in our coming and going. Open 24 hours, daily. A toll fee ($1.50 American, $1.75

Canadian) is collected before entering on both sides of the Detroit River.

U.S.-Canada Bridge

Blue Water International Bridge
At end of I-94 going east, Port Huron
313-984-3131

We like to take this less-trafficked bridge into Canada when we are going to Eastern Ontario. On the way back to the U.S., we always stop for an ice cream cone at the London Farm Dairy Bar (2136 Pine Grove Avenue, 984-5111), just south of the foot of the bridge. Above the dairy sign, a giant cow with horns looks out at the traffic.

SP T   Carillon Tower

Burton Memorial Tower
300 block of South Thayer Street, Ann Arbor
313-764-2539

Visitors can climb to the top floor of the carillon tower, one of the landmarks on the University of Michigan campus, during concerts from 12-12:30 p.m. weekdays when school is in session. Way up there you'll have a bird's-eye view of Ann Arbor and will also see and hear 55 bells, the world's third heaviest carillon instrument. Carillon concerts are also held at 7 p.m. seven selected Mondays, June–August.

SP T H-main floor   Farmhouse

Cobblestone Farm
2781 Packard, Ann Arbor
313-994-2928

Location: On Packard Road, between Platt and Stone School Roads
Hours: 1-4 p.m., Thursday-Sunday, May-October
Admission: $5 family rate, $1.50 adults, 75 cents children 3 to 17 and seniors, under 3 free
Ages: 5 and up
Plan: Short visit
Parking: Free, behind the barn

Lunch: Picnic area near playground. Many restaurants in nearby Briarwood Mall or on UofM campus.
Facilities: Bathrooms. Gift shop with handcrafted toys and concession, located in Cobblestone Farm Center. Playground on site.

Cobblestone Farm is a living farm museum that tells the story of nineteeth-century Michigan farm life through a variety of restored, authentically furnished buildings: the elegant Ticknor-Campbell house, a pioneer log cabin, and a replica of an 1880s barn, full of animals. Costumed guides lead public tours through the house; the other buildings are open for browsing. A playground is on the grounds. Children will benefit most from a pre-arranged group tour. Throughout spring and fall, there are weekend festivals and Living History programs which offer demonstrations of 19th century crafts.

SP T H   Historic Home

Cranbrook House and Gardens

380 Lone Pine Road, Bloomfield Hills
313-645-3149

Location: Enter off Lone Pine Road, just west of Cranbrook Road
Hours: Home tour: 11 a.m. and 1:15 p.m. Thursday. Groups of 15 or more can schedule special tours.
   Garden: 10 a.m.-5 p.m., Monday-Saturday. 11 a.m.-5 p.m., Sunday, May-October.
Admission: Home tour and garden: $6, children under 5 free.
   Gardens: $2 adults, $1.50 children and seniors, under 5 free.
Ages: Home tour: older children. Garden walk: all ages.
Plans: Short visit for each
Parking: Along Lone Pine Road or across the street in Christ Church parking lot
Lunch: Vending machines in the Cranbrook Institute of Science, or find restaurants in nearby Birmingham or along Woodward Avenue or Telegraph Road.
Facilities: Bathrooms in house

Cranbrook House is an English manor house designed by Albert Kahn and built in the early 1900s for *The Detroit News* publisher and Cranbrook founders, George Booth and his wife, Ellen Scripps Booth. Older children will enjoy learning about the life of these two influential people. The gardens surrounding the home offer 40 acres of formal plantings, woods, pine forest walks, and two lakes. The gardens are a perfect way to experience seasonal changes. Kids love scampering along the paths and ducking into the pine forest.

SP T   Historic Home

Crocker House

15 Union Street, Mount Clemens
313-465-2488

Location: Cass Avenue and Gratiot
Hours: 10 a.m.-4 p.m., Tuesday-Friday; 1-4 p.m., first Sunday of each month. Closed in January. Increased hours during December. Group tours available.
Admission: $1 adults, 50 cents children
Ages: 8 and up
Plan: Under one hour
Parking: On street
Lunch: Restaurants in town
Facilities: Bathrooms. Small gift shop with Victorian replica toys and other inexpensive items.

Older children with an interest in the Victorian age will enjoy Crocker House's authentically furnished rooms and costumed mannequins. They will also enjoy the home's special Christmas exhibits and decorations during December.

SP T H   Historic Village & Train

Crossroads Village/Huckleberry Railroad

G-5055 Branch Road, Flint
313-736-7100
1-800-648-7275

Location: Just north of Flint. Follow I-475 off either I-75 or I-69 to Carpenter Road (exit 11).
Hours: 10 a.m.-5:30 p.m., Monday-Friday. 11 a.m.-6:30 p.m., weekends and holidays. Train departs hourly 11 a.m.-4p.m., weekdays. Noon-5 p.m., weekends and holidays. Christmas at Crossroads: 3:30-9:30 p.m., Fridays, Saturdays, Sundays, November 25-December 30.

Admission: $7.75 adult, $5.25 children 4 to 12, $6.75 seniors, 3 and under free. Group rates and family membership available.
Ages: 3 and up
Plan: Half day visit
Parking: Free lot adjacent to village
Lunch: Small cafe, ice cream parlor, picnic area, cider mill
Facilities: Bathrooms. General store features country and handcrafted items, dolls and candy. Depot Souvenir Shop offers train memorabilia and novelty items.

Crossroads Village and Huckleberry Railroad offer families a perfect summer outing. Take a 45-minute ride on the full-size steam train. Walk the nineteenth-century village streets and explore 26 beautifully restored buildings, including three working mills, a toy maker's barn, one-room schoolhouse, and general store. Duck into the Opera House for a half-hour magic show. Costumed guides, hands-on experiences, craft demonstrations, and a ride on a restored ferris wheel and carousel add to children's enjoyment. Christmas at Crossroads Village is a festive time with over 70,000 sparkling lights, Santa's workshop, and sleigh rides.

SP T   Historic Home

Curwood Castle
224 Curwood Castle Drive, Owosso
517-723-8844

Location: One block east and two blocks north of M-52 and M-21 intersection. Owosso is located west of Flint and northeast of Lansing
Hours: 1-5 p.m., Tuesday-Sunday. Group tours can be pre-arranged for the morning.
Admission: Free. Donations accepted. Group tours have nominal fee.
Ages: All ages
Plan: Short visit
Parking: Free on site
Lunch: Drive into downtown Owosso
Facilities: Bathrooms inside castle. Surrounding the castle is a park that includes an old log cabin and a footbridge over the Shiawassee River.

Curwood Castle is the former work studio of James Oliver Curwood, a famous writer of adventure books. He built the castle in 1922, based on a romantic reproduction of a Norman chateau. Children will love climbing up to the top of the towering turret and looking out the windows at the rushing Shiawassee River below.

SP T H   Historic Buildings

Dearborn Historical Museum: McFadden Ross House and Exhibit Annex

915 South Brady, Dearborn
313-565-3000

Location: Just north of Michigan Avenue
Hours: 9 a.m.-5 p.m., Monday-Saturday, May-October. 1-5 p.m., Monday-Saturday, November-April.
Admission: Free
Ages: All ages
Plan: Short visit
Parking: Use lot adjacent to buildings
Lunch: Nearby Fairlane Town Center has a wide variety of restaurants both inside the mall and on the grounds
Facilities: Bathrooms, gift shop

The 1800s come to life in three buildings. The first two are located on Brady Street. The Mc-Fadden-Ross House contains domestic and period exhibits; the Exhibit Annex has craft shops, wagons, and buggies. The Commandant's Quarters, located at the corner of Michigan and Monroe, houses military exhibits and period rooms.

Caboose

Depot Town Caboose

23½ Cross Street, Ypsilanti
313-483-4256
313-482-4920

While shopping or browsing in Ypsilanti's restored Depot Town shops, be sure to let the kids climb on board the shiny red caboose and play "engineer."

SP T   Detroit-Windsor Tunnel

Detroit-Windsor Tunnel
100 East Jefferson, Detroit
313-567-4422

Young children won't believe you at first when
you tell them they are driving under the Detroit
River. Older children will be amazed that such a
tunnel could ever be built. It's a Detroit landmark
that makes your trip to Windsor begin as an adventure. The tunnel is located at the foot of Ran-
dolph and Jefferson. Open 24 hours, daily. A toll
fee ($1.50 American, $1.75 Canadian) is collected
before entering on both sides of the Detroit River.

SP T   One-Room Schoolhouse

Dewey School
11501 Territorial Road, Stockbridge
517-851-8247

Location: Mayer and Territorial Roads, just off
M-106, south of Stockbridge. Located close to
the Waterloo Area Farm Museum.
Hours: 1-4 p.m., Sunday, June-August. 1-4 p.m.,
Saturday and Sunday, September-first weekend
in October. Special "Rural Schooldays" tour avail-
able during May and September.
Admission: $1 per person, children under 5
free. $1 per child for group tours.
Ages: Second grade and up for school tours.
Plan: Under one hour
Parking: Free lots adjacent to schoolhouse
Lunch: Picnic area in nearby Waterloo Recre-
ation Area
Facilities: Gift counter with old-fashioned
school supplies.

Children can become nineteenth-century school-
children in this one-room historic schoolhouse.

SP T H   Auto Baron Home

Edsel and Eleanor Ford House
100 Lake Shore Road, Grosse Pointe Shores
313-884-4222
313-884-3400 (recorded information)

Location: Off I-94, Vernier Road Exit. Go east to Lake Shore Drive (Jefferson).
Hours: One-hour tours are offered noon, 1, 2, 3 and 4 p.m., Wednesday-Sunday. Group tours by appointment. Grounds are open 11:30 a.m.-5 p.m., May-October.
Admission: $4 adults, $3 seniors, $2 children. $2 per person, grounds only, May-October
Ages: 7 and up
Plan: Short visit
Parking: Free, on site
Lunch: A tea tent on the grounds, selling drinks, sandwiches, and snacks is available May-October. Picnicking on the grounds is allowed.
Facilities: Bathrooms in guard house. Books and postcards are on sale in home's main lobby.

Friendly, engaging tour guides help children find many things of interest in the Edsel and Eleanor Ford home, such as the ever-present view of Lake St. Clair, curious and beautiful decorative pieces, and a many-sided mirror in the Art Deco study that gives off infinite images. Best of all, the tour offers an inside look into one of Detroit's first families. After the 50-minute tour, walk or drive over to the Play House. For most children, this will be the highlight of the visit. Built to resemble the mansion, this playhouse is created in three-quarter size with furnishings to match. Adults will feel like Alice in Wonderland. Special art exhibits, teas, and holiday and summer children's shows are offered.

SP T   Railcar

Eisenhower Presidential Car
7203 US-12, Onsted (Irish Hills)
517-467-2300

Location: In front of Stagecoach Stop, U.S.A., off US-12
Hours: 12:30-5:30 p.m., Tuesday-Friday. 12:30-6:30 p.m., Saturday and Sunday, June-August. Closed Monday. Self-guided tours. Group tours available.
Admission: Admission is included in Stagecoach Stop, U.S.A. fee: $7 adults, $6 children 12 and under, 3 and under free. Group rates available.
Ages: 5 and up
Plan: Under one hour. With Stagecoach Stop, plan on a half day visit.

Parking: Free on site
Lunch: Restaurant in Stagecoach Stop, fudge shop adjacent to railroad car, picnic areas
Facilities: Bathrooms. Gift Shop in Stagecoach Stop.

Once known as the "White House on Wheels," this railroad car was used by President Eisenhower from 1952 to 1960. Today it houses Eisenhower memorabilia and offers children a look at the conditions of coach travel. Kids will especially enjoy seeing where Eisenhower slept and ate.

SP T H   Historic Farmstead

Ella Sharp Museum
3225 Fourth Street, Jackson
517-787-2320

Location: 4½ miles south of I-94 and US-127 intersection
Hours: 10 a.m.-5 p.m., Tuesday-Friday. Noon-5 p.m., Saturday. Closed Sundays, Mondays, and holidays. Planetarium show: 3 p.m., Sunday, September-June.
Admission: $5 family, $2.50 adults, $2 seniors, $1 children under 12. Family membership available.
Ages: 2 and up
Plan: Half day visit
Parking: Free on site
Lunch: Granary Restaurant: 11 a.m.-2:30 p.m., Tuesday-Friday. Noon-4 p.m., Saturday. Ice cream parlor: 11 a.m.-2:30 p.m., Tuesday-Friday. Noon-4 p.m., Saturday. Adjacent Ella Sharp Park has picnic area and playground.
Facilities: Bathrooms, drinking fountain. Gift shop full of kids' toys, games, books, tapes, jewelry, and science items.

The Ella Sharp Museum is a historic complex with a vision of the future. The cornerstone of the complex is the beautifully restored nineteenth-century Merriman-Sharp family farmhouse. Tours are scheduled on the hour and half hour, daily until 4:30 p.m. Children will enjoy learning about the life of Jackson's most famous lady, seeing the toys and dolls in the children's room, and walking up to the rooftop cupola. There are many other authentically furnished, restored buildings along Farm Lane: the Eli Stilson log house, country store, print shop, schoolhouse, barn, woodworking and broom-making shops.

The modern galleries include the Hurst Planetarium, Art Gallery, Heritage Hall's Native American exhibits, and the Discovery Gallery with hands-on exhibits that will delight children.

H	Detroit Landmark

Fisher Building
3011 West Grand Boulevard, Detroit
313-874-4444

Point out the Fisher Building's green tiled roof to the kids, and it will always be a point of reference for them. Once in the lobby, crane your necks upwards to see the impressive mosaic, marble, and tiled ceiling; shop and browse, but don't forget the fun stuff. Take the kids through the skywalks and tunnels (the Fisher Building is connected to the GM Building, New Center One, and Hotel St. Regis) and up and down New Center One's glass elevators. Park in Crowley's lot.

T	Auto Baron Home

Fisher Mansion/Bhaktivedanta Center
383 Lenox, Detroit
313-331-6740

Location: This site is off the beaten track. Take I-94 east to Cadieux exit. Go south to East Jefferson, then west to Dickerson. Follow Dickerson south. Dickerson becomes Lenox Avenue at Essex Street. After one block on Lenox, look for the Fisher Mansion on your right.
Hours: Noon-9 p.m., Friday and Saturday. Noon-8 p.m., Sunday. One-hour tours: 12:30, 2, 3:30, and 6 p.m., Friday, Saturday, and Sunday. Group tours available during the week.
Admission: $5 adults, $4 seniors and students, $3 children, children 10 and under free when accompanied by adult
Ages: 8 and older
Plan: Short visit
Parking: Free, use second gate
Lunch: Govinda's, located in the elegant dining room, offers gourmet vegetarian cuisine as well as kid-pleasing desserts.

Facilities: Bathrooms. East Indian grocery and gift shop with made-in-India items, books, snacks, and incense.

Children with a vivid imagination will love this home, built by Auto Baron Lawrence Fisher in the 1920s, in a highly opulent and decorative style. Everywhere there are carved wooden faces, painted ceilings, gold inlaid patterns, and detailed tiles. Children will enjoy the indoor boatwells, the secret doors, and haunting mirrors.

The mansion, now cultural center for Krishna Consciousness followers, also has a remarkable collection of Indian paintings, tapestries, masks and sculptures. Children are welcomed on the tours and encouraged to ask questions. There are two audio-visual presentations, one 10 minutes, the other 20 minutes, both with Krishna religious content. The theme and message of both go over the heads of children, but they might enjoy the colorful costumes and images.

SP T   Lighthouse

Fort Gratiot Lighthouse
2800 Omar Street, Port Huron
313-984-2602

Location: I-94 and Hancock Street
Hours: Tours by appointment only.
Admission: Free
Ages: 6 and up
Plan: Under one hour
Parking: Free lot to the right of lighthouse
Lunch: Picnic area behind lighthouse
Facilities: Bathrooms

Kids will enjoy climbing up the spiral staircase and romping around the outside picnic area of this oldest lighthouse in operation in the United States.

SP T H   Fort

Fort Malden National Historic Park
100 Laird Avenue
Amherstburg, Ontario, Canada
519-736-5416

Location: From tunnel, take Riverside Drive (Highway 18) to Amherstburg. Turn right at Alma

Street, left at Laird Street. Approximately 25 minutes from tunnel.

Hours: 10 a.m.-5 p.m., daily, year-round
Admission: Free
Ages: All ages
Plan: Short visit
Parking: Free lot in front of fort
Lunch: Picnic areas along fort's grassy avenues
Facilities: Visitor center, bathrooms, benches along Detroit River

Built in 1796 by the British, Fort Malden saw action during the War of 1812. Today, her four remaining buildings sit among rolling hills and grassy avenues. Kids will enjoy almost everything about this fort. The slide history is only six minutes long; costumed guides demonstrate musket firing and other nineteenth-century military routines. Children are allowed to try on military costumes. Best of all, the hills and avenues are perfect for running and rolling. After your visit, drive down a block to Austin "Toddy" Jones Park, located at the corner of Laird Avenue South and North Street. Here you'll find creative slides and swings, plus a wooden fort climber.

H	Detroit Landmark

Fox Theatre
2211 Woodward, Detroit
313-567-6000

Golden ornaments, red marble pillars, sculptured animals with jeweled eyes, glittering chandeliers —these are only a few of the details which make the Fox a majestically exotic former movie palace. Try to catch a family show, which will have more modestly priced tickets than the major attractions.

H	Historic Theater

Gem Theatre
58 East Columbia, Detroit
313-963-9800

This small, 450-seat, intimate theater has been authentically restored to its former 1920s glory days. Come in and take a peek and stay for a cabaret-style musical revue.

| H | Detroit Landmark |

GM Building
3044 West Grand Boulevard, Detroit
313-556-6200

Take the skywalk from the Fisher Building into
this landmark building, and you'll be surrounded
by cars. The kids will enjoy eating at an old-fashioned cafeteria with old-fashioned prices, located
on the basement level of the building, and open to
the public only after 1 p.m. Monday-Friday. Take
the tunnel back to the Fisher Building for Stroh's
ice cream.

| H | Detroit Landmark |

Greektown
Monroe Street near Beaubien, Detroit
313-965-3800 (Hot line)

Come to Greektown hungry and sample baklava,
shish kabob, and flaming cheese. Monroe Street
is lined with Greek bakeries, Greek restaurants,
ice cream parlors, fudge shops, and gourmet
bakeries. Trappers Alley, a festival marketplace
opening onto Monroe Street, has a People Mover
station on the third level.

| SP T H | Historic Village |

Greenfield Village
20900 Oakwood Boulevard, Dearborn
313-271-1976 (24-hour information)
313-271-1620

Location: Michigan Avenue and Southfield
Freeway
Hours: 9 a.m.-5 p.m., daily, mid-March-first
week in January. Closed Thanksgiving Day and
Christmas Day.
Admission: $11.50 adults, $10.50 seniors,
$5.75 children 5 to 12, under 5 free. Family mem-
berships and annual passes available. Additional
fees for Steam Train Ride, Suwanee Steamboat,
Carousel and Carriage Tours
Ages: All ages

Plan: Full day
Parking: Free, adjacent to museum and village
Lunch: The Eagle Tavern for full dinners, Suwanee Restaurant at Suwanee Park for cafeteria selection, Main Street Lunch Stand for light refreshments, Covered Bridge Lunch Stand for snacks. Picnicking is allowed throughout the village. I recommend bringing a picnic lunch and adding snacks as the day wears on.
Facilities: Bathrooms, drinking fountains, stroller rental. Three gift shops. The well-stocked Great American Emporium, located at the entrance, has many reproductions of old-fashioned children's toys, books, and craft items.

Greenfield Village is one of the Detroit area's best-known sites. Its restored homes, workshops, and stores offer a glimpse into America's past and a look at inventors Thomas Edison, the Wright Brothers, and Henry Ford, men who revolutionized our world. The village is too large to see everything on one visit with small children. Your best bet is to concentrate on the sure-fire child-pleasers. Take the 30-minute round-trip train ride and visit the Firestone Farm, a working farm where costumed interpretive guides live and work according to a nineteenth-century schedule. The nearby demonstration barns, particularly glass blowing and printing, appeal to children and offer vivid memories. Ride the Suwanee Steamboat and the restored carousel, then buy an ice cream, and call it a day. You can always come again. There are many theme weekends throughout the summer and fall and Christmas festivities in December.

SP T H   Historic Village

Greenmead Museum and Historical Village

38125 Eight Mile Road, Livonia
313-477-7375

Location: Newburgh and Eight Mile Roads
Hours: 1-4 p.m., Sunday, May-December. The grounds are open daily during daylight hours. Group tours available by appointment.
Admission: $2 adults, $1 seniors, children are free. Grounds free.
Ages: 5 and up
Plan: Short visit

Parking: Free on site
Lunch: Picnic tables in park
Facilities: Outhouses available during spring. Gift shop with variety of old-fashioned toys and trinkets.

This small historic nineteenth-century village includes Hill House, 2 other houses, a church, general store, and interpretive center. Kids will enjoy the interpretive center's ten-minute slide show, the general store's penny candy, and the restored buildings' furnishings and costumed mannequins. The on-site park has a small playground. There are special programs and decorations at Christmas.

SP T   Auto Baron Home

Henry Ford Estate-Fairlane
4901 Evergreen
University of Michigan-Dearborn
313-593-5590

Location: Michigan Avenue and Evergreen Road
Hours: Home tours: 1:30-4:30 p.m., Sunday year-round. On the hour 10 a.m.-3 p.m., except at noon, Monday-Saturday, April-December. Guided nature tour of grounds: year-round, call for reservations. Self-guided nature tour: year-round, maps available from parking lot vending machine. Breakfast with Santa and Santa's Workshop are held in December.
Admission: Home tour: $6 adults, $5 children and seniors.
Ages: 8 and up for home tour. 2 to 10 years for Breakfast with Santa and Santa's Workshop.
Plan: Home tour: 1½ hours.
Parking: Free lot across from estate
Lunch: Pool restaurant: 11 a.m.-2 p.m., Monday-Friday, year-round; picnic areas
Facilities: Bathrooms. Gift shop with Ford-related items, old-fashioned toys, and books.

For children, the main attraction on this estate is the white clapboard miniature farmhouse, full of hands-on, nineteenth-century clothes, games, toys, and miniature farm and household implements. Parents need to duck while entering the farmhouse; children fit perfectly.

The 1½ hour tour of the Ford mansion might be too much for little children, but older children will enjoy walking single file through a 16-foot deep underground tunnel connecting the main house with the electric power house, peeking into the indoor bowling alley, and being allowed to sit on the unauthentic furniture as the tour guide speaks.

SP T   Fort

Presently closed due to budget cuts; hopes to re-open soon. Call to schedule tours.

Historic Fort Wayne

6325 West Jefferson, Detroit
313-297-9360

The 83-acre fort includes the National Museum of Tuskegee Airmen (*see* Museums),` Great Lakes Indian Museum (*see* Museums), a restored 1880 Victorian Commanding Officer's House, visitor center, and the Spanish-American War Guard-house.

T   Lightship

Huron Lightship Museum

Pine Grove Park, Port Huron
313-982-0891

Location: Pine Grove Avenue, just north of downtown business district
Hours: Summer: 1-4:30 p.m., Wednesday-Sunday. September, April, and May: 1-4:30 p.m. Saturday and Sunday. Additional hours are available by appointment only.
Admission: $1 adults, 50 cents seniors and students, 6 and under free
Ages: All ages. Main deck is stroller accessible.
Plan: Under one hour
Parking: Concessions available during the summer; downtown Port Huron offers a variety of restaurants. For ice cream, visit the London Farm Dairy Bar.
Facilities: Public restrooms in the park.

Before the days of electrically lighted buoys, lightships were used to warn ships of shallow water and help them steer their course. The Huron Lightship, built in 1920, was anchored six miles north of the Blue Water Bridge and retired from active duty in 1971. It is the last lightship to operate on the Great Lakes. Two decks (levels) are open to the public in a self-guiding tour.

SP T   Historic Farmstead

John Freeman Walls Historic Site

Puce Road, Maidstone Township
Ontario, Canada
519-258-6253 (office, not site)

Location: Take Highway 401 east, exit Puce Road north. The site is approximately two miles north on Puce Road, 20 minutes from Windsor-Detroit border.
Hours: 10 a.m.-5 p.m., daily, May 15-Labor Day. School and group tours available by appointment.
Admission: $7 family of four, $3 adults, $2 seniors, $2 children, under 5 free. Group rates available.
Ages: All ages
Plan: Short visit
Parking: Free on site
Lunch: Picnic area
Facilities: Bathrooms. Gift shop with Canadian and Underground Railroad crafts and souvenirs.

Former slave John Freeman Walls and his wife escaped to freedom and settled in Maidstone Township in 1846. Their farmstead became an important terminal on the Underground Railroad. This historic site features a train caboose museum of Underground Railroad history and African art, a 1798 log cabin, and 1846 log cabin. A movie about Underground Railroad history is also shown. The site makes history vividly come to life. Movie is available.

SP T H   Historic Village

John R. Park Homestead

360 Fairview Avenue, Essex
Ontario, Canada
519-738-2029

Location: Essex County Road 50 between Kingsville and Colchester. From Windsor, take Highway 18 southeast to Road 50 (45 minutes southeast of Windsor).

Hours: 11 a.m.-5 p.m., daily, end of June–mid-September. 11 a.m.-4 p.m., Sunday-Friday, mid-September–mid-October. 11 a.m.-4 p.m. Monday-Friday, mid-October–June. Group tours available, call at least two weeks in advance.
Admission: $9 family, $2.50 adults, $2 children 4 to 16, 3 and under free
Ages: 5 and up
Plan: Short visit
Parking: Free, on site
Lunch: Picnic area, cold drinks and snack foods for sale
Facilities: Bathrooms. Gift shop with wooden toys and candy sticks.

The John R. Park Homestead, including Park's home and several restored buildings—shed, smoke house, ice house, outhouse, blacksmith shop, sawmill, and livestock stable—offer children a hands-on look into nineteenth-century life. Costumed guides demonstrate and involve children in seasonal crafts such as candle dipping, spinning, butter churning, and nineteenth-century games. Children will also enjoy the short introductory slide show presentation. Many special seasonal events celebrate maple syrup, fall harvest, and Christmas.

H	Restored Shopping Plaza

Kerrytown Plaza
407 North Fifth Avenue, Ann Arbor
313-662-4221

Specialty shops and restaurants are located in this charming setting of restored nineteenth-century buildings. Kids will love the aromas coming from the specialty foods shops and market. Little Dipper Candle Shop lets children dip their own candles ($1.25/pair; Monday-Friday. Groups should call for reservation, 313-994-3912). On Wednesday and Saturday mornings, the adjacent Farmers' Market is bustling with activity.

SP T H	Auto Baron Home

Meadow Brook Hall and Knole Cottage
Oakland University, Rochester
313-370-3140

Location: On Adams Road, five miles north of I-75

Hours: July–Labor Day: 10:30 a.m.-5 p.m., Monday-Saturday and 1-5 p.m., Sunday. Rest of year: 1-5 p.m., Sunday only. Last tour is at 3:45 p.m. Christmas walk: 10 a.m.-4 p.m. or 10 a.m.- 8 p.m., depending on the day, late November-early December.

Admission: $5 adults, $3 children 4–12, under 3 are free. Christmas walk: $6 adults, Monday-Friday. $8 adults, Saturday and Sunday. $4 children 12 and younger.

Ages: 8 and up

Plan: Short visit (indoor tour takes approximately two hours)

Parking: Free lot adjacent to mansion

Lunch: Summer Tea Room open 11:30 a.m.–3 p.m., July–Labor Day. Available for groups at other times by prior reservations.

Facilities: Bathrooms. Small gift counter with Meadow Brook Hall stationery.

Matilda Dodge Wilson, widow of auto baron John Dodge, built her 100-room Tudor mansion in the 1920's for approximately $4 million. Meadow Brook Hall is Michigan's Biltmore, a magnificent tribute to a bygone era, decorated richly with authentic furnishings. The two-hour tour is not appropriate for small children, but patient older children will be rewarded with visual architectural delights and interesting anecdotes. Meadow Brook Hall's grounds are lovely at every season, and children will want to walk into the woods to explore the Knole Cottage, a six-room playhouse built to three-quarter size for Matilda and John Wilson's daughter. During the Christmas walk, Santa presides over Knole Cottage, and children are encouraged to visit during daylight hours. Car buffs won't want to miss "Concours d'Elegance," the classic, antique, and sports car show, the first Sunday in August.

SP T   Historic Village

Mill Race Historical Village

Griswold, north of Main Street, Northville
313-348-1845

Location: 4 miles west of I-275

Hours: 2-5 p.m., Sundays, June-October. Grounds always open. Pre-arranged tours available all year. School groups can spend a day in

the Wash Oak School, October-November or April-May.
Admission: Donation, fee for tours
Ages: 8 and up
Plan: Short visit
Parking: Free on site
Lunch: Picnic sites on grounds
Facilities: Bathrooms in main house, small gift shop

This historic village includes a restored nineteenth-century home with exhibits of local history, plus several other restored homes and buildings —church, inn, school, and blacksmith shop—all on a seven-acre site along Mill Pond. Children will enjoy the one-room schoolhouse and gazebo.

SP T H   Historic Buildings

Navarre-Anderson Trading Post and Country Store Museum
North Custer Road at Raisinville Road
Monroe
313-243-7137

Location: Four miles west of Monroe on North Custer at the Raisinville Bridge
Hours: 1-5 p.m., Wednesday–Sunday, Memorial Day-Labor Day. Group tours available.
Admission: Free
Ages: All ages
Plan: Under one hour
Parking: Free adjacent to Country Store Museum
Lunch: Restaurants in town
Facilities: Bathrooms. Country store offers penny candy and souvenirs.

The restored and furnished trading post, built in 1789, is the oldest residence in Michigan. The Country store is typical of the early 1900s general store. Children will enjoy choosing penny candy.

SP T H   Historic Home

Park House Museum
214 Dalhousie Street, Amherstburg
Ontario, Canada
519-736-2511

Location: Highway 18 and Rankin Avenue

Hours: Summer: 10 a.m.-5 p.m., daily. Winter: 11 a.m.-5 p.m., Tuesday-Friday, and Sunday. Closed Monday and Saturday.
Admission: $5 family, $2 adults, $1.50 seniors, 50 cents children 6 to 16, under 6 free. Family membership available.
Ages: 7 and up
Plan: Short visit
Parking: Free on street
Lunch: Picnic area, restaurants, bakery, and ice cream parlor on Dalhousie Street
Facilities: Bathrooms. Gift shop with books and tinware.

Park House, the oldest house within a 250 mile radius, was built in Detroit in 1796 and later moved across the river. The first floor has been restored to show what life was like in the 1850s. Costumed guides demonstrate early domestic life, including tinsmithing and printing. Children will be interested in the doctor's and ship captain's offices, the children's nursery full of toys, and the sewing room. Upstairs, there are pioneer and local history exhibits. Best of all, Park House is located in the Navy Yard, along the Detroit River, a wonderful place to picnic and boat watch in the summer.

SP T H   Historic Home

Pine Grove Historical Museum
405 Oakland, Pontiac
313-338-6732

Location: ½ mile north of Y-Track Drive
Hours: 9 a.m.-4 p.m., Monday-Friday. Group tours available.
Admission: $3 adults, $1.50 children 16 and younger and seniors
Ages: 6 and up
Plan: Short visit
Parking: Free on site
Lunch: Carriage house doubles as a lunchroom. Picnicking is allowed on the museum's four acres.
Facilities: Bathrooms. Gift shop with old-fashioned, hand-made toys and items, ranging in price from 25 cents to $20.

At Pine Grove, the home of Michigan Governor Moses Wisner, children are encouraged to step back into the past. The Greek Revival home is chock full of authentic furnishings, clothing, and home implements. The four-acre estate also includes a fully equipped summer kitchen, smoke house, root cellar, and one-room schoolhouse. Costumed guides lead group tours and offer children hands-on experiences.

H   Detroit Landmark

Renaissance Center

Jefferson Avenue, Detroit
313-568-5600

Kids will love walking through the three futuristic silver towers that have come to symbolize Detroit. Park in the structure off Beaubien, ride the People Mover in a circle, and disembark at the RenCen station. Stores and restaurants are located on Levels 1 and 2. Visit the Westin's eight-story atrium lobby filled with plants, observation lookouts, and reflecting pools. Don't leave without viewing "The World of Ford," a display of the newest in Ford and Lincoln-Mercury cars (Tower 300, Level 2. 10 a.m.-6 p.m., Monday-Friday. Noon-5 p.m., Saturday).

SP T   Historic Farmhouse

Rochester Hills Museum at Van Hoosen Farm

1005 Van Hoosen Road, Rochester
313-656-4663

Location: One mile east of Rochester Road off Tienken Road, five miles north of M-59
Hours: 1-4 p.m., Wednesday-Sunday
Admission: $2 adults, $1 seniors, 50 cents children
Ages: 8 and up
Plan: Short visit, includes driving tour of Stoney Creek Village
Parking: Free on site
Lunch: Picnic area along Stoney Creek
Facilities: Bathrooms. Gift shop with local history books, stationery, craft items.

The Sarah Van Hoosen Jones homestead is a low, rambling estate nestled in the middle of historic Stoney Creek Village. Authentic furnishings and household implements make nineteenth-century rural Michigan come to life. Children will especially enjoy the doctor's office and farm office, the kitchen with its 1902 washing machine and old-fashioned ice box, and the child's bedroom, furnished with toys, games, clothes, and child-sized furniture. The grounds and gazebo are ideal for an afternoon romp. There are special annual events, including Christmas activities and summer camp. Archaeological digs are in progress on the site.

SP T H   Historic Village & Car Museum

Southwestern Ontario Heritage Village

Essex County Road 23, Essex
Ontario, Canada
519-776-6909

Location: From Detroit-Windsor bridge, take Highway 3 east to 23 south. The village is just south of the Highway 19 and 23 junction.
Hours: 11 a.m.-5 p.m., Wednesday-Sunday, April-June and September-November. 11 a.m.-5 p.m., daily, July-August. Group tours available. Special times available for school groups.
Admission: $8 family, $3 adults, $2 seniors, $1.50 children, under 5 are free.
Ages: All ages
Plan: Short visit
Parking: Free on site
Lunch: Picnic tables in village park. Refreshment stand available during special events.
Facilities: Bathrooms in car museum. Souvenirs and candy in general store.

Southwestern Ontario Heritage Village's ten turn-of-the-century buildings—a railway station, schoolhouse, church, general store, shoe repair–barber shop, home, three log cabins, and barnyard buildings—are located in the midst of 54 wooded acres. A transportation museum documents the early settlers' travel from snowshoes and wagons to modern automobiles. The buildings, artifacts, and museum make history come to life for children. Special events are the Teddy Bear Reunion and Steam Engine Show.

T H   Restored Shopping Plaza

Trappers Alley (The Alley)

Monroe and Beaubien, Greektown, Detroit
313-963-5445

Location: Corner of Monroe and Beaubien, five
blocks north of the Renaissance Center, in the
heart of Greektown
Hours: 10 a.m.-9 p.m., Monday-Thursday. 10
a.m.-midnight, Friday and Saturday. Noon-7 p.m.,
Sunday. Fifteen-minute historic tours available;
call ahead.
Admission: Free
Ages: All ages
Plan: Short visit
Parking: Street parking is very difficult to find.
Use the rear parking lot on Lafayette. $1 first ½
hour, $1 second ½ hour, 50 cents each additional
hour.
Lunch: Fast-food booths with tables and chairs,
plus sit-down restaurants
Facilities: Bathrooms. Many gift and clothing
stores. People Mover Station located on third
level.

A fur tannery in the 1850s, Trapper's Alley is now
three levels of aromatic food booths, colorful gift
shops, and hanging sculpture. Children will enjoy
the carnival atmosphere. It is also a convenient
People Mover station.

SP T   Historic Farmhouse

Trenton Historical Museum

306 St. Joseph, Trenton
313-675-2130
313-675-1286 (group tours)

Location: Corner of Third and St. Joseph
Hours: 1-4 p.m. Saturday, year-round. 1-4 p.m.
Saturday and Sunday, December. Groups should
call to schedule tours.
Admission: Free
Ages: School age and up
Plan: Under one hour
Parking: Free on street
Lunch: Full selection of fast food restaurants lo-
cated one block away on West Jefferson. Also
restored Old Trenton Hotel offers elegant fare.
Facilities: Bathrooms; some gift items for sale.

Visit the two-story Victorian home, built in 1881 and authentically furnished to illustrate the times. Children will enjoy the home's children's toys, old music box and phonograph, cannonball and kitchen implements, as well as the carriage shed's old hearse, carriage, arrowheads, and tools.

SP T   Historic Village

Troy Museum and Historic Village Green

60 West Wattles, Troy
313-524-3570

Location: Corner of Wattles (Seventeen Mile Road) and Livernois
Hours: 9 a.m.-5:30 p.m., Tuesday-Saturday. 1-5 p.m., Sunday.
Admission: Free
Ages: 6 and up
Plan: Under one hour
Parking: Lot west of the museum
Lunch: Lots of restaurants in the area
Facilities: Bathrooms. Gift shop with old-fashioned toys, candy sticks, coloring books.

The Troy Museum offers several special exhibits each year of curious local artifacts. While young children might find these static exhibits boring, they will enjoy the village green's restored and furnished buildings. Buy each of the little historians a candy stick and roam around out back. You'll find a gazebo, pioneer log cabin, one-room school house, wagon shop, print shop, and the Greek Revival home of early pioneer Solomon Casewell.

SP T   African American History

Underground Railroad - Second Baptist Church

441 Monroe Avenue, Detroit
313-961-0920

Location: Monroe at Beaubien in Greektown
Hours: Pre-arranged tours by appointment only.
Admission: Free, donations accepted
Ages: 8 and older

Plan: Short visit. Tour lasts approximately one hour.
Parking: Use lots west and north of the church; the church will validate the parking ticket.
Lunch: Nearby Greektown
Facilities: Bathrooms, drinking fountain.

The Second Baptist Church was one of several Detroit stations on the famous Underground Railroad. Between 1836 and 1865, more than 5,000 fugitive slaves passed through the 12-by-13-foot windowless cellar room. For many, it was their last stop on the road to Canada and to freedom. The tour begins with an introduction in the chapel and then continues down a narrow staircase into the once-barren room. Colorful murals depict freedom routes and famous abolitionists. Church historian/tour guide Nathaniel Leach makes the era come to life. Sitting in the actual hiding room is quite an emotional experience.

SP H   Historic Inn & Barn

Walker Tavern Historic Complex
US-12, Brooklyn
517-467-4414

Location: Just north of US-12 on M-50, across the street from the Brick Walter Tavern, now an antique mart. Continue west on US-12 to antique store and flea market territory.
Hours: 10 a.m.-5 p.m., daily, Memorial Day-Labor Day
Admission: Free
Ages: 8 and older
Plan: Under one hour
Parking: Free lot
Lunch: Picnic tables and grills
Facilities: Outhouses

You can learn some interesting facts at the Walker Tavern Visitor Center. Built in the 1830s, the Walker Tavern was a regular stop on the Great Sauk Trail, the stagecoach route traveling between Detroit and Chicago. One hundred years ago, it took five days to get to Chicago from Detroit; it cost 25 cents a night and 25 cents for a meal at the tavern. Although the visitor center's exhibits are colorful and easy-to-read, they will only interest older children with a yen for history. Children of all ages will find the site's other two buildings very interesting. There's a blacksmith shop in the reconstructed barn and the Walker Tavern has been restored to look like an authentic 1840s inn, with furnished barroom, parlor, and dining room-kitchen.

SP T H   One-Room Schoolhouse

Washburn Schoolhouse

300 Dorothy Street, South Lyon
313-437-1735

Location: Just south of downtown South Lyon, in McHattie Park
Hours: 1-5 p.m., Thursday and Sunday. Call to arrange school and group tours.
Admission: Free
Ages: Elementary school children and up
Plan: Under one hour
Parking: Frèe parking in lot adjacent to museum
Lunch: Family-owned restaurants and fast-food franchises are located in town, on Lafayette and Lake Streets.
Facilities: Bathrooms, gift counter in the Witch's Hat Depot Museum.

Children get a taste of the nineteenth-century as they sit at small wooden desks in the restored schoolhouse, practicing their lessons on slates.

SP T   Historic Farmstead

Waterloo Area Farm Museum

9998 Waterloo-Munith Road, Stockbridge
517-596-2254

Location: I-94 west to exit 153. Take Clear Lake Road to Waterloo, then follow signs three miles to farm.
Hours: 1-4 p.m., Tuesday-Sunday, June-August. 1-4 p.m., Saturday and Sunday, September-early October. Last tour at 3:30 p.m.
Admission: $2.50 adults, $2 seniors, 75 cents children 5 to 11, under 5 free. Family memberships available. Ticket allows entrance to Dewey School.
Ages: 6 and up
Plan: Short visit
Parking: Free lot adjacent to farmhouse
Lunch: Picnic area on grounds and in nearby Waterloo Recreation Area

Facilities: Outhouses. Gift shop with lots of crafts and Made-in-Michigan items and toys.

The Waterloo Museum consists of an 1850s farmhouse, log cabin, and outbuildings—ice house, barn, bake house, windmill, milk cellar, and farm repair shop—that were once part of the homestead of German immigrant Jacob Ruehle. Like many families of the time, the Ruehles were industrious, thrifty, and imaginative. Their personalities live on in the homestead, furnished in detail with authentic clothing, furniture, tools, and implements. Kids will enjoy the 100-year-old gadgets, including a sausage stuffer, honey extractor, rug beater, and copper boiler. There's even a dog treadmill attached to a churn so the family pet could help make butter. Tour guides encourage young visitors to polish silver with white ash and try on the child-sized yoke with hanging buckets used to carry water up to the house from the stream. Special events are Pioneer Day in October and Christmas on the Farm in December. Three on-site programs, as well as the Dewey one-room schoolhouse tour, are available to area school children.

T	Historic Home

Willistead Manor

1899 Niagara Street, Windsor
Ontario, Canada
519-255-6545

Location: Niagara Street at Kildare Road
Hours: 1-4 p.m., First and third Sunday of each month, January-June. 1-4 p.m., Sunday-Wednesday, July-August. 1-4 p.m., Sunday, and 7-9 p.m., Wednesday, December. No tours December 24-26, 31. Last tour begins at half hour before closing.
Admission: $2.50 adults, $2 seniors, $1 children
Ages: 6 and up
Plan: Short visit
Parking: Free on site
Lunch: Many restaurants along Riverside Drive in downtown Windsor.
Facilities: Bathrooms. Christmas Shoppe in the Coach House during Christmas touring schedule.

Willistead Manor will fuel imaginative children with the stuff of great stories. The elaborately furnished home of Edward Chandler Walker, son of distillery founder Hiram Walker, spares no expense in details and materials. There are elaborate hand-carved wooden mantels, colorful furnishings, draperies, and an impressive staircase. Children will love the home's secret doorways and walk-in safe. Fifteen acres of park land offer families a wonderful place to romp.

SP T H	Grist Mill

Wolcott Mill
Kunstman Road, Ray Township
313-749-5997

Location: Kunstman Road, north of Twenty-Nine Mile Road, between Van Dyke and North Avenue in Ray Township, just outside of Romeo.
Hours: 10 a.m.-5 p.m. Monday-Friday. 10 a.m.-7 p.m., Saturday and Sunday, May-October. 10 a.m.-5 p.m., daily, April and November. Groups may also schedule tours by advance appointment.
Admission: Free
Ages: School age
Plan: Short visit; 1½ hour tour
Parking: Vehicle entry fee: $2 daily, $10 annual.
Lunch: Picnic tables
Facilities: Bathrooms

The restored 140-year-old Wolcott Mill offers imaginative displays on the milling industry, pioneer life, and farming, and many children's pioneer workshops throughout the year.

7
SCIENCE AND NATURE

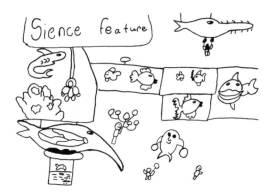

This chapter helps you cater to your children's innate curiosity about the world. Watch them soar through space at area planetariums and explore science and their environment with hands-on exhibits and activities at area science museums and nature centers. Take a family stroll through the seasons along marked trails; visit eternal summer in area conservatories lush with tropical ferns and arid cacti. Feed corn kernels to a hungry goat; watch a baby calf suckle; witness electric eels at feeding time. It's all happening at area zoos, nature centers, and petting farms.

Abbreviations: SP—site offers school programs; T—site offers group tours; H—wheelchair accessible.

SP T H   Planetarium

Abrams Planetarium
Michigan State University, East Lansing
517-355-4676, 517-355-4672 (ask the astronomer)

Location: Near Shaw and Farm Lanes, MSU campus
Hours: Building: 8:30 a.m.-Noon, 1-4:30 p.m., Monday-Friday. Planetarium shows: 8 p.m., Friday and Saturday, 2:30 and 4 p.m., Sunday.

Weekday shows for groups by appointment. Christmas show during December.

Admission: $3 adults, $2.50 students and seniors, $2 12 and under. Group rates and family memberships available.

Ages: All ages. Some shows require minimum age.

Plan: Short visit

Parking: In front of building. Free on weekends. 50 cents weekdays.

Lunch: Burger King and vending machines located in the Michigan Union, corner of Abbott and Grand River. Many other restaurants on Grand River Avenue, across from campus.

Facilities: Bathrooms. Gift shop with astronomy-related novelties, books, star maps.

The Abrams Planetarium's 360-degree domed sky theater, post-show sky talks, and blacklight space art gallery will introduce children to the wonders of the universe.

SP T H   Hands-On Science Museum

Ann Arbor Hands-On Museum
219 East Huron Street, Ann Arbor
313-995-5439

For full information, see Museums

SP T H   Greenhouses

Anna Scripps Whitcomb Conservatory
Belle Isle Park, Detroit
267-7133, 267-7134

Location: On Belle Isle

Hours: 10 a.m.-5 p.m., daily, year-round.

Admission: $1 adults, 50 cents children. Admission also allows entry to Aquarium.

Ages: All ages

Plan: Under one hour

Parking: Free on site

Lunch: Picnic area, nearby concession stands (summer only)

Facilities: Bathrooms

Each room offers children a temperate climate with lush tropical flowers, greens, and unusual cacti. Point out the orange and banana trees; listen for chirping birds. The conservatory is a particulary nice place to visit during the winter. Kids can skip from room to room, soaking in the warmth.

`SP T H`   Working Farm

Bellairs Hillside Farm and the Sheep Shed

8351 Big Lake Road, Clarkston
313-625-1181, 313-625-2665

Location: Dixie Highway and I-75
Hours: Noon-5 p.m. Tuesday-Saturday. Groups of six or more by appointment only.
Admission: Free, $1 tour packet per family
Ages: 5 and over
Plan: Short visit
Parking: Free, near farmhouse
Lunch: Picnic tables
Facilities: Bathrooms. Gift shop with wool and sheepskin clothing items, plus spinning craft supplies.

In season, kids can pet the lambs, and watch sheep being sheared and goats milked at this family-run working farm. On special days there are also spinning demonstrations, plus samples of Scotch broth and summer sausage. The Bellairs family enjoys introducing children to sheep and their products. Sheepshearing Days are held in May and October. Lamb Walks at Easter. Barn walks and Christmas Shopping open house in December.

`SP T H`   Aquarium

Belle Isle Aquarium

Belle Isle Park, Detroit
313-267-7159

Location: On Belle Isle
Hours: 10 a.m.-5 p.m., daily. Electric eel feeding shows: 10:30 a.m., 12:30, and 2:30 p.m. daily. Additional 4:30 p.m. feeding on Sunday.
Admission: $1 adults, 50 cents children. Admission also allows entry to conservatory.
Ages: All ages
Plan: Short visit

Parking: Free on site
Lunch: Picnic areas and concessions during the summer
Facilities: Bathrooms located in nearby building. Gift shop with shells and other marine items.

The green-tiled, domed building is the nation's oldest aquarium, built in 1904. Murky and still, it echoes with an underwater sensation and houses more than 200 species of fish, reptiles, and amphibians. Kids become transfixed by the exotic and the frightening aquatic creatures gliding about in 50 well-labeled tanks. Electric eel feeding shows are worth seeing. As the eels are fed, their current turns on a lightbulb and sounds a horn.

SP T H   Wildlife & Plants, Trails

Belle Isle Nature Center

Belle Isle Park, Detroit
313-267-7157

Location: On east end of Belle Isle
Hours: 10 a.m.-4 p.m., Wednesday-Sunday. Closed Mondays and Tuesdays.
Admission: Free. Donations welcome.
Ages: 5 and up
Plan: Under one hour
Parking: Free, adjacent to center
Lunch: Picnic area across the street
Facilities: Bathrooms, nature trails

Nature Center displays, exhibits, films, slide programs, and live native animals, plus two nature trails, help children better understand their environment. Kids will also be interested in the Injured Animal Shelter, which houses injured native animals and is located adjacent to the center.

SP T H   Zoo

Belle Isle Zoo

Belle Isle Park, Detroit
313-267-7160

Location: On Belle Isle
Hours: 10 a.m.-5 p.m., daily, May 1-October 31. Sea lion feedings at 11 a.m. and 4 p.m., daily.
Admission: $2 adults, $1 seniors, 50 cents 2 to 12, under 2 are free

Ages: All ages
Plan: Short visit
Parking: Free on site
Lunch: Snack stands
Facilities: Bathrooms, souvenir stand

Belle Isle Zoo's elevated boardwalk is ¾ mile long with a refreshment stand mid-way. It offers families with small children a wonderfully unique way to view over 130 animals, take a walk, and have a snack, all at the same time. Kids will love the exotic animals: pink flamingoes, kangaroos, sea lions, and the siamangs—unusual, hooting apes.

SP T H   Working Dairy Farm

Calder Brothers Dairy Farm

9334 Finzel Road, Carleton
313-654-2622

Location: South Stoney Creek and Finzel Roads. Carleton is about 70 minutes south of downtown Detroit, off I-75 south.
Hours: 10 a.m.-8 p.m., Monday-Saturday. 11 a.m.-8 p.m., Sunday. Closes at 9 p.m. during the summer. Call ahead to schedule tours.
Admission: Free for farm visit. $4.25 per person for pre-arranged tour.
Ages: All ages
Plan: Short visit
Parking: Free on site
Lunch: Picnic tables. A full-service ice cream parlor featuring Calder Brothers ice cream, plus a farm store selling Calder Brothers dairy products: milk bottled in glass, chocolate milk, buttermilk, sour cream, butter, eggs, and egg nog.
Facilities: Bathrooms. Farm store also sells jellies, jams, and hand-woven baskets.

Visit a true working dairy farm. The kids will enjoy petting and watching the animals—lots of cows, plus peacocks, dogs, burros, and geese. Buy milk in bottles and enjoy delicious handmade ice cream. Pre-arranged tours include milking a cow by hand, bottle feeding a calf, watching a cow being machine-milked, and watching how milk is stored for transport to the Calder Brothers processing plant. Each tour participant also receives a complimentary ice cream cone.

SP T H   Nature Center, Trails

Carl F. Fenner Arboretum

2020 East Mt. Hope Avenue, Lansing
517-483-4224

Location: Trowbridge Road exit off I-496, south
on Harrison Road, west on Mt. Hope Avenue
Hours: Grounds: 8 a.m.-dusk, daily. Nature Cen-
ter Building: 9 a.m.-4 p.m., Tuesday-Friday. 10
a.m.-5 p.m., Saturday. 11 a.m.-5 p.m., Sunday
Admission: Free
Ages: All ages
Plan: Short visit
Parking: Free on site
Lunch: Picnic area
Facilities: Bathrooms. Nature center gift shop
(open on the weekends) sells nature-oriented col-
oring books, story books, magnifying glasses,
polished stones.

For a 5-cent donation, children can buy packets
of crackers to throw to the birds, geese, and
squirrels living within the Fenner Arboretum's 120
acres. Walking along the easy trails you'll also
find an herb garden, waterfowl pond, replica of a
pioneer cabin, and if you're lucky, you'll catch a
glimpse of the arboretum's American bison. The
nature center houses displays, touch-me exhibits, and live Michigan animals. Seasonal events
are the Maple Syrup Festival in March and the
Apple Butter Festival in October.

SP T H   Petting Farm

Charles L. Bowers Farm

1219 East Square Lake Road, Bloomfield Hills
313-645-4830

Location: Off I-75 between Adams and Squirrel
Roads
Hours: Pre-arranged tours available 10 a.m.-3
p.m., weekdays. Open Barn Days, free to the
public two Saturdays in fall and spring.
Admission: $2 per person for tour
Ages: Preschool to 12th grade
Plan: Short visit
Parking: Free on site
Lunch: Lots of restaurants located on Telegraph
Road

Facilities: Bathrooms

Children will cherish the Charles L. Bowers School Farm experience, offered as part of a group tour or during the several Open Barn Days throughout the year. They can observe and participate in many rural activities—milking cows, churning butter, harvesting crops, spinning wool, feeding barnyard animals, preserving food, making cheese, and going on a hayride.

SP T H   Planetarium

Children's Museum Planetarium
67 East Kirby, Detroit
313-494-1210

Location: In the Cultural Center, just north of the Detroit Institute of Arts. A prancing silver horse sculpture made of chrome car bumpers sits on the front lawn.
Hours: Planetarium demonstrations: 11 a.m. and 1 p.m., Saturday. Afternoons only during the summer.
Admission: $1
Ages: Geared to elementary school-age children
Plan: Under one hour
Parking: Use metered parking along Kirby or park in the Science Center lot on John R ($3) and walk a block to the museum
Lunch: Eat across the street in the DIA Kresge Court Cafe
Facilities: Bathrooms, drinking fountain. Gift shop with lots of handmade and unique toys and gifts.

Planetarium shows are held in a small intimate second-story room. With a sense of humor and wonder, they offer explanations of seasonal wonders, folk tales, and legends relating to the night sky. They are wonderful first-time experiences for young children.

SP T H   Greenhouses, Petting Farm

Colasanti's Tropical Gardens
Ruthven, Ontario, Canada
519-326-3287

Location: Off Highway 3, approximately 25 miles from the Ambassador Bridge

Hours: 8 a.m.-5 p.m., Monday-Thursday. 8 a.m.-7 p.m., Friday-Sunday.
Admission: Free
Ages: All ages
Plan: Short visit
Parking: Free on site
Lunch: Picnic table area and snack bar with hot dogs, soft drinks, ice cream, and snacks
Facilities: Bathrooms. Almost all of the hundreds of species of tropical plants and cacti are for sale (only bulbs and citrus can't be brought back through U.S. customs).

Enter a tropical rain forest or warming desert, and see 15 greenhouses full of brilliant tropical flowers and unusual cacti. Mixed in with these fragrant and colorful plants are exotic birds and a barnyard of animals to pet and play with, from sheep and goats to an ostrich and bison. On the weekends, pony rides for children are available for $1.

SP T H   Working Dairy Farm

Cook's Farm Dairy

2950 Seymour Lake Road, Ortonville
313-627-3329

Location: Take I-75 north to M-15 north. Go east on Seymour Lake Road one mile.
Hours: Summer: 9 a.m.-10 p.m., Monday-Saturday. 2-10 p.m., Sunday. Winter: 9 a.m.-8 p.m., Monday-Saturday. 2-8 p.m., Sunday. Call to schedule tours for groups of ten or more.
Admission: Free for grounds and farm store. $2 per person for tour, includes a complimentary ice cream cone and glass of Cook's chocolate milk.
Ages: All ages
Plan: Short visit. Tour takes approximately one hour.
Parking: Free on site
Lunch: Picnic tables. Ice cream parlor with Cook's ice cream, farm store with Cook's dairy products—all made on premises.
Facilities: Outhouses. Farm store also sells seasonal items such as honey and pumpkins.

After visiting Cook's Farm Dairy, toddlers will have no problem telling you what a cow says. Cows are everywhere, lounging on the grass, nosing up against the fence. You can visit the cows in the barn and treat the family to an ice cream cone, or call ahead for the tour and still enjoy an ice cream cone. The informal tours start in the cow barn. After meeting newborn calves, you are taken into the production plant for a dry run of the process that turns cows' milk into ice cream and chocolate milk. The tour ends in the ice cream parlor/farm store with a complimentary cone and glass of chocolate milk.

SP T H   Hands-On Science Museum

Cranbrook Institute of Science
500 Lone Pine Road, Bloomfield Hills
313-645-3200

For full information, see Museums

SP T H   Planetarium

Cranbrook Institute of Science Planetarium
500 Lone Pine Road, Bloomfield Hills
313-645-3200

Location: Use the entrance to the Cranbrook Educational Community, the farthest east off Lone Pine Road between Lahser and Cranbrook Roads. You'll know you're there when you see the stegosaurus.
Hours: Lasera Shows: 7:30, 8:30, 9:30, 10:30 p.m., Friday. 2:15, 3:45, 8:30, 9:30, 10:30, 11:30 p.m., Saturday. 2:15 and 3:45 p.m., Sunday. Planetarium Shows: 12:30, 1:30, 3, 7:30 p.m., Saturday. 1:30 and 3 p.m., Sunday. Additional shows are added during holidays and school vacations.
Admission: $4 adults, $3 children ages 3 to 17 and seniors, children under 3 free. Family membership available. Group rates available on weekdays. Planetarium: $1 additional, members free. Lasera: $1.50 additional, for daytime shows. $2 after 6 p.m.
Ages: 5 and up for most lasera and planetarium shows. 3 and up are admitted to the holiday show, "Ornaments."
Plan: Shows are approximately one hour
Parking: Free on site
Lunch: A lunch room with vending machines
Facilities: Bathrooms, drinking fountain on lower level. Two gift shops offer a wonderful

selection of science toys. The Dino Shop specializes in dinosaur gifts; the lobby shop has everything else.

Cranbrook Institute of Science offers creative, colorful, and educational stargazing shows, and sound and light lasera shows in a state-of-the-art planetarium. Older children and teens will especially enjoy the lasera shows set to rock music.

SP T H   Hands-On Science Museum

Detroit Science Center
5020 John R, Detroit
313-577-8400

For full information, see Museums

SP T H   Omnimax Theater

Detroit Science Center Space Theater
5020 John R, Detroit
313-577-8400

Location: One mile east of Woodward on the corner of Warren and John R
Hours: The Space Theater shows Omnimax movies every hour . 10:30 a.m.-1:30 p.m., Monday-Friday. 12:30-5:30 p.m., Saturday and Sunday. Closed major holidays.
Admission: Omnimax Theater is included in general admission: $6.50 adults and children 13 and up, $4.50 children 12 and under and seniors, under 4 free. Family membership gives you free admission to Cranbrook Institute of Science and Lansing's Impression 5 Museum.
Ages: All ages, but preschoolers might be uncomfortable with the Omnimax movie's motion and speed
Plan: Movies vary from 30 minutes to one hour
Parking: Lot adjacent to entrance, off John R, $3 all day parking
Lunch: Eat in the DIA's Kresge Court Cafe Wednesday-Sunday.
Facilities: Bathrooms and drinking fountain on exhibit floor. Gift shop near entrance has great science, dino, and space items.

Omnimax's 360-degree domed screen will fill your senses and immerse you in the middle of the action. You might be soaring above the earth, caught in a windstorm, or rushing down a waterfall. Nature's most beautiful images are caught in vivid breadth and color.

SP T H   Zoo

Detroit Zoological Park

8450 West Ten Mile Road, Royal Oak
313-398-0900

Location: Ten Mile and Woodward Avenue. Entrance off Woodward, north of Ten Mile.
Hours: 10 a.m.-5 p.m., daily, May-October. 10 a.m.-4 p.m., Wednesday-Sunday, November-April.
Daily Feeding Schedule: Penquins: 10:30-noon; Polar Bears: 2-2:30 p.m.; Sea Lions: 11 a.m. and 3 p.m.; Elephants: 1 p.m. May 1-Labor Day.
Admission: $6 adults, $4 seniors, $3 children 2 to 12, under 2 free. Includes zoo train (trains operate daily May 1 through October 1, weekends through November 1, then shut down until May 1). Family membership and group rates available.
Ages: All ages
Plan: Half day visit
Parking: $3 cars, $6 buses. Use parking garage across from entrance
Lunch: Picnic areas, tables, food concessions
Facilities: Bathrooms, drinking fountains, gift concessions. Kids Kabs (strollers) $3+$1 deposit/day. Roller Chairs (fits an adult or 3 kids) $5/day+$1 deposit.

The Detroit Zoo offers families several attractions all rolled into one admission. There are wonderful outdoor exhibits of animals both exotic and exciting, including the "Chimps of Harambee," a four-acre African rain forest environment. There are indoor exhibits—the bird house, reptile house, and penguinarium. For small children, there's a barnyard full of farm animals and the zoo train you can ride from one end of the zoo to the other as much as you want. The Log Cabin Learning Center (located near the train station on the far end of the zoo) offers lots of hands-on experiences for learning about animals up close. Special events occur throughout the year, including the Zoo Boo at Halloween.

SP T H   Nature Center, Trails

Dinosaur Hill Nature Preserve and Den

333 North Hill Circle, Rochester
313-656-0999

Location: Tienken and Rochester Roads
Hours: Nature den: 9 a.m.-2 p.m., Monday. 9 a.m.-5 p.m., Tuesday-Friday. Noon-3 p.m., Saturday and Sunday, Labor Day-2nd weekend in June. 9 a.m.-3 p.m., Monday-Friday. 10 a.m.-3 p.m., Saturday. Noon-3 p.m., Sunday, 3rd week in June-Labor Day. Trails: dawn to dusk. There are trail maps in the metal mailbox attached to the den.
Admission: Free. A fee is charged for group tours, classes, and special events.
Ages: All ages
Plan: Short visit
Parking: Free on street
Lunch: Picnic area
Facilities: Bathrooms. Squirrel Corner Gift Shop offers many inexpensive nature and dinosaur related items.

This gem of a city park sits quietly in the corner of a tidy neighborhood. In spite of its name, Dinosaur Hill is not a repository of dinosaur bones, but 16 heavily wooded acres full of trails and the Dinosaur Den, a combination nature center-library-classroom-gift shop. The den is full of nests, eggs, stuffed birds, small forest animals, butterflies, an aquarium, and fossils. There are lots of hands-on artifacts and small eye lenses to encourage a closer look. The den offers classes, summer camp, birthday parties, and special seasonal events.

SP T   Nature Center, Trails

Drayton Plains Nature Center

2125 Denby Drive, Drayton Plains
313-674-2119

Location: ¼ mile west off Dixie Highway, on Hatchery Road
Hours: Grounds only: sunrise to dusk, daily. Interpretive Center: 10 a.m.-4 p.m., Saturday. Noon-4 p.m., Sunday. Group tours are available

at mutually convenient times and can be arranged by calling ahead.

Admission: Grounds and interpretive center free. Minimum fee for group tour.
Ages: School age children and up
Plan: Short visit. Tours are approximately 1½ hours.
Parking: Free on site
Lunch: Picnic tables on site
Facilities: Bathrooms. Nature store with field guides, books, and coloring books for children.

Once the old state fish hatchery, Drayton Plains Nature Center sits on 137 acres on the banks of the Clinton River. Prairie, woods, and wetland make up its varied topography. Families can enjoy the outdoors year-round on 4½ miles of marked nature trails. There are a variety of touch-and-see nature exhibits inside the Interpretive Center, including large fish tanks displaying local fish, such as blue gill and bass. There are a variety of group tour programs; one of the most popular includes a brief visit to a pioneer log cabin on the grounds.

SP T H   Trails

E.L. Johnson Nature Center
3325 Franklin Road, Bloomfield Hills
313-339-3497

Location: On Franklin Road, south of Hickory Grove, north of Long Lake Road
Hours: 8 a.m.-dusk, Monday-Friday. 10 a.m.-4 p.m., most weekends. Children and families can sign up for classes run by the Bloomfield Hills Parks and Recreation. Special pre-arranged tours are also available.
Admission: Free for trails, minimum fee for programs
Ages: All ages
Plan: Under one hour
Parking: Free on site
Lunch: Telegraph Road offers a variety of fast-food restaurants
Facilities: Bathroom in visitor center

This 32-acre site offers families a quiet trail through wooded terrain, dappled with wild flowers and a meandering stream. There are also wild animals—foxes, ducks, deer, and owls—that make their home in the woods.

SP T H   Hands-On Science Museum

Ella Sharp Museum— Discovery Gallery

3225 Fourth Street, Jackson
517-787-2320

For full information, see Historic Sites

SP T H   Education Center, Trails

For-Mar Nature Preserve and Aboretum and De Waters Education Center

5360 East Potter Road, Burton
313-736-7100

Location: Northeast of downtown Flint in Burton
Hours: Education Center: Hours vary; call for an appointment. Nature Preserve and Arboretum: 8 a.m.-sunset, daily. For a guided hike, call for an appointment.
Admission: Free. Guided nature hikes, $1.
Ages: All ages
Plan: Short visit
Parking: Free
Lunch: Picnicking on grounds is prohibited.
Facilities: Bathroom inside education center

For a first-hand look at nature, take a guided naturalist walk through the nature preserve's 380 acres; a handicapped-accessible trail is also available. The De Waters Education Center offers a demonstration bee-hive, and please-touch-me nature games, exhibits, and displays.

T H   Conservatory and Trails

Hidden Lake Gardens

M-50, Tipton
517-431-2060

Location: On M-50, five miles west of junction of M-50 and M-52
Hours: 8 a.m.-dusk, daily April-October. 8 a.m.-4 p.m., daily November-March.

Admission: $3 weekends and holidays, $1 weekdays. Family memberships available.
Ages: All ages
Plan: Short visit
Parking: Free on site
Lunch: Picnic tables
Facilities: Bathrooms. Gift shop in visitor center has science items, "Hidden Lake" and Michigan State t-shirts and sweatshirts.

Walk the scented trails, feed swans, picnic amid tall pine trees, drive through six miles of winding roads, and wander through the conservatory's unique tropical and arid plants. Hidden Lake Gardens, owned by Michigan State University and full of Spartan spirit, is a peaceful spot to stop on your way west across the state.

`SP T H`   Greenhouse, Gardens

Horticultural Gardens
Michigan State University, East Lansing
517-355-0348

Location: Bogue and Wilson Streets, across from the Veterinary Clinic, on the MSU campus
Hours: Greenhouse: 8 a.m.-5 p.m., Monday-Friday, year-round. Gardens: Dawn-dusk.
Admission: Free
Ages: All ages
Plan: Under one hour
Parking: Lot adjacent to gardens. $1 parking token can be purchased inside greenhouse.
Lunch: Burger King and vending machines are located in the Michigan Union, corner of Abbott and Grand River. Many other restaurants are located on Grand River Avenue, across from campus.
Facilities: Bathrooms in greenhouse

The Horticultural Center includes a garden of beautiful annuals and perennials and a teaching greenhouse, full of seasonal flowers and greens.

`SP T`   Trails

Howell Nature Center
1005 Triangle Lake Road, Howell
517-546-0249

Howell Nature Center is primarily a wildlife rehabilitation center, housing injured wildlife.

While the center does not offer public hours, it does offer some scheduled school or group tours, school outreach programs, nature trails, and cross-country ski trails in the winter. Call ahead to schedule tours, school programs, and use of trails.

SP T H   Nature Interpretive Centers

Huron-Clinton Metroparks Nature Centers

The following metroparks have nature centers with hands-on exhibits for children, live Michigan animals, nature trails, and year-round programs. Vehicle permits $2 daily, $15 annual. General hours: 10 a.m.-5 p.m., daily during the summer. 1-5 p.m., Monday-Friday. 10 a.m.-5 p.m., weekends, during the school year. School groups should call for appointment. Call 1-800-47-PARKS or the individual nature center for more information. *See* Parks.

Indian Springs Nature Center
5200 Indian Trail, Clarkston
313-625-7280

Kensington Nature Center and Farm Center
2240 West Buno Road, Milford
313-685-1561

Hudson Mills Visitor Center
8801 North Territorial Road, Dexter
313-476-8211
(No nature center; naturalist will accommodate pre-arranged school and scout groups)

Metro Beach Nature Center
Metropolitan Parkway, Mt. Clemens
313-463-4332

Oakwoods Nature Center
Huron River Drive, Flat Rock
313-782-3956

Stony Creek Nature Center
4300 Main Park Road, Washington
313-781-4621

SP T H Hands-On Science Museum

Impression 5 Museum

200 Museum Drive, Lansing
517-485-8116

For full information, see Museums

SP T H Nature Center

Independence Oaks Nature Center

9501 Sashabaw Road, Clarkston
313-625-6473

Location: 2½ miles north of I-75 on Sashabaw
Road
Hours: 10 a.m.-6 p.m., daily, Memorial Day-Labor Day. 10 a.m.-5 p.m., Tuesday-Sunday, school
year. Trail hours: 8 a.m.-dusk. Family classes and
programs are offered year-round. Call ahead to
book groups.
Admission: Park entry fee, free admission to
nature center
Ages: All ages
Plan: Short visit
Parking: On site
Lunch: Picnic areas available on rental basis
Facilities: Bathrooms. Amphitheater located
adjacent to nature center.

Children will enjoy the discovery area's miniaturized exhibits and life-sized dioramas designed
especially for hands-on learning. They will also
enjoy looking through the windows and observing
wildlife in the center's outdoor feeding station
and exploring the constellations in Starlab, a
portable planetarium. A 200-seat amphitheatre
offers many year-round family programs.

SP T H Bird Sanctuary

Jack Miner Bird Sanctuary

Kingsville, Ontario, Canada
519-733-4034

Location: Three miles north of Kingsville, off Division Road (Road #29)
Hours: 9 a.m.-5 p.m., Monday-Saturday, year-round. October and November are peak migration months. Grounds are open 8 a.m.-sundown.

Admission: Free
Ages: All ages
Plan: Short visit
Parking: Free on site
Lunch: Picnic area
Facilities: Bathrooms, playground

Thousands of Canadian geese stop off at the Jack Miner Sanctuary during October and November on their way south. Children are encouraged to feed the waterfowl with handfuls of grain from the barley bucket located near the sanctuary's pond. Try to plan your trip for early morning or late afternoon. The geese come in for breakfast between 7 and 8 a.m. At 4 p.m., the geese put on an "airshow." They take off and land when a three-wheeled, all-terrain vehicle drives through the flocks.

SP T H   Petting Farm

Kiwanis Children's Farm
Lake Chipican Drive, off Christina Street
Sarnia, Ontario, Canada
519-332-0330, ext. 209

Location: Christina Street and Cathcart Boulevard, 1 mile north of Highway 402
Hours: 9:30 a.m.-8 p.m., June-August. 7:30 a.m.-4:30 p.m., September-May.
Admission: Free
Ages: All ages
Plan: Short visit
Parking: Free on site
Lunch: Picnic areas, concessions
Facilities: Bathrooms, playground

Within Cantara Park along Lake Huron is the small petting farm, perfect for young children. The farm has both domestic animals and poultry. Adjacent to the farm are three historic buildings: a pioneer log cabin, smoke house, and carriage house.

SP T H   Working Farm

Langenderfer Farm
11840 Strasburg Road, Erie
313-856-4283

Location: Take Telegraph Road six miles south of Monroe to Woods Road. Go west one mile to Strasburg Road. Go south ¼ mile to farm.
Hours: 9 a.m.-5 p.m., Monday-Saturday, March-June. Fall hours vary. Farm is open to the public. Call ahead for a tour.
Admission: $3.50 per person for tour includes beverage and homemade doughnut.
Ages: All ages
Plan: Short visit
Parking: Free on site
Lunch: Indoor picnic area
Facilities: Bathrooms

Visit during the spring and learn how eggs are incubated to produce chicks and ducklings. Visit during the fall and enjoy a pumpkin and Halloween experience. *See* Michigan at work.

SP T H   Conservation, Nature Center

Leslie Science Center and Project Grow

1831 Traver Road, Ann Arbor
313-662-7802

Location: Traver Road and Barton Drive, east of Plymouth Road
Hours: Grounds open sunrise-dusk, daily. Call two weeks ahead for tours of display area.
Admission: Free
Ages: 3 and up
Plan: Under one hour
Parking: Free on site
Lunch: Restaurants are located nearby on UofM campus.
Facilities: Bathrooms in main residence. Project Grow office has t-shirts and homegrown honey.

Leslie Science Center is a site for conservation related experiences, training, and education. Children will enjoy the indoor observation beehive and worm box. The center holds spring and fall festivals, workshops, birthday parties, and summer camp. Project Grow sponsors area community gardens.

SP T H   Nature Center, Trails

Lloyd A. Stage Outdoor Education Center

6685 Coolidge Highway, Troy
313-524-3567

Location: ¾ mile north of Square Lake Road, on Coolidge Highway
Hours: 8:30 a.m.-4:30 p.m., Tuesday-Saturday. Noon-8 p.m., Sunday, Memorial Day-Labor Day. Scout and school groups are encouraged to call to arrange programs and tours.
Admission: Free
Ages: All ages
Plan: Short visit. Tours are approximately 1½ hours.
Parking: Free on site
Lunch: Picnic area
Facilities: Bathrooms. Gift shop with bird books, feeders, t-shirts, and notecards.

Lloyd A. Stage Outdoor Education Center includes 99 acres of rolling meadow, forest, and stream, plus a farm site and Interpretive Center. The Interpretive Center houses exhibits, dioramas, hands-on displays, and a gift shop. The self-guided nature trails are well marked and maps are available. The center also offers year-round family classes and outings. A Junior Naturalist Club is available for children. Maple Sugar Festival and Rent-a-Maple program in March.

SP T H   Planetarium

Longway Planetarium

1310 East Kearsley Street, Flint
313-760-1181

Location: Flint's Cultural Center, exit Longway Boulevard off I-475
Hours: Office 8 a.m.-5 p.m., Monday-Friday. Call for Laser and Planetarium shows; their hours vary.
Admission: $5 depending on show. Group rates available.
Ages: All ages, but age requirements varies with show; call ahead
Plan: Short visit
Parking: Free on site

Lunch: Picnicking on planetarium lawn is permitted in warm weather
Facilities: Bathrooms. Gift shop with space, hologram, and star gazing gifts—gyroscopes, prisms, star explorers.

The Longway Planetarium is a treat for children of all ages. Be sure to call ahead to time your visit to one of their planetarium shows or laser shows set to rock music. Kids will also like the two 55-foot space murals lining the circular outer wall of the planetarium. Created with luminescent paint on black canvas, the murals make you feel as if you are looking out into space.

SP T H   Petting Farm

Maybury State Park Petting Farm
20145 Beck Road, Northville
313-349-8390

Location: Entrance off Eight Mile Road, six miles west of I-275
Hours: Park: 8 a.m.-10 p.m., daily year-round. After Labor Day, park closes at dusk. Farm: 10 a.m.-5 p.m., daily year-round.
Admission: Minimal fee for farm tour.
Ages: Preschool to 11 years
Plan: Short visit
Parking: $3.50 vehicle entrance fee. $15 yearly permit fee.
Lunch: Picnic area
Facilities: Outhouses, nearby playground. Hayrides at riding stables by reservation, bike trails, cross-country ski rentals and trails.

Super-sized bunnies, honking geese, and shy turkeys share the spacious two-story barn with cows, pigs, and goats. Visit during early spring and you'll be rewarded with a new crop of animal babies. You'll also meet Farmer Beemer, the Maybury Park ranger, who's usually on hand to answer questions. Maybury playground, with one the area's best wooded all-purpose climbers, is nearby—if you can pry your little ones away from the animals.

SP T H   Space Museum

Michigan Space Center

2111 Emmons Road, Jackson
517-787-4425

For full information, see Museums

SP T H   Natural History Museum

MSU Museum

101 West Circle Drive
Michigan State University Campus
East Lansing
517-355-2370

For full information, see Museums

SP T H   Petting Farm

Mott Farm

6140 Bray Road, Flint
313-760-1795

Location: Just north of Flint. Follow I-475 off either I-75 or I-69 to Carpenter Road (exit 11). Same entrance as Crossroads Village/Huckleberry Railroad.
Hours: 10 a.m.-5 p.m., Monday-Friday. 10 a.m.-6:30 p.m., Saturday and Sunday, May 1-November 1
Admission: $1 adult, 50 cents children, 3 and under free. Group rates available.
Ages: Preschool to early elementary
Plan: Short visit
Parking: Free on site
Lunch: Picnic areas
Facilities: Port-a-johns

Mott Petting Farm's two barns are full to the brim with animals gentle enough to pet and feed. Children will enjoy a quick visit to the farm before or after a visit to Crossroads Village/Huckleberry Railroad.

`SP T H`   Nature Center, Trails

Ojibway Park and Nature Center

5200 Matchette Road, Windsor
Ontario, Canada
519-966-5852

Location: Next to Windsor Raceway off Highway 3
Hours: Trails: 5 a.m.-midnight. Center: 10 a.m.-5 p.m., daily
Admission: Free
Ages: All ages
Plan: Short visit
Parking: Free in adjacent lots
Lunch: Picnic tables
Facilities: Restrooms; bird books and birdseed for sale

Ojibway Park offers an 160-acre forest and prairie clearing with shady picnic areas. The nature center is devoted to exhibits and displays on wildlife. Children are encouraged to handle the displays and get to know the center's snakes and turtles.

`SP T`   Zoo

Potter Park Zoo

1301 South Pennsylvania Avenue, Lansing
517-483-4221

Location: 4 blocks south of I-496
Hours: Zoo buildings: 9 a.m.-7 p.m., daily, Memorial Day-Labor Day. 9 a.m.-5 p.m. daily, after Labor Day. Park: 8 a.m.-dusk, daily, year-round.
Admission: $2 adults, $1 children.
Ages: All ages
Plan: Short visit
Parking: $1.50 vehicle admission
Lunch: Picnic areas and food concessions (summer only)
Facilities: Bathrooms, gift concessions

Children will enjoy visiting this zoo located in hilly Potter Park. They'll find a variety of animals as well as activities. There are 400 animals, including large cats, primates, an elephant, and wallaby, a penguinarium, farmyard with farm animals, small children's contact center, playground, and in the summer, pony and camel rides.

SP T H   Zoo, Petting Farm

Ruby Farms

6567 Imlay City Road, Ruby
313-324-2662

Location: Just northwest of Port Huron
Hours: 11 a.m.-5 p.m., Wednesday-Sunday,
September-Christmas
Admission: Small fee
Ages: Especially geared for preschool and early
elementary
Plan: Short visit
Parking: Free on site
Lunch: Cider mill/restaurant
Facilities: Bathrooms, gift shop

Ruby Farms offers city children a chance to frolic
in the country, pet and feed a variety of farm animals, as well as watch several exotic zoo-type
animals. The farm offers fresh cider from its cider
mill/restaurant, and in November and December,
cut-your-own Christmas trees.

SP T H   Nature Center, Trails

Seven Ponds Nature Center

3854 Crawford Road, Dryden
313-796-3419

Location: North of Pontiac, east off M-24 on
Dryden Road
Hours: 9 a.m.-5 p.m., Tuesday-Sunday. 2 p.m.
Sunday family programs or nature walks, year-
round.
Admission: $5 family, $1.50 adults, 75 cents
children
Ages: All ages
Plan: Short visit
Parking: Free on site
Lunch: Picnic area
Facilities: Bathrooms. Gift shop-bookstore with
children's books and bird-feeding supplies.

Children are encouraged to touch and explore at
the Seven Ponds Nature Center. Inside the Interpretive Building, there are natural history
collections of skins, insects, and minerals, a
touch table for handling items, and an observation beehive for close inspection of bee activity.
Outside, there are trails.

SP T H   Fishing

Spring Valley Trout Farm

12190 Island Lake Road, Dexter
313-426-4772

Location: I-94 west to exit 167 (Dexter), then four miles west of Dexter to Island Lake Road
Hours: Spring and fall: 9 a.m.-6 p.m., Saturday and Sunday. Memorial Day-Labor Day: 9 a.m.-6 p.m., Wednesday-Sunday.
Admission: $2 for 6 years and older, under 6 free. You pay per pound for all you catch; fish can't be thrown back into the pond. Fish are packaged in ice free of charge. There is a small fee for cleaning the fish.
Ages: 2 and up for fishing
Plan: Short visit
Parking: Free on site
Lunch: Vending machines, snacks, picnic areas with grills
Facilities: Bathroom, white pine lodge

For a first fishing experience, you can't beat Spring Valley Trout Farm. With admission, you are given all the equipment you need—life jacket (for children under 11), pail, poles, hooks, and worms. Helpful staff members show you how to cut off a section of worm, snag it on the hook, and toss your line into the spring-fed pond. The fact that you are guaranteed a catch is the most amazing part for children (and you'll notice adults get very excited, too). For little ones, there is a small children's pond. They can also feed the 20,000 or more trout fingerlings in the trout farm's rearing areas—fish food is available in the lodge for 10 cents.

SP T   Planetarium

Starlab

Independence Oaks Nature Center
9501 Sashabaw Road, Clarkston
313-625-6473

Location: 2½ miles north of I-75 on Sashabaw Road. Skylab is set up inside a nature center classroom.

Hours: By appointment only; for school and civic groups. Families are welcome to sign up for workshops or attend evening "Star Parties," held four times a year, at the beginning of each new season.
Admission: $50/first program; $40 additional show
Ages: 1st grade and up
Plan: 45-minute show
Parking: On site. Park entry fee.
Lunch: Covered picnic sites nearby
Facilities: The nature center includes a please-touch-me exhibit room and 10-miles of outdoor trails.

SP T H   Nature Center

Sterling Heights Nature Center

42700 Utica Road, Sterling Heights
313-739-6731

Location: Van Dyke and Utica Roads, one block east of Van Dyke
Hours: 10 a.m.-5 p.m., Monday-Thursday and Saturday. 1-5 p.m., Sunday. Closed Friday. Tours may be pre-scheduled at convenient times.
Admission: Free
Ages: 3 and up
Plan: Short visit
Parking: Free on site
Lunch: Picnicking is permitted. Auditorium may be used as a lunchroom.
Facilities: Bathrooms

The Sterling Heights Nature Center, part of the city's parks and recreation department, sits on seven acres overlooking the Clinton River. The display room features hands-on natural science experiences. There are live snakes, turtles and fish, nature puzzles, mystery boxes, and animal skins. Family nature movies are shown 7:30 p.m., Tuesday and Wednesday. Nature classes and programs are also offered for children and adults.

SP T H   Nature Preserve, Trails

University of Michigan-Dearborn Environmental Study Area

News and Information, Dearborn
313-593-5338

Location: On the grounds of the Henry Ford Fairlane Estate, 4901 Evergreen Road, west of Fairlane Town Center
Hours: Dawn-Dusk
Admission: Free
Ages: All ages
Plan: Short visit
Parking: Lot adjacent to Ford estate power-house
Lunch: Picnicking is not allowed. The Ford estate's Pool Restaurant is open 11 a.m.- 2 p.m., Monday-Friday, year-round. Many restaurants are available in Fairlane Town Center.
Facilities: Self-guided nature trails, maps available for small fee in parking lot boxes

Nature lovers are encouraged to visit the sprawling nature area on the Rouge River that was once part of Henry Ford's estate. Special seasonal nature hikes are held throughout the year and a special family treasure hunt-nature walk, "The Wizards Were Here," is also available.

SP T H   Natural History Museum

University of Michigan Exhibit Museum
1109 Geddes Avenue, Ann Arbor
313-763-6085
313-764-0478 (group tours)

For full information, see Museums

SP T H   Planetarium

University of Michigan Exhibit Museum Planetarium
1109 Geddes, Ann Arbor
313-764-0478

Location: Fourth floor of the UofM Exhibit Museum, corner of Geddes and Washtenaw Avenues on the U of M campus
Hours: 10:30 and 11:30 a.m., Saturday; tickets go on sale at 9 a.m. 2, 3, and 4 p.m., Saturday and Sunday; tickets go on sale at 1 p.m. Special Christmas Shows are offered during December and at extra times during vacation week. Groups may pre-arrange shows at convenient times.

Admission: $2 for Saturday morning shows. $2.50 for Saturday and Sunday afternoon shows.
Ages: All ages for Saturday morning shows. Age 5 and up for Saturday and Sunday afternoon shows.
Plan: Shows are approximately 35 minutes
Parking: Use street meters or Fletcher Street parking lot
Lunch: Many restaurants on campus
Facilities: Bathrooms. Gift shop with many inexpensive dinosaur and natural history items.

While most families come to the Exhibit Museum to see dinosaurs, the planetarium offers another trip into the exciting realm of natural science and creates a realistic image of the night sky on its 360° dome. Shows are imaginative and most interesting for children 5 and up.

SP T H   Greenhouse, Trails

University of Michigan
Matthaei Botanical Gardens

1800 North Dixboro Road, Ann Arbor
313-998-7061

Location: Take US-23 north, exit at Geddes Road, and turn right. At Dixboro Road, turn left. Gardens are 1½ miles on your right.
Hours: Conservatory: 10 a.m.-4:30 p.m., daily. Grounds: 8 a.m.-sunset. Group tours available. Call three weeks in advance.
Admission: $1 for conservatory. Under 6 free. Grounds are free.
Ages: All ages
Plan: Short visit
Parking: Free on site
Lunch: You'll find restaurants going west on Geddes or driving into UofM's campus
Facilities: Bathrooms. Gift shop with t-shirts, mugs, and botanical items.

It's perpetual summer in the Matthaei Botanical Gardens Conservatory. Lush tropical plants with vivid reds and pinks, exotic banana and lemon trees, and huge exotic cacti capture children's attention. They will also enjoy peering into two ponds full of gliding koi. Four outdoor trails are marked for a self-guided stroll revealing seasonal changes. Maps are available in the conservatory.

SP T H   Nature Center

Waterloo Geology Center

Waterloo Recreation Area, McClure Road
Chelsea
313-475-3170

Location: Off McClure Road in the Waterloo
Recreation Area
Hours: 9 a.m.-5 p.m., daily
Admission: $3.50 daily vehicle pass
Ages: All ages
Plan: Short visit. The nature trails have walking
times of 20 minutes to one hour.
Parking: Free on site
Lunch: Picniking sites are located on the far east
side of the recreation area
Facilities: Bathrooms, gift shop

While the emphasis is on rocks, the center also
offers children a chance to see stuffed animals
and birds and honeybee hives. There are several
nature trails, plus a geology trail with many large
examples of rocks found in the around the Waterloo Recreation Area.

SP T H   Nature Center/Trails

Woldumar Nature Center

5539 Lansing Road, Lansing
517-322-0030

Location: Southwest Lansing, 1 mile north of
I-96, off Lansing Road exit.
Hours: Trails: Dawn-dusk. Center: 9 a.m.-5 p.m.,
Monday-Friday; weekend hours vary.
Admission: Trails: 50 cents/person. Center is
free. Fee for special seasonal events. $1.50/per-
son (minimum $20) for 2-hour naturalist-led pro-
gram.
Ages: All ages
Plan: Short visit
Parking: Free in lot
Lunch: Space available for groups only
Facilities: Bathrooms and gift shop in nature
center

The 188-acre nature preserve offers a variety of
habitats, including a Beech and Maple hard-
woods forest, Spruce and Pine plantation, Grand
River frontage and pond, as well as a variety of

wildlife—deer, fox, and great blue herons. The nature center offers animal mounts, a bird feeding observation area, and reading room.

8
SEASONAL
HARVEST

Here are enough farmers' markets, u-pick farms, and cider mills to keep you out of doors and full of fresh foods all year long. Kids love bustling farmers' markets. Take your little red wagon to pull the kids and the crops, and be sure to peek under produce-laden tables; you just might find bunnies hidden in crates.

Or pick the produce yourself at Michigan's u-pick farms. Many offer a variety of activities during harvest season, from blue-grass music and hay rides to petting farms and candle dipping. How can you resist freshly picked strawberries in June, raspberries in July, peaches in August, or apples, cider, and donuts in September? During October, many farms offer Halloween activities plus pumpkin and gourd picking. Beginning Thanksgiving weekend, tree farms offer Christmas activities—a visit with Santa, a sleigh ride, and a chance to choose your own Christmas tree. "Quick Look Lists" list farms according to their u-pick crop. Use these lists for handy reference.

Farmers' Markets

Ann Arbor Farmers' Market

407 North Fifth Street, Ann Arbor
313-761-1078
313-662-4221

Location: Next door to Kerrytown, Catherine and Fifth Streets
Hours: 7 a.m.-3 p.m., Saturday and Wednesday, May 1-Christmas. 8 a.m.-3 p.m., Saturday, January-May.

Eastern Market

2934 Russell, Detroit
313-833-1560

Location: 2 blocks east of I-75, take Mack Avenue exit
Hours: 5 a.m.-noon, Monday-Friday. 5 a.m.-6 p.m., Saturday, year-round.

The area's largest, most boisterous, and aromatic farmers' market. You'll find freshly baked goods, wonderful specialty stores, live animals, and a crush of colorful people. Arrive early Saturday morning to be sure of a parking space.

Monroe Farmers' Market

20 East Willow, Monroe
313-242-6522

Location: In back of Elias Brothers Big Boy on Monroe Street
Hours: 6 a.m.-noon, Tuesday and Saturday, spring-fall

Mount Clemens Farmers' Market

37685 South Gratiot, Mount Clemens
313-469-2525

Location: Downtown Mt. Clemens.
Hours: 9 a.m.-9 p.m., Monday-Saturday. 9 a.m.-7 p.m., Sunday, year-round

Plymouth Farmers' Market

Plymouth
313-453-1540 (Chamber of Commerce)

Location: At "The Gathering," across from Kellogg Park, on Penniman and Main Streets
Hours: 7:30 a.m.-12:30 p.m., Saturday, first week in May to mid-October

Pontiac Farmers' Market

Pontiac
313-858-9807

Location: Pontiac Lake Road, west of Telegraph
Hours: 6:30 a.m.-1 p.m., Tuesday, Thursday, Saturday, May 1-November 1. After November 1, Thursday and Saturday only.

Royal Oak Farmers' Market

316 East Eleven Mile Road, Royal Oak
313-548-8822

Location: One mile east of Woodward, three blocks east of Main Street
Hours: 7 a.m.-1 p.m., Tuesday, Thursday, Friday, and Saturday, June-September. 7 a.m.-1 p.m. Tuesday, Friday, and Saturday, May and October, November-Christmas. 7 a.m.-1 p.m. Saturday only, December 26-April.

Windsor City Market

Chatham Street East, Windsor
Ontario, Canada
519-255-6260

Location: On the corner of Pitt and McDougall Streets, a few blocks from the tunnel exit in Windsor
Hours: 7 a.m.-4 p.m., Tuesday-Thursday. 7 a.m.-6 p.m., Friday. 5 a.m.-4 p.m., Saturday, year-round.

Ypsilanti Farmers' Market

Depot Town, Ypsilanti
313-483-1480

Location: In Depot Town, Cross Street just east of Huron River Drive
Hours: 7 a.m.-3 p.m., Wednesday and Saturday.

U-Pick Farms and Cider Mills

Here is a sampling of the most popular farms and cider mills in the greater Detroit area. To help you find the site closest to your home, check the county in which each farm or cider mill is located. Also, be sure to call ahead for directions and hours. Hours vary depending on the season, the crop, and the weather.

Alber Orchard and Cider Mill

13011 Bethel Church Road, Manchester
313-428-7758

Location: Washtenaw County
Hours: 9 a.m.-6 p.m., daily, September–December
Activities: Cider mill, farm store, donuts

Almar Orchards

1431 Duffield, Flushing
313-659-6568

Location: Genesee County
Hours: 9 a.m.-6 p.m., Monday-Saturday; noon-6 p.m., Sunday, September–October
Activities: Cider mill

Altermatt's Farm

16580 Twenty-Five Mile Road, Washington
313-781-3428

Location: Macomb County
Hours: Strawberries: 7 a.m.-dusk, June-August. 9 a.m.-dusk, September-November. Farm market: May-November.
Activities: U-pick strawberries and early raspberries, farm market with seasonal vegetables, pumpkins, gourds and flowers.

Amon Orchards

7404 North US-31, Traverse City
616-938-1644
616-938-9160

Location: Grand Traverse County
Hours: Mid-July–mid-August
Activities: U-pick cherries, farm tours, and farm market.

Apple Charlie's and South Huron Orchard and Cider Mill

38035 South Huron Road, New Boston
313-753-9380

Location: Wayne County
Hours: 8 a.m.-dark, September–October
Activities: U-pick apples, cider mill

Art Hazen

1144 Peavy Road, Howell
517-548-1841

Location: Livingston County
Hours: 8 a.m.-8 p.m., daily, July–September
Activities: U-pick blueberries

Ashton Orchards and Cider Mill

3925 Seymour Lake Road, Ortonville
313-627-6671

Location: Oakland County
Hours: August–March
Activities: Cider mill and farm market

Asplin Farms Cider Mill

12190 Miller, Lennon
313-621-4780

Location: Genesee County
Hours: Noon-5 p.m., Tuesday-Thursday. Noon-11 p.m., Friday. 10 a.m.-5 p.m., Saturday and Sunday. Closed Monday. Mid-September–mid-December. Country Music Jamboree inside cider mill, 6:30-11 p.m. Friday, April-December.
Activities: Cider mill; beginning Thanksgiving weekend: u-pick Christmas trees, and weekend horse-drawn wagon rides.

Blake's Big Apple Orchard

71485 North Avenue, Armada
313-784-9710

Location: Macomb County
Hours: 9 a.m.-6 p.m., daily, April-December
Activities: U-pick strawberries, cherries, apples, pumpkins, raspberries, peaches and Christmas trees. Group tours, produce store, fudge shop, bakery, animal petting farm, wagon rides, and train rides through the orchard on weekends.

Blake's Orchard and Cider Mill

17985 Armada Center Road, Armada
313-784-5343

Location: Macomb County
Hours: 9 a.m.-6 p.m., daily, June-December
Activities: U-pick strawberries, cherries, vegetables, raspberries, pumpkins, apples and pears, wagon and pony rides, cider mill, Christmas trees, farm market, weekend activities, group tours

Bowerman's Westview Orchards

65075 Van Dyke, Romeo
313-752-3123

Location: Macomb County
Hours: 8 a.m.-7 p.m. daily, July
Activities: U-pick cherries

Brookwood Fruit Farm

7845 Bordman Road, Almont
313-798-8312

Location: Lapeer County
Hours: 8 a.m.-6 p.m. daily, July–November.
Activities: U-pick cherries, peaches, pears, apples, red raspberries, plums

Coon Creek Orchard

78777 Coon Creek Road, Armada
313-784-5062

Location: Macomb County
Hours: 8 a.m.-6 p.m., daily, late June-end November.
Activities: U-pick cherries, peaches, raspberries, apricots, plums, pears, grapes, apples, pumpkins, cider mill, farm market, gift shop

Crossroads Village Cider Mill

G-5055 Branch Road, Flint
313-736-7100

Location: Genesee County
Hours: 10 a.m.-5:30 p.m., Monday-Friday. 11 a.m.-6:30 p.m., Saturday and Sunday. Labor Day-Christmas.
Activities: Cider press demonstration. The mill is part of the Huckleberry Railroad/Crossroads Village complex.

Davies Orchard and Cider Mill

40026 Willow Road, New Boston
313-654-8893

Location: Wayne County
Hours: 9 a.m.-7 p.m., daily, mid-September–end-October
Activities: U-pick apples, cider mill, donuts, honey.

DeGroot's Strawberries

4232 Bull Run Road, Gregory
517-223-9311

Location: Livingston County
Hours: 8 a.m.-8 p.m., June-July
Activities: U-pick strawberries

Deneweth's Pick Your Own Strawberry Farms

16125 Twenty-Two Mile Road, Shelby Township
313-247-5533

Location: Macomb County
Hours: 7 a.m.-dusk, June-July
Activities: U-pick strawberries, wagon rides to and from field

Dexter Cider Mill

3685 Central Street, Dexter
313-426-8531

Location: Washtenaw County
Hours: 8 a.m.-5 p.m., Late August-Thanksgiving
Activities: Cider press demonstrations, donuts

Diehl's Orchard and Cider Mill

1478 Ranch, Holly
313-634-8981

Location: Oakland County
Hours: 9 a.m.-6 p.m. daily, August-October 30. 9 a.m.-5 p.m. daily, October 31-December 31. 9 a.m.-5 p.m., Monday-Saturday; 1-6 p.m., Sunday, January 1-August 1.
Activities: Country shop with cider, donuts, apples, jams, jellies, popcorn. Wagon rides and entertainment on weekends during fall; Ciderfest last weekend in September.

Driver's Berry Farm

Doane Road, South Lyon
313-437-1069
313-437-1606

Location: Livingston County
Hours: 9 a.m.-8 p.m., daily during July
Activities: U-pick raspberries

Erie Orchards

1235 Erie Road, Erie
313-848-4518

Location: Monroe County
Hours: 9 a.m.-7 p.m., Monday-Saturday. Noon-6 p.m., Sunday, mid-July-Christmas
Activities: U-pick blueberries, peaches, apples, pumpkins, and Christmas trees. Cider press and donut-making demonstrations. Weekend entertainment, pony rides, animal petting farm and hayrides. Group and school tours available.

Erwin Orchards

61019 Silver Lake, South Lyon
313-437-4701

Location: Oakland County
Hours: 9 a.m.-6:30 p.m., daily
Activities: U-pick apples, pumpkins. Group tours, wagon rides, country store. Erwin Orchards grows dwarf apple trees, just the right height for young pickers.

Foreman Orchards and Cider Mill

50050 West Seven Mile Road, Northville
313-349-1256

Location: Wayne County
Hours: 9 a.m.-7 p.m., daily, July 1-end of December
Activities: Large country store with apples, seasonal candies, baked goods, and gifts; cider-press demonstrations

Franklin Cider Mill

7450 Franklin Road, Franklin
313-626-2968

Location: Oakland County
Hours: 8:30 a.m.-6 p.m., daily, Saturday before Labor Day-Saturday after Thanksgiving
Activities: Cider-press demonstrations, food stand selling apples, seasonal foods, donuts

Frank's Orchard

6146 Dexter-Ann Arbor Road, Dexter
313-662-5064

Location: Washtenaw County
Hours: 3 p.m.-dark, Monday-Friday; 8 a.m.-8 p.m. Saturday and Sunday, mid-September–mid-November.
Activities: U-pick apples, cider mill, fall foods

Goodison Cider Mill

4295 Orion, Lake Orion
313-652-8450

Location: Oakland County
Hours: 11 a.m.-6 p.m., Monday-Friday. 9 a.m.-6 p.m., Saturday and Sunday. Labor Day–December
Activities: Cider-press demonstrations, donuts, jams & jellies

Greenock Mills

10470 Rushton Road, South Lyon
313-437-5900

Location: Livingston County

Hours: 10 a.m.-6 p.m., Thursday-Sunday, mid-September–mid-November
Activities: Cider and donuts, small museum with antique clothes and toys

Hazen's Blueberries

350 Wise Road, Commerce
313-363-4072

Location: Oakland County
Hours: 8 a.m.-8 p.m., daily, July-September
Activities: U-pick blueberries

Hilltop Orchards and Cider Mill

11468 Hartland Road, Fenton
313-629-9292

Location: Livingston County
Hours: 10 a.m.-5:30 p.m., daily, September-Christmas
Activities: Cider, donuts, antique market

Howell's Apple Ranch

811 North State Street, Stanton
517-831-4918

Location: Montcalm County
Hours: 8 a.m.-6 p.m., Monday-Saturday, August-November
Activities: Cider mill and homemade donuts, fall goodies, farm market, retail apples

Hy's Cider Mill

6350 Thirty-Seven Mile Road, Romeo
313-798-3611

Location: Macomb County
Hours: 11 a.m.-6 p.m., Saturday and Sunday. September-Thanksgiving
Activities: U-pick apples, cider, donuts, gift shops, and wagon rides for apple pickers

Jefferys

3805 Cribbins Road, Goodells
313-324-2874

Location: St. Clair County

Hours: 10 a.m.-7 p.m., Monday-Saturday; noon-5 p.m. Sunday, July
Activities: U-pick blueberries

Koan's Orchards
12183 Beecher, Flushing
313-659-8720

Location: Genesee County
Hours: 8 a.m.-6 p.m., Monday-Saturday; 9 a.m.-6 p.m. Sunday, mid-September–winter
Activities: Cider mill, donuts, farm market

Lakeview Farm and Cider Mill
12075 Island Lake, Dexter
313-426-2782

Location: Washtenaw County
Hours: 9 a.m.-5 p.m., Tuesday-Sunday. Closed on Monday, September 15-November 15
Activities: Watch cider and donuts being made, fall harvest items, pumpkins

McCarron's Orchard
7456 West Carpenter, Flushing
313-659-3813

Location: Genesee County
Hours: 9 a.m.-6 p.m. Monday-Saturday; 11 a.m.-5 p.m., Sunday, August-Christmas. 9 a.m.-6 p.m. Friday and Saturday; 11 a.m.-5 p.m. Sunday, January-April
Activities: Cider mill, fruit market, bakery specializing in homemade fruit pies

Makielski Berry Farm
7130 Platt Road, Ypsilanti
313-572-0060

Location: Washtenaw County
Hours: 8 a.m.-8 p.m., daily during season
Activities: U-pick early and fall raspberries, pumpkins

Martinsville Cider Mill
Greenfield Village, Dearborn
313-271-1620

Location: Wayne County
Hours: 9 a.m.-5 p.m., daily during the season
Activities: Cider-pressing demonstrations. The cider mill is one of Greenfield Village's historic buildings.

Masters Orchard and Cider Mill

10241 East Richfield, Davison
313-653-5677

Location: Genesee County
Hours: 9 a.m.-6 p.m., daily, September-January
Activities: Cider mill

Meyer Berry Farm

48120 West Eight Mile Road, Northville
313-349-0289

Location: Oakland County
Hours: Strawberries in June, pumpkins in October
Activities: U-pick strawberries and pumpkins

Middleton Berry Farm

2120 Stoney Creek Road, Oakland
313-693-6018

Location: Oakland County
Hours: Hours vary depending on crop. June-October
Activities: U-pick strawberries, spring and fall raspberries, and pumpkins, petting farm, wagon rides. Group tours available.

Middleton Cider Mill

46462 Dequindre, Utica
313-731-6699

Location: Macomb County
Hours: 9 a.m.-6 p.m., daily September, October, and November
Activities: Cider-press demonstrations, pony rides, wild geese and ducks, donuts, candy

Miller's Big Red

4900 West Thirty-Two Mile Road, Romeo
313-752-7888

Location: Macomb County
Hours: 9 a.m.-6 p.m., daily, May–early-December
Activities: U-pick strawberries and apples, hayrides, u-pick pumpkins, cider mill, fresh product, and flowers. Girl Scout merit badge program.

Montrose Orchards

12473 Seymour, Montrose
313-639-6971

Location: Genesee County
Hours: 8 a.m.-6 p.m., daily, June-August
Activities: U-pick strawberries, cherries, blueberries

Morton's Strawberry Farm

Michigan Avenue (US 12), Saline
313-429-9342 (hot line)

Location: Washtenaw County
Hours: 8 a.m.-8 p.m., daily, June
Activities: U-pick strawberries

Navarre Strawberry Farm

1485 Bates Lane, Monroe
313-241-0723

Location: Monroe County
Hours: 8 a.m.-8 p.m. daily, May-July and September
Activities: U-pick asparagus, strawberries, raspberries

Obstbaum Orchards and Cider Mill

9252 Currie Road, Northville
313-349-5569

Location: Washtenaw County
Hours: 10 a.m.-6 p.m., Saturday and Sunday, mid-September–Thanksgiving
Activities: U-pick apples, cider and donuts, farm market with candies, butters, syrups, preserves, dried flowers and wreaths

Paint Creek Mill

4480 Orion Road, Rochester
313-651-8361

Location: Oakland County
Hours: Cider Mill: 9 a.m.-6 p.m., daily, September-Christmas. 11 a.m.-6 p.m. Tuesday-Sunday, March-September. Restaurant: 5-10 p.m., Tuesday-Saturday. 9 a.m.-2 p.m., Sunday, year-round.
Activities: Cider-press demonstrations, donuts, baked goods, candy, honey. Large mill water wheel and trails.

Pankiewicz Farms Cider Mill

10387 Lindsey Road, Richmond
313-727-9051

Location: Macomb County
Hours: Weekends only, mid-September–mid-October
Activities Cider and donuts

Parmeter Cider Mill

714 Baseline Road, Northville
313-349-3181

Location: Wayne County
Hours: 10 a.m.-8 p.m., daily, Saturday before Labor Day-Sunday before Thanksgiving
Activities: Cider-press demonstrations, country store with cider, donuts, caramel apples, honey, jam, candy

Plymouth Orchards and Cider Mill

10685 Warren Road, Plymouth
313-455-2290

Location: Washtenaw County
Hours: 9 a.m.-8 p.m., daily, late August-day before Thanksgiving
Activities: U-pick apples, pumpkins. Cider-press demonstrations, petting farm, wagon rides, country market. Group tours available.

Porters Orchard and Cider Mill

12160 Hegel, Goodrich
313-636-7156

Location: Genesee County
Hours: 9 a.m.-6 p.m., Monday-Saturday; 1:30-6 p.m. Sunday, mid-August–mid-April
Activities: Cider mill

Preiss Sod and Strawberry Farm
8211 Clyde Road, Fenton
313-632-7107

Location: Livingston County
Hours: 8 a.m.-8 p.m., daily June
Activities: U-pick strawberries

Pumpkin Factory
48651 Harris, Belleville
313-461-1835

Location: Wayne County
Hours: 9 a.m.-9 p.m., daily, October
Activities: Halloween costumes, u-pick pumpkins, gift shop

Pumpkin Patch
32285 Sibley Road, New Boston
313-753-4586

Location: Wayne County
Hours: 9 a.m.-9 p.m., October
Activities: U-pick pumpkins, hayrides, pony rides, petting farm

Ray Schultz Farm
10090 Martz Road, Ypsilanti
313-483-1370

Location: Washtenaw County
Hours: 7 a.m.-7 p.m., June-July
Activities: U-pick strawberries

Ridgemere Berry Farm
2824 Clyde Road, Highland
313-887-5976

Location: Oakland County
Hours: 9 a.m.-dark, Monday-Saturday, June, September, October

Activities: Group tours available ("Raspberry Hayrides" include picking raspberries, a raspberry sundae, hayride, and pumpkin). Ten-minute slide show of Ridgemere Berry Farm, hayrides, u-pick strawberries, fall raspberries and pumpkins, country store.

Rochester Cider Mill

5212 Rochester Road, Rochester
313-651-4224

Location: Oakland County
Hours: 9 a.m.-6 p.m., daily, September-October. 9 a.m.-5 p.m., daily, November-December.
Activities: Group tours available. Cider press and donut-making demonstrations, petting farm, antique tools and farm equipment on display, farm store with caramel apples, candy, apples, and other fall goodies.

Rowe's Produce Farm

10570 Martz Road, Ypsilanti
313-482-8538

Location: Washtenaw County
Hours: 7 a.m.-8 p.m., during June.
Activities U-pick strawberries

Roy Long

Bogie Lake Road, Commerce Township
313-360-3774

Location: Oakland County
Hours: 8 a.m.-8 p.m. daily, May-June
Activities: U-pick asparagus, strawberries

Ruby Farms

6567 Imlay City Road, Ruby
313-324-2662

For full information, see Science and Nature

Sandy Acres Blueberry Farm

38093 Judd Road, Belleville
313-753-9969

Location: Wayne County

Hours: 8 a.m.-6 p.m., Tuesday-Saturday; 10 a.m.-6 p.m. Sunday, closed Monday, July
Activities: U-pick blueberries

Spicer Orchard Farm Market and Cider Mill

10411 Clyde Road, Fenton
313-632-7692

Location: Livingston County
Hours: U-pick: 9 a.m.-6 p.m., July-December; farm store open year-round
Activities: U-pick cherries, raspberries, apples, farm market, country craft store, cider mill, cider and donut-making demonstrations

Stony Creek Orchard and Cider Mill

2961 West Thirty-Two Mile Road, Romeo
313-752-2453

Location: Macomb County
Hours: 9:30 a.m.-6 p.m., daily, early September-Christmas. 9:30 a.m.-5:30 p.m., Wednesday-Sunday, January-March.
Activities: U-pick apples, farm market with cider, donuts, jams. Christmas trees during December.

Stotz's Pumpkin Farm

3767 Lewis Avenue, Ida
313-269-2510

Location: Monroe County
Hours: 9 a.m.-6:30 p.m., Monday-Saturday; 11 a.m.-6:30 p.m., Sunday, October-November.
Activities: Group tours available. Halloween "Spook House," farm animals, pumpkin characters, gift shop, pumpkins for sale.

Symanzik's Berry Farm

8146 East Baldwin Road, Goodrich
313-636-7714

Location: Genesee County
Hours: 7 a.m.-9 p.m., Monday-Thursday; 7 a.m.-5 p.m. Friday-Sunday, June-July. 9:30 a.m.-6 p.m., daily, August-September. 9 a.m.-6 p.m., daily, October.

Activities: Group tours available. U-pick strawberries, late raspberries, and pumpkins, petting farm, play area, picnic tables, hayrides.

Tom Walker's Grist Mill
(Parshallville Cider Mill)
8507 Parshallville Road, Fenton
313-629-9079

Location: Livingston County
Hours: 10 a.m.-6 p.m., daily, September–mid-November
Activities: Cider press demonstrations, donuts

Uncle John's Cider Mill
8614 North US-27 Street, St. Johns
517-224-3686

Location: Clinton County (30 minutes north of Lansing)
Hours: 9 a.m.-6 p.m., daily, mid-June-January 1
Activities: U-pick pumpkins, cider-press demonstration, gift shop, baked goods, apples, wagon rides, Halloween family fun house, weekend bands and craft shows, Christmas trees and holiday gift items.

Upland Hills Farms
481 Lake George Road, Oxford
313-628-1611

Location: Oakland County
Hours: Pumpkin Festival: 10 a.m.-5 p.m., Saturday and Sunday, October
Activities: Pumpkin Festival: Hayride, u-pick pumpkins, playground, puppet show, haunted house, petting farm, pony rides, country store, fall goodies.

Uptegraff's Orchard
5350 North Gale, Davison
313-653-4577

Location: Genesee County
Hours: 10 a.m.-6 p.m., daily, August-late fall
Activities: U-pick apples, cider mill, farm market

Verellen Orchards

63260 Van Dyke, Romeo
313-752-2989

Location: Macomb County
Hours: 6:30 a.m.-7 p.m. Monday-Friday; 7 a.m.-7 p.m. Saturday; 7 a.m.-6 p.m. Sunday, June-July
Activities: U-pick strawberries, cherries

Warner's Orchard and Cider Mill

5970 Whitmore Lake Road, Brighton
313-229-6504

Location: Livingston County
Hours: 9 a.m.-6 p.m. Tuesday-Saturday; 11 a.m.-6 p.m., Sunday; closed Monday, August-December.
Activities: U-pick apples, cider mill, farm store donut making demonstrations on weekends

Wasem Fruit Farm

6580 Judd Road, Ypsilanti
313-482-2342

Location: Washtenaw County
Hours: 9 a.m.-6 p.m., daily., September-Halloween
Activities: U-pick apples

Weier's Cider Mill

603 West Thirteenth Street, Monroe
313-242-7396

Location: Monroe County
Hours: 8 a.m.-5 p.m., daily, September–mid-November
Activities: Cider mill

Westcroft Gardens

21803 West River Road, Grosse Ile
313-676-2444

Location: Wayne County
Hours: 8 a.m.-5 p.m. Monday-Friday, August-October
Activities: U-pick raspberries

Wiard's Orchards

5565 Merritt Road, Ypsilanti
313-482-7744

Location: Washtenaw County
Hours: 9 a.m.-6 p.m., daily. Country Fair: Saturday and Sunday, September-October
Activities: U-pick apples, pumpkins, petting farm, craft booths, entertainment, train, pony and wagon rides, country store with seasonal goodies, cider-press demonstrations

William Lutz

11030 Macon Road, Saline
313-429-5145

Location: Washtenaw County
Hours: Dawn-dusk, 9 days during October, for those who pay one fee to "rent-a-tree" and then are welcome to all the apples that the tree produces. The last Sunday in October is open to the public for a final "clean sweep" of the orchards. Apples then are priced by the bushel.
Activities: Rent-a-tree program

Windy Ridge Orchard and Cider Mill

9375 Saline-Milan Road, Saline
313-429-7111

Location: Washtenaw County
Hours: 10 a.m.-6 p.m., Saturday and Sunday, weekend after Labor Day, weekend after Halloween
Activities: U-pick apples and pumpkins, hayrides, cider and donuts, retail apples, antiques

Wolcott Orchards

3284 West Coldwater Road, Mt. Morris
313-789-9561

Location: Genesee County
Hours: 9 a.m.-6 p.m., daily, year-round
Activities: Apples, cider-press demonstration, bakery, gift shop, weekend hayrides. Group tours available. Apple Festival last weekend in September.

Yates Cider Mill

1990 East Avon Road, Rochester
313-651-8301

Location: Oakland County
Hours: 9 a.m.-7 p.m., daily, September and October. 9 a.m.-5 p.m., daily, November.
Activities: Group tours available weekdays for a minimum charge. Cider-press demonstration, donuts, apples and seasonal foods, fudge shop, picnic area, water wheel, trails.

Zabinsky Blueberry Farm

10810 Beach Road, Dexter
313-426-2900

Location: Washtenaw County
Hours: 8 a.m.-8 p.m., mid-July–Labor Day
Activities: Hook your bucket to the piece of rope around your waist and you're ready to pick blueberries. The farm supplies every picker with rope and bucket.

Quick-Look Lists

During the spring, summer and fall, Michigan's farms are bursting with berries, apples, pumpkins, cider and Christmas trees. Here is a listing of u-pick farms and cider mills arranged to help you see at a glance which farms offer which crops. Often, farms close or change their u-pick policy depending on that season's weather conditions. PLEASE CALL AHEAD TO VERIFY HOURS AND LOCATION.

U-Pick Summer Fruits

Strawberries
Season: Mid-June–early July
Altermatt's Farm, Washington. 313-781-3428.
DeGroot's Strawberries, Gregory. 517-223-9311.
Deneweth's Pick Your Own Strawberry Farms, Shelby Township. 313-247-5533.
Meyer Berry Farm, Northville. 313-349-0289.
Middleton Berry Farm, Oakland. 313-693-6018.
Montrose Orchards, Montrose. 313-639-6971.
Morton's Strawberry Farm, Saline. 313-429-9342.
Navarre Strawberry Farm, Monroe. 313-241-0723.
Preiss Sod and Strawberry Farm, Fenton. 313-632-7107.

Ray Schultz Farm, Ypsilanti. 313-483-1370.
Rowe's Produce Farm, Ypsilanti. 313-482-8538.
Roy Long, Commerce Township. 313-360-3774.
Symanzik's Berry Farm, Goodrich. 313-636-7714.
Verellen Orchards, Romeo. 313-752-2989.

Blackberries and raspberries
Season: Early July
Altermatt's Farm, Washington. 313-781-3428.
Coon Creek Orchard, Armada. 313-784-5062.
Driver's Berry Farm, South Lyon. 313-437-1606.
Makielski Berry Farm, Ypsilanti. 313-572-0060.
Middleton Berry Farm, Oakland. 313-693-6018.
Navarre Strawberry Farm, Monroe. 313-241-0723.

Cherries
Season: July 15-August 15 for sweet and sour cherries
Amon Orchards, Traverse City. 616-938-9157.
Blake's Big Apple Orchard, Armada. 313-784-9710.
Blake's Orchard and Cider Mill, Armada. 313-784-5343.
Bowerman's Westview Orchards, Romeo. 313-752-3123.
Brookwood Fruit Farm, Almont. 313-798-8312.
Coon Creek Orchard, Armada. 313-784-5062.
Montrose Orchards, Montrose. 313-639-6971.
Spicer Orchards Farm Market and Cider Mill, Fenton. 313-632-7692.
Verellen Orchards, Romeo. 313-752-2989.

Blueberries
Season: Mid-July–early September
Art Hazen, Howell. 517-548-1841.
Erie Orchards, Erie. 313-848-4518.
Hazen's Blueberries, Commerce. 313-363-4072.
Jefferys Blueberries, Goodells. 313-324-2874.
Montrose Orchards, Montrose. 313-639-6971.
Sandy Acres Blueberry Farm, Belleville. 313-753-9969.
Zabinsky Blueberry Farm, Dexter. 313-426-2900.

Peaches
Season: August-September
Blake's Big Apple Orchard, Armada. 313-784-9710.
Brookwood Fruit Farm, Almont. 313-798-8312.
Coon Creek Orchard, Armada. 313-784-5062.
Erie Orchards, Erie. 313-848-4518.

Fall Raspberries
Season: Late August-October
Blake's Big Apple Orchard, Armada. 313-784-9710.
Blake's Orchard and Cider Mill, Armada. 313-784-5343.
Brookwood Fruit Farm, Almont. 313-798-8312.
Coon Creek Orchard, Armada. 313-784-5062.
Makielski Berry Farm, Ypsilanti. 313-572-0060.
Middleton Berry Farm, Oakland. 313-693-6018.
Ridgemere Berry Farm, Highland. 313-887-5976.
Symanzik's Berry Farm, Goodrich. 313-636-7714.
Westcroft Gardens, Grosse Ile. 313-676-2444.

U-Pick Apples

Season: Late-August–November
Apple Charlie's and South Huron Orchard and Cider Mill, New Boston. 313-753-9380.
Blake's Big Apple Orchard, Armada. 313-784-9710.
Blake's Orchard and Cider Mill, Armada. 313-784-5343.
Brookwood Fruit Farm, Almont. 313-798-8312.
Coon Creek Orchard, Armada. 313-784-5062.
Davies Orchard and Cider Mill, New Boston. 313-654-8893.
Erie Orchards, Erie. 313-848-4518.
Erwin Orchards, South Lyon. 313-437-4701.
Frank's Orchard, Dexter. 313-662-5064.
Hy's Cider Mill, Romeo. 313-798-3611.
Miller's Big Red, Romeo. 313-752-7888.
Obstbaum Orchards and Cider Mill, Northville. 313-349-5569.
Plymouth Orchards and Cider Mill, Plymouth. 313-455-2290.
Spicer Orchards Farm Market and Cider Mill, Fenton. 313-632-7692.
Stony Creek Orchard and Cider Mill, Romeo. 313-752-2453.
Uptegraff's Orchards, Davison. 313-653-4577.
Warner's Orchard and Cider Mill, Brighton. 313-229-6504.
Wasem Fruit Farm, Ypsilanti. 313-482-2342.
Wiard's Orchards, Ypsilanti. 313-482-7744.
William Lutz, Saline. 313-429-5145.

U-Pick Pumpkins

Season: October
Blake's Big Apple Orchard, Armada. 313-784-9710.
Blake's Orchard and Cider Mill, Armada. 313-784-5343.
Coon Creek Orchard, Armada. 313-784-5062.

Erie Orchards, Erie. 313-848-4518.
Erwin Orchards, South Lyon. 313-437-4701.
Kensington Metropark Farm Center, Milford. 313-685-1561.
Meyer Berry Farm, Northville. 313-349-0289.
Middleton Berry Farm, Oakland. 313-693-6018.
Plymouth Orchards and Cider Mill, Plymouth. 313-455-2290.
Pumpkin Factory, Belleville. 313-461-1835.
Pumpkin Patch, New Boston, 313-753-4586.
Ridgemere Berry Farm, Highland. 313-887-5976.
Symanzik's Berry Farm, Goodrich. 313-636-7714.
Uncle John's Cider Mill, St. Johns. 517-224-3686.
Upland Hills Farms, Oxford. 313-628-1611.
Wiard's Orchards, Ypsilanti. 313-482-7744.
Windy Ridge Orchard and Cider Mill, Saline. 313-429-7111.

Cider Mills

Season: Late August-December
Alber Orchard and Cider Mill, Manchester. 313-428-7758.
Almar Orchards, Flushing. 313-659-6568.
Apple Charlie's and South Huron Orchard and Cider Mill, New Boston. 313-753-9380.
Ashton Orchards and Cider Mill, Ortonville. 313-627-6671.
Asplin Farms Cider Mill, Lennon. 313-621-4780.
Blake's Orchard and Cider Mill, Armada. 313-784-5343.
Coon Creek Orchard, Armada. 784-5062.
Crossroads Village Cider Mill, Flint. 313-736-7100.
Davies Orchard and Cider Mill, New Boston. 313-654-8893.
Dexter Cider Mill, Dexter. 313-426-8531.
Diehl's Orchard and Cider Mill, Holly. 313-634-8981.
Erie Orchards, Erie. 313-848-4518.
Foreman Orchards and Cider Mill, Northville. 313-349-1256.
Franklin Cider Mill, Franklin. 313-626-2968.
Frank's Orchard, Dexter. 313-662-5064.
Goodison Cider Mill, Lake Orion. 313-652-8450.
Greenock Mills, South Lyon. 313-437-5900.
Hilltop Orchards and Cider Mill, Fenton. 313-629-9292.
Howell's Apple Ranch, Stanton. 517-831-4918.
Hy's Cider Mill, Romeo. 313-798-3611.
Koan's Orchards, Flushing. 313-659-8720.
Lakeview Farm and Cider Mill, Dexter. 313-426-2782.

Martinsville Cider Mill, Greenfield Village, Dearborn. 313-271-1620.

Masters Orchard and Cider Mill, Davison. 313-653-5677.

McCarron's Orchard, Flushing. 313-659-3813.

Middleton Cider Mill, Utica. 313-731-6699.

Miller's Big Red, Romeo. 313-752-7888.

Obstbaum Orchards and Cider Mill, Northville. 313-349-5569.

Paint Creek Cider Mill, Rochester. 313-651-8361.

Pankiewicz Farms Cider Mill, Richmond. 313-727-9051.

Parmeter Cider Mill, Northville. 313-349-3181.

Plymouth Orchards and Cider Mill, Plymouth. 313-455-2290.

Porters Orchard and Cider Mill, Goodrich. 313-636-7156.

Rochester Cider Mill, Rochester. 313-651-4224.

Spicer Orchards Farm Market and Cider Mill, Fenton. 313-632-7692.

Stony Creek Orchard and Cider Mill, Romeo. 313-752-2453.

Tom Walker's Grist Mill, Fenton. 313-629-9079.

Uncle John's Cider Mill, St. Johns. 517-224-3686.

Uptegraff's Orchard, Davison. 313-653-4577.

Warner's Orchard and Cider Mill, Brighton. 313-229-6504.

Weier's Cider Mill, Monroe. 313-242-7396.

Wiard's Orchards, Ypsilanti. 313-482-7744.

Windy Ridge Orchard and Cider Mill, Saline. 313-429-7111.

Wolcott Orchards, Mt. Morris. 313-789-9561.

Yates Cider Mill, Rochester. 313-651-8301.

U-Pick Christmas Trees

The abundance of Christmas tree farms in Southern Lower Michigan makes it easy for families to pick and cut their own tree. Many farms also offer a variety of holiday attractions, including horse-drawn wagon rides, visits with Santa, craft shops and refreshments. So start a new family tradition. Dress warmly; bring a saw in case the farm doesn't supply one; bring twine to secure the tree to your car, and don't forget to bring along your camera. Most Christmas tree farms open the last weekend in Thanksgiving and stay open through Christmas Eve, but call ahead to be sure trees are still available.

Arend Tree Farms, 3512 Notten Road, Grass Lake. 313-475-7584.

Arend Tree Farms 2 & 3, 12870 South M-50, Brooklyn. 517-592-2006.

Asplin Farms, 12190 Miller Road, Lennon. 313-621-4780.

Baldwin Road Tree Farm, Baldwin Road between Indianwood and Seymour Lake Road, Oxford. 313-652-2381.

Blake's Big Apple Orchard, 71485 North Avenue, Armada. 313-784-9710.

Blake's Orchard and Cider Mill, 17985 Armada Center Road, Armada. 313-784-5343.

Boughan's Tree Farm #1, 44020 Hull Road, Belleville. 313-699-5062.

Boughan's Tree Farm #2, 15851 Martinsville Road, Belleville. 313-699-6483, 313-697-9600.

Broadview Christmas Tree Farm, 4380 Hickory Ridge Road, Highland. 313-887-8733.

Camp Oakland, 930 East Drahner Road, Oxford. 313-628-2561.

Candy Cane Christmas Tree Farm #1, 2401 Farnsworth Road, Lapeer. 313-628-8899.

Candy Cane Christmas Tree Farm #2, 4780 Seymour Lake Road, Oxford. 313-628-8899.

Chaprnka Tree Farm, 10421 West Coldwater Road, Flushing. 313-659-9329.

Christmas Tree Lane, 4311 Fishville Road, Grass Lake. 517-522-8231.

Cohoctah Tree Works, Durand Road, Cohoctah. 517-546-0711.

Coldsprings Farm, 4250 Park Lake Drive, Dexter. 313-475-7584.

Erie Orchards, 1235 Erie Road, Erie. 313-848-4518.

Fodor's Christmas Tree Farm, 3738 Burtch Road, Grass Lake. 517-522-4982.

Green Tee, 2233 Oakville Waltz Road, New Boston. 313-654-6427.

Hillside Farm, 4714 U.S. 12, Tipton. 313-274-0681.

Howell Nature Center, 1005 Triangle Lake Road, Howell. 517-546-0249.

Huff Tree Farm, 1500 Wardlow, Highland. 313-887-4230.

Huron Christmas Farm, 32100 King Road, New Boston. 313-753-9288.

Kelley's Frosty Pines, 7600 Hitchcock Road, White Lake. 313-698-1674.

Marlin Bliss Tree Farm, 13437 Todd Road, Ida. 313-269-2346.

Matthes Evergreen Farm, 13416 Lulu Road, Ida. 313-269-6244.

Mosher Tree Farm, 7155 North Territorial Road, Dexter. 313-426-5271.

Noel Tree Co., M-36 and Arnold Road, Gregory. 313-522-3991.

Pampered Pines, 4248 Rabidue and Brott Road, Goodells. 313-324-2913.

Pleasant Knoll Tree Farm, 3080 Oak Grove Road, Howell. 517-546-2954.

R.L.B. Tree Farm, 8133 McKinley Road, Flushing. 313-639-7416.

Ruby Tree Farm, 6567 Imlay City Road, Ruby. 313-324-2662.

Runyan's Country Tree Farm, 10235 Webster Road, Clio. 313-687-2476.

Sherwood Forest, 4981 Adams, Rochester. 313-652-4920.

Skyhorse Station Evergreen Plantation, 11000 Roberts Road, Stockbridge. 517-851-7017.

Smiths Farm, 7242 East Mt. Morris Road, Otisville. 313-653-6187.

Stony Creek Orchard and Cider Mill, 2961 West Thirty-Two Mile Road, Romeo. 313-752-2453.

Sun Tree Farms, 3640 Judd Road, Saline. 313-429-3666.

Thornhollow Tree Farm, 44387 Hull Road, Belleville. 313-699-3709.

Tollander Tree Farm #1, 5690 Griswold Road, Port Huron. 313-985-8951.

Tollander Tree Farm #2, 7747 Imlay City Road, Port Huron. 313-985-8951.

Tollander Tree Farm #3, Bryce Road between Rabidue and Cribbins Roads, Port Huron. 313-985-8951.

Trim Pines Farm, 4357 East Baldwin, Grand Blanc. 313-694-9958.

Uncle John's Cider Mill, 8614 North US-27 Street, St. Johns. 517-224-3686.

Waldock Tree Farm, 5665 Crofoot, Howell. 517-546-3890.

Warren's Tree Farm, 8366 Spicer Road, Brighton. 313-231-4335.

Wenzel's Tree Farm, 8475 Bishop Road, Brighton. 313-233-7903.

9
PARKS

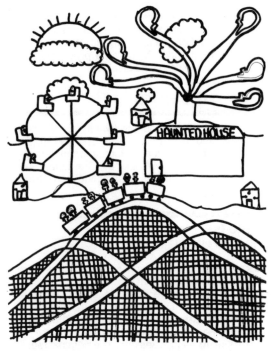

Beaches, picnic tables, creative playgrounds, and wild water slides—the map of southeastern lower Michigan is dotted with city, county, state, and national parks. The Detroit Parks and Recreation Department operates over 200 neighborhood parks and play lots, including Belle Isle and the newly developed riverfront parks. The Huron-Clinton Metropolitan Authority operates 13 popular metroparks offering a wide range of seasonal activities from nature centers and beaches to boat ramps and toboggan runs.

Macomb County's Freedom Hill is an outdoor concert site; Oakland County's eight developed parks offer wave-action pools, beaches, and cross-country skiing. Wayne County's seven parks criss-cross the county, and the Michigan State Department of National Resources oversees parks offering family beaches, horseback riding, and a petting farm. Michigan's national parks include Isle Royal, Pictured Rocks, and Sleeping Bear Sand Dunes. There are also Windsor City Parks and Canadian National Parks within a short drive.

This chapter also includes a sampling of adventure parks and water parks. Be sure to check your city's parks and recreation department for a catalog of seasonal activities, classes, family events, vacation camps, sports leagues, and neighborhood parks. Many area programs offer activities for children with disabilities.

Detroit Parks

For general information and location of city playgrounds and play lots, call 313-224-1180. For specific Detroit Parks and Recreation events and activities, call the 24-hour "Leisure Line," 313-252-2200-3501. Here is a sampling of Detroit's best family parks.

Belle Isle
313-267-7115

Location: East Jefferson at Grand Boulevard, 2½ miles east of the RenCen
Hours: Grounds are open 24 hours, daily. All buildings are open year-round. Food concessions and the zoo are open April-October. Check individual listings for specific hours of buildings.
Admission: All facilities charge a nominal fee.
Facilities: Playscape—a creative playground, Aquarium, Dossin Great Lakes Museum, Nature Center, Anna Scripps Whitcomb Conservatory, Zoo. *For full information, see* Museums *and* Science and Nature.

You'll see the giant slide as you drive across the bridge onto the island. It's part of Playscape, an imaginative playground made up of timbers of all sizes and shapes, a fireman's pole, tree house, suspended bridge, tire swings, and other play equipment. Visit Belle Isle just for this playground —open all year—or be sure to leave time at the end of your visit to the other sites. Your kids won't want to leave unless you promise they'll be back soon.

Chene Park
313-393-0066

Location: Along the Detroit River between

Chene and DuBois Streets, just east of the RenCen

Hours: Outdoor amphitheater offers a summer season of concerts and programs
Admission: Free
Facilities: Outdoor amphitheater hill in the summer, outdoor ice skating in the winter

Hart Plaza
313-224-1184

Location: Jefferson Avenue, along the Detroit River, just west of the RenCen
Hours: Always open
Admission: Free
Facilities: Outdoor plaza, Noguchi fountain, benches, walkway along the river, summertime food concessions, wintertime ice skating

Hart Plaza epitomizes summertime in the city. It's home to the ethnic festivals each summer weekend from May to Labor Day, Freedom Festival activities during the July Fourth weekend, and the Montreux Jazz Festival in early September. Even on a day without a festival, the plaza is busy and lively. Kids will enjoy running around the Noguchi fountain's "shower" and walking along the river, watching for barges. During the winter, families can ice-skate on a large outdoor rink.

Presently closed due to budget cuts; hopes to reopen soon. Call to schedule group tours.

Historic Fort Wayne
6325 West Jefferson, Detroit
313-297-9360

St. Aubin Park
313-259-4677

Location: Atwater and St. Aubin, along the Detroit River, just east of the RenCen
Hours: Always open
Admission: Free
Facilities: Creative play area, marina, picnic areas, river overlooks, bicycle paths and walkways

This brand-new riverfront family park has an imaginative, marine-inspired children's playground.

Huron-Clinton Metroparks

Thirteen metroparks, with over 23,491 acres of parkland, offer a wide variety of recreation for residents of Livingston, Oakland, Macomb and Wayne counties. The parks are open year-round, but call ahead; hours may vary from park to park and for different activities and seasons. Young children enjoy the "tot lots," fantasy playground villages located at the following metroparks: Hudson Mills, Lake Erie, Lower Huron, Metro Beach, and Willow. Families also enjoy visiting the well-staffed, hands-on nature centers located at Indian Springs, Kensington (which also has a farm center), Metro Beach, Oakwoods, and Stony Creek. Of special interest is Wolcott Mill Metropark, site of a historic grist mill.

Vehicle permits are required ($2 daily, $15 annual, $8 senior citizen annual). Huron-Clinton Metropolitan Authority is located at 13000 High Ridge Drive, Brighton. For toll-free information, call 1-800-47-PARKS.

Delhi Metropark

East Delhi Road, Ann Arbor
Call Hudson Mills Metropark for information
313-426-8211

Fifty-acre park along the Huron River, five miles northwest of Ann Arbor. Picnic sites with shelters and stoves, playfields, fishing sites, swings, and slides. Canoe rentals available May-September. Call Skip's Canoe Livery, 313-769-8686.

Dexter-Huron Metropark

Huron River Drive, Dexter
Call Hudson Mills Metropark for information,
313-426-8211

A riverside park with 122 acres, 7½ miles northwest of Ann Arbor. Shady picnic sites with tables and stoves, swings, slides, playfields, and fishing sites.

Hudson Mills Metropark
8801 North Territorial Road, Dexter
313-426-8211

A multi-purpose park of 1,504 acres, located 12 miles northwest of Ann Arbor, on North Territorial Road at the crossing of the Huron River. Picnic sites, swings, slides, tot lot, playing fields, hike-bike trail, nature trail, fishing. The Activity Center has food service, tennis, basketball and shuffleboard courts, softball diamond, and bicycle rental in summer. During the winter, the Activity Center offers ski rental, two ice rinks, indoor food service, and cross-country ski trails.

Huron Meadows Metropark
8765 Hammel Road, Brighton
313-231-4084

A 1,540-acre park, located six miles south of Brighton. Picnic sites and Golf Center building with food service, driving range, and 18-hole golf course. During the winter, there is cross-country skiing and ski rental.

Indian Springs Metropark
5200 Indian Trail, Clarkston
313-625-7280

A 2,224-acre park located near Clarkston, nine miles northwest of Pontiac. A six-mile bike-hike trail, picnic sites, 18-hole golf course, nature trails, and nature center. During the winter, there is cross-country skiing and ski rental.

Kensington Metropark
2240 West Buno Road, Milford
313-685-1561

This 4,337-acre multi-purpose park, located near Milford and Brighton, offers summertime boat rental, 18-hole golf course, bike-hike trail, picnic sites, fishing sites, the Island Queen—a 66-passenger sternwheeler, two beaches with bath-houses, heated showers, playgrounds, and food service. The Farm Center (including hay/sleigh rides and food service) and Nature Center are open year-round. During the winter, the park offers cross-country ski trails and rentals, ice-skating, tobogganing, and sledding.

Lake Erie Metropark

32481 West Jefferson, Rockwood
313-379-5020

A 1,597-acre park located in Brownstown Township between Gibraltar and Rockwood, along Lake Erie. During the summer, the park offers picnic sites, wooden playscape, nautical tot lot, marina, and entertainment. The "Great Wave," a large wave-action pool with bathhouse, food service building, and wet shop is open 9:30 a.m.-8 p.m., daily, Memorial Day-Labor Day. Cross-country skiing, rental, and ice-skating during the winter.

Lower Huron Metropark

17845 Savage Road, Belleville
313-697-9181

A 1,256-acre park located along the Huron River near Belleville, with shorefishing, picnic-playfield sites, 18-hole golf course, playscape, nature trails, tennis courts, basketball courts, volleyball, and horseshoe equipment. The swimming pool with water slide, bathhouse, and food service is open 9:30 a.m.-7 p.m., weekdays; 10:30 a.m.-8 p.m., weekends and holidays, Memorial Day-Labor Day. Winter facilities include cross-country ski trails and three ice rinks.

Metro Beach Metropark

Metropolitan Parkway, Mount Clemens
313-463-4581

A 770-acre park located along Lake St. Clair, five miles southeast of Mount Clemens. Summer facilities include Olympic-size swimming pool, putt-putt golf, 18-hole golf course, shuffleboard and horseshoe courts, beach, boat ramp, beach shop, food service, voyageur canoe tours, and trackless train. A nature center, bike-hike trails, and tot lot village are open all year. Cross-country ski trails and rental, ice-skating and ice-fishing are available during winter.

Oakwoods Metropark

Willow Road, Flat Rock
313-782-3956

A 1,719-acre park located five miles northeast of Flat Rock and adjacent to Willow Metropark offers a nature center, interpretive trails, and voyageur canoe tours.

Stony Creek Metropark

4300 Main Park Road, Washington
313-781-4242

A 4,461-acre·park located six miles north of Utica and northeast of Rochester. Two beaches with bathhouses, heated showers, food service, picnic sites, swings and slides, bike-hike trails, bike rentals, 18-hole golf course, boat launching, voyageur canoe tours, sailboard rental and lessons, nature trails, and nature center. During winter, cross-country skiing and rental.

Willow Metropark

South Huron, Huron Township
313-697-9181 (Lower Huron Metropark)

A 1,531-acre park located between Flat Rock and New Boston offers shuffleboard, tennis and basketball courts, food service, playfields, 18-hole golf course, and picnic sites with tables and stoves. The large tot lot is open April-October. The Olympic-size swimming pool is open 9:30 a.m.-7 p.m., weekdays; 10:30 a.m.-8 p.m., weekdays and holidays, Memorial Day-Labor Day. Winter facilities include cross-country ski trails and rental, snack bar, and sledding hill.

Wolcott Mill Metropark

Kunstman Road,
north of Twenty-Nine Mile Road
between Van Dyke and North Avenue
in Ray Township
313-749-5997

A 2,380-acre park located along the banks of the north branch of the Clinton River, between Twenty-Six and Thirty-One Mile Roads in Macomb County. The park includes a 140-year-old gristmill open to the public 10 a.m.-5 p.m., Monday-Friday. 10 a.m.-7 p.m., Saturday and Sunday, May-October. 10 a.m.-5 p.m., daily April and November.

Macomb County Parks and Recreation

See Freedom Hill *in* That's Entertainment

Michigan National Parks and Lakeshore

Michigan's three national parks—Isle Royale National Park, Sleeping Bear Dunes National Lakeshore, and Pictured Rocks National Lakeshore—offer us a rugged and beautiful Michigan.

Isle Royale National Park
87 North Ripley, Houghton
906-482-0984

Isle Royale is the least accessible of the three parks. 48 miles off the coast of Michigan, in Lake Superior, it can only be reached by ferry or seaplane from Houghton or by ferry from Copper Harbor—June–September, reservations required. An isolated wilderness park, only 45 miles long, its rocky coastline, dense forests, off-shore islands, lakes, and streams are untamed by man and offer a safe habitat for wolf and moose. The park is open mid-April–October, with full services mid-June–Labor Day. 165 miles of hiking trails, camping and housekeeping cabins, or Rock Harbor Lodge accommodations are available. A visit to Isle Royale requires planning.

Pictured Rocks National Lakeshore
For information:
Munising Falls Interpretive Center
400 East Munising Avenue, Munising
906-387-3700
Grand Sable Visitor Center
M-58, Grand Marais
906-494-2660

Pictured Rocks National Lakeshore, 40 miles of

spectacular, multi-colored, naturally-sculpted rock formations, is best viewed by boat. From Lake Superior, the massive, painted rocks assume many shapes and their precipices and deep gorges attest to the erosive action of ice, waves, and wind.

The main entrance to the park is located at Munising Falls Interpretive Center. Hours: 8 a.m.-6 p.m., daily, July 1-September 7. 9 a.m.-4:30 p.m., daily, the rest of the year. The Grand Sable Visitor Center, in Grand Marais, is open 8:30 a.m.-5:30 p.m., daily. July-Labor Day. For more information on Pictured Rocks boat cruises, *see* Beyond Southeastern Michigan.

Sleeping Bear Dunes National Lakeshore

Visitor Center
M-72, Empire
616-326-5134

The highest sand dunes west of the Sahara, Sleeping Bear Dunes National Lakeshore towers 500 feet above the water and lies along 33 miles of Lake Michigan's shore and includes the Manitou Islands. Unlike the Sahara, you don't need a camel to get around. There are 35 miles of hiking and cross country skiing trails. Or drive the 6-mile Pierce Stocking Scenic Drive, open mid-April–mid-November, for wonderful views from the top of the bluffs overlooking Lake Michigan. Kids love throwing off their shoes and sinking into the warm sand as they crawl their way up the mountain and over the top, walking all the way to Lake Michigan. The Visitor Center is open 9 a.m.-5 p.m., daily, year-round. *See* Beyond Southeastern Michigan.

Michigan State Parks

Michigan State parks dot the map offering sandy beaches, forest trails, and recreation facilities. Parks are open 8 a.m.-10 p.m., daily, year-round. Vehicle permits are required ($3.50 daily, $1 daily for seniors, $15 annual). Administrative offices are located in Lansing. Department of Natural Resources: 517-373-1220. Michigan State Parks: 517-373-1270. Here is a sampling of popular parks in southeastern lower Michigan.

Bald Mountain Recreation Area

1330 East Greenshield Road, Lake Orion
313-693-6767

This 4,637-acre park offers picnic sites, playground, beach, beach house and concession, boat rental, hiking and cross-country skiing trails.

Dodge No. 4 State Park

4250 Parkway, Waterford
313-666-1020

A 139-acre park located off Cass Elizabeth Lake Road offering picnic sites, playground, beach, beach house and concession, boat rental, cross-country skiing, ice-skating, and snowmobiling.

Highland Recreation Area

5200 East Highland Road, Milford
313-887-5135

This 5,524-acre park offers picnic sites, playground, beach, beach house and concession, bridle paths, cross-country ski trails.

Island Lake Recreation Area

12950 East Grand River, Brighton
313-229-7067

This 3,466-acre park offers picnic sites, canoe rental, playground, beach, beach house, and concession.

Lakeport State Park

7605 Lakeshore Road, Lakeport
313-327-6765

A 565-acre park along Lake Huron offering picnic sites, playground, beach, beach house and concession.

Maybury State Park

20145 Beck Road, Northville
313-349-8390

This 944-acre park offers picnic sites, bike and

hiking trails, living farm, cross-country ski rental and trails, playscape, horse trails and riding stables.

Pontiac Lake Recreation Area

7800 Gale Road, Pontiac
313-666-1020

A 3,700-acre park with picnic sites, playground, beach, beach house and concession, archery range, horse trails and riding stables.

Proud Lake Recreation Area

3500 Wixom Road, Milford
313-685-2433

A 3,614-acre park offering hiking trails, picnic sites, playground, beach, beach house and concession.

Sterling State Park

2800 State Park Road, Monroe
313-289-2715

This 1,000-acre park offers picnic sites, playground, beach, beach house and concession.

Oakland County Parks

Eight developed parks in Oakland County offer family beaches, picnic sites, boat rental, wave-action pools and water slides, nature trails, and much more. Parks are open year-round. Summer hours are 8 a.m. to one hour after sunset, daily. Winter hours are 8 a.m.-sunset, 9 a.m.-4 p.m. for golf courses, weather permitting. But call ahead; hours may vary from park to park and for different activities and facilities.

Daily weekday vehicle pass is $3.50 for Oakland County residents, $7 for non-residents. Daily weekend and holiday vehicle pass is $4.50 for residents, $8 for non-residents. Annual vehicle pass is $16 for residents, $26 for non-residents. For general information, 313-858-0906.

Addison Oaks

1480 West Romeo Road, Leonard
313-693-2432

A 793-acre park located 13 miles north of Rochester that offers camping, swimming, picnicking, boat rental, fishing, hiking and nature study, plus winter snowmobile trails, sledding and tobogganing hills, ice-fishing, and ice-skating.

Glen Oaks

30500 Thirteen Mile Road, Farmington Hills
313-851-8356

This 18-hole golf course, located between Orchard Lake and Middlebelt Roads, offers cross-country skiing and equipment rental in the winter.

Groveland Oaks

14555 Dixie Highway, Holly
313-634-9811

A 360-acre park located at Dixie Highway and Grange Hall Road that offers a sandy beach, swimming lake, plus a flume water slide that splashes into Stewart Lake. There are also camping, picnicking, and boat rental facilities.

Independence Oaks

9501 Sashabaw Road, Clarkston
313-625-0877

This 1,062-acre park located on Sashabaw Road, 2½ miles north of I-75, offers ten miles of marked nature and ski trails, a nature interpretive center, 200-seat amphitheater, boat rental, picnicking, fishing, swimming, and ice-skating, and many facilities for the handicapped.

Red Oaks

1455 East Thirteen Mile Road, Madison Heights
313-585-6990

Keep cool bucking the waves and whoosing around the curves in Red Oak's large wave-action pool and two water slides. Food service and inner tube and raft rental are available.

Springfield Oaks

12451 Andersonville Road, Davisburg
313-625-8133

The Youth Activities Center and outdoor arenas host August's annual 4-H Fair; the golf course offers cross-country skiing in the winter.

Waterford Oaks

2800 Watkins Lake Road, Pontiac
313-858-0913
313-858-0918 (wave pool)
313-858-5433 (tennis complex)
313-858-0915 (BMX track)

This 145-acre park located between Watkins and Scott Lake Roads offers a wave-action pool; giant two-flume "Slidewinder" water slides; bicycle motorcross track; games complex with platform tennis, tennis, volleyball, shuffleboard, and horseshoe courts; activities center; picnicking; hiking trail.

White Lake Oaks

991 South Williams Lake Road, White Lake
313-698-2700

An 18-hole golf course with cross-country skiing and rental during the winter.

Wayne County Parks

For exact location, activities, and hours of each park, call the main information number, 313-261-1990, 9 a.m.-5 p.m., weekdays. Administrative offices are at 33175 Ann Arbor Trail, Westland, open 8 a.m.-4:30 p.m., Monday-Friday. Park grounds are open dawn to dusk daily.

Bell Creek Park and
Lola Valley Park

Redford

Neighboring parks along the Bell branch of the Rouge River, Bell Creek offers softball and baseball diamonds and tennis courts; Lola Valley offers natural beauty and picnic tables.

Elizabeth Park

Trenton
313-671-5220 (Pony ranch)

The state's oldest county park offers softball and baseball diamonds, tennis courts, tourist lodge, speed-skating rink, pony and sleigh rides, concessions, and an entertainment pavilion.

Lower Rouge Parkway

Dearborn to Canton Township

This 12-mile parkway along three Rouge River forks offers baseball and softball diamonds, football and soccer field, tennis courts, picnic tables, and nature trails.

Middle Rouge Parkway

(commonly known as Edward Hines Park)
Dearborn to Northville

This 17½-mile parkway along the scenic banks of the Middle Rouge River offers softball and baseball diamonds, bike, hike, and bridle paths, picnicking sites, tennis courts, football and soccer fields, fishing, a wooded arboretum, plus sledding and toboggan hills, ice-skating, and cross-country skiing in winter.

Veterans Memorial Park

Hamtramck

Tennis courts, baseball and softball diamonds, playground and baseball stadium.

Warren Valley Golf Course

Dearborn Heights

A 36-hole course with cross-country skiing, rental, and lessons in winter.

William P. Holliday Forest and Wildlife Preserve

Westland

Picnicking and 12 miles of marked nature trails.

Windsor City Parks and Canadian National Parks

Take a family walk through downtown Windsor's city parks and explore Canada's national parks located in Southern Ontario.

Coventry Gardens and Peace Fountain

Two miles east of downtown Windsor
on Riverside Drive East
at Pillette Road
519-255-6270

During the summer, the Peace Fountain is illuminated with ever-changing patterns of colored lights and water.

Fort Malden National Historic Park

100 Laird Avenue, Amherstburg
519-736-5416

For full information, see Historic Sites

Navy Yard Park

Dalhousie Street, Amherstburg

Behind the historic Park House Museum on Dalhousie Street in Amherstburg, just east of the Amherstburg Boblo Dock, overlooking the Detroit River. There are park benches for picnicking and old anchors for creative photos of the kids.

Point Pelee National Park

South of Leamington, Ontario
519-322-2371 (recorded information)
519-322-2365 (visitor center)

Location: From Detroit, take the Ambassador Bridge to Windsor. From Windsor, follow Route 3 to Leamington. Prominent signs give directions to the park. About an hour's drive from the bridge.

Hours: Grounds and nature trails, 6 a.m.-10 p.m., daily May-Labor Day. Visitor center, 10 a.m.-6 p.m., daily. Rest of year: Visitor center 10 a.m.-5 p.m. daily. Boardwalk, 11 a.m.-4 p.m., daily. Trails, 11 a.m.-6 p.m., daily. Closed January 1 and December 25.

Admission: Daily vehicle permit, $5; Seasonal vehicle permit $11.75 (Canadian dollars)

Ages: All ages

Plan: Full day

Parking: On site

Lunch: Picnic sites

Facilities: Visitor center with exhibits and theater, boardwalk, observation tower, nature trails. Canoe and bicycle rental April-Labor Day. Ice-skating and cross-country skiing during winter, weather permitting.

This well-kept park becomes a bird-watcher's paradise in early May, and August through October as migratory birds stop along their routes. Monarch butterflies are also plentiful during mid-September. A wide variety of activities are available throughout the year that appeal to children of all ages.

Queen Elizabeth II Gardens, Jackson Park

Tecumseh Road and Ouellette Street
Windsor
519-255-6270

This formal flowering garden located five minutes from the tunnel includes a six-acre rose garden with 450 different varieties. Kids will enjoy the maze-like shrubbery and the grounded Lancaster Memorial Bomber, a large World War II Royal Air Force Bomber.

Adventure Parks

Amusement rides, family entertainment, a trip back to the wild west and to prehistoric times— Michigan's adventure parks offer hours of fun for children of all ages.

Boblo Island

3509 Biddle, Wyandotte
313-284-6116 (hot-line)
313-284-2288 (group sales)
519-252-4444 (Windsor)

Location: There are two docks. Gibraltar dock —I-75 south to exit 29A. Amherstburg, Ontario, dock—Off Kings Highway 18.
Hours: Park is open 10 a.m.-6 p.m. weekdays, Memorial Day-July 3. 10 a.m.-9 p.m., daily after Fourth of July weekend. Gibralter boats begin departures at 9 a.m. Amherstburg boats begin departures at 10 a.m.
Admission: Tickets cover both boat ride and admission to the Island Theme Park. They vary in price depending on dock.
Ages: All ages
Plan: Full day
Parking: $3 Gibraltar and Amherstburg dock
Lunch: Food concessions, restaurants, picnic sites
Facilities: Bathrooms, rides, food, and gift concessions

Boblo is Detroit's floating pleasure island, with enough rides and fun to last an entire day. For children under 48 inches "Kids Kingdom" offers kiddie rides, a petting farm and live animal show. Children of all ages will want to watch the special-effect show in the Carrousel Theatre and the Olympic High Dive show in the center of the park. Even if your kids are too old for the kiddie areas, but too young for the really scary rides, they'll enjoy the train, Pirate Ship, and Log Flume.

Illuminated Cascades
Sparks Foundation County Park

1992 Warren Avenue, Jackson
517-788-4320 day
517-788-4227 night

Location: Exit 138 at junction of I-94 and US-127
Hours: Illuminated Cascades: 7:30-11 p.m., daily Memorial Day-Labor Day. All other park facilities: Sunrise-sunset, Memorial Day-Labor Day.
Admission: For falls, $2 adults and children 6 and up, children 5 and under free. Group rates available.
Ages: All ages

Plan: Half day visit; spend an evening
Parking: Free on site
Facilities: Picnic and playground areas, paddle-boats and miniature golf, Cascades museum and gift shop.

Summer evenings, the Cascades, a 500-foot hill of six spraying fountains, comes to life in vivid color. Live bands, fireworks, and entertainment add to the thrill. Families can also enjoy paddle-boats, miniature golf, and other park facilities.

Mixer Playground
Fuller Park

1519 Fuller Road, Ann Arbor
313-994-2780

Location: Fuller Road and Malden Lane
Hours: Dawn to dusk, daily
Admission: Free
Ages: All ages; purposely designed to offer wheel chair accessibility
Plan: Short visit
Parking: Free in lot adjacent to playground
Lunch: Small snack bar
Facilities: The Fuller Park pool is open Memorial Day–mid-September.

Mixer Playground is a barrier-free, two-story, creative wooden playscape with slides and crawl spaces. Built entirely by community volunteers, the play area is designed to offer accessibility to all children.

Penny Whistle Place

G-5500 Bray Road, Flint
313-736-7100
1-800-648-7275

Location: I-475 and Carpenter Road (exit 11)
Hours: 10 a.m.-7 p.m., daily, Memorial Day-Labor Day, weather permitting.
Admission: $2.75, children ages 2-3 $1, under 1 are free. Group rates available.
Ages: 3-10 year olds
Plan: Half day visit
Parking: Free on site
Lunch: Concessions, picnic tables
Facilities: Bathrooms, drinking fountains, benches for parents

At Penny Whistle, a creative playground, children can explore, climb, and become daring adventurers in a safe environment. Toddlers play in a sandbox with creative dump trucks large enough to sit on, zoom down the Tube Slides, and march around the Punch Bag Forest. Older children will love diving into layers of orange balls in the Ball Crawl, soaring over an abyss in the Cable Glide, and pumping water and sound at the Music Pump. Parents can sit up close to watch, give their children a hand, or become adventurers themselves. Attendants are also on hand to help children.

Prehistoric Forest

US-12, Onsted (Irish Hills)
517-467-2514

Location: On US-12 in Irish Hills
Hours: 10 a.m.-6 p.m., daily, Memorial Day-Labor Day
Admission: $4 adults, $3 children 4 to 16, 3 and under free.
Ages: Preschoolers
Plan: Short visit
Parking: Free on site
Lunch: Picnic sites. Stagecoach Stop U.S.A. is down the road.
Facilities: Bathrooms, gift shop

Prehistoric Forest, a kitschy representation of Mesozoic life, is for dinophiles with a taste for the tacky. The safari train takes you "deep" into the forest where more than 40 prehistoric beasts dwell in different stages of decomposition. Some are tall and ferocious, their scales barely covering chicken wire frames. For young children, such details don't count; they'll be amazed and delighted.

Stagecoach Stop, U.S.A.

7203 US-12, Onsted (Irish Hills)
517-467-2300

Location: On US-12 in Irish Hills, seven miles west of M-50 and M-52 intersection
Hours: 10:30 a.m.-5:30 p.m., Tuesday-Friday; 10:30 a.m.-6:30 p.m., Saturday and Sunday, June-August. Closed Mondays.

Admission: $7 adults, $6 children 12 and under, 3 and under free. Includes admission to Eisenhower Presidential Car. Group rates available.
Ages: All ages
Plan: Half day visit
Parking: Free on site
Lunch: Restaurant, ice cream parlor, concessions, fudge shop, picnic tables
Facilities: Bathrooms, gift shop

Walk along an 1880s Wild West town. Visit the general store, carriage house, saw mill, and blacksmith shop. Take a wild game train ride. Visit the petting farm and kiddie rides. Don't be surprised if the townsfolk get rowdy and a street fight begins. Just sit on the bleachers and see who's going to win.

Water Parks

Buck the wild waves, whoosh around the curves of a monster slide, and take a bumper boat ride—Michigan's water parks keep you cool.

Four Bears Water Park
3000 Auburn Road, Utica
313-739-5863

Location: Auburn Road, between Ryan and Dequindre, seven miles east of I-75, just off M-59
Hours: 11 a.m.-7 p.m., daily, Memorial Day-Labor Day.
Admission; $11.95 over 48 inches, $5.95 under 48 inches, under 3 years and over 65 years free. Group rates and season pass available.
Ages: All ages
Plan: Full day visit
Parking: Free. Next to entrance and across the street.
Lunch: Restaurant, vending machines, concessions, picnic tables
Facilities: Bathrooms, beach house with showers and lockers. Gift shop selling beach paraphernalia and Four Bears souvenirs.

Wear your bathing suit, pack a change of clothes and a picnic lunch, and plan on a full day of water activities at Four Bears. Young children will enjoy the kiddie rides, playground, petting zoo, elephant or camel rides, bumper boats and miniature water slide. Older children will want to play miniature golf, practice their swings at the batting cages, take a turn on the 50-foot triple water slide, or ride the go-carts. The whole family will enjoy the petting zoo, paddle boats, and man-made lake. Four Bears is the area's best full-service water park and well worth the admission price.

Groveland Oaks Water Slide

5990 Grange Hall Road, Holly
313-634-9811

Location: Groveland Oaks County Park, Dixie Highway at Grange Hall Road
Hours: 8 a.m.-9 p.m., daily, Memorial Day-Labor Day
Admission: Water slide 50 cents/ride or $5/day. Oakland County residents vehicle entry fee $3.50 weekday ($4.50 weekend); non-residents $7 weekday ($8 weekend).
Ages: Recommended 5 and up
Plan: Half day-full day visit
Parking: Free on site
Lunch: Concession stands
Facilities: Bathrooms, beach, paddleboat, canoe, rowboat and waterbug (1-person paddle-boat) rental

Groveland Oaks offers an added attraction to family beach visits. Now you can ride a water slide and splash right into the lake.

Lake Erie Metropark Wave Pool

32481 West Jefferson, Rockwood
313-379-5020

Location: Brownstown Township between Gibraltar and Rockwood, along Lake Erie
Hours: Memorial Day-Labor Day: 9:30 a.m.-8 p.m., daily.
Admission: $3. $1.50 twilight (5 p.m.-closing). Raft rental $1.50 per raft. $2 daily vehicle permit, $10 annual vehicle permit.
Ages: All ages. Small children need to be closely supervised.
Plan: Half day-full day visit
Parking: Free on site
Lunch: Snack bar and picnic tables adjacent to pool area

Facilities: Bathrooms, coin lockers, wet shop with beach paraphernalia and rafts

Throughout the day, the pool alternates periods of three-foot waves with intervals of calm. Be sure to arrive early enough to rent a raft. It's more fun to ride the wild waves on a raft.

Red Oaks Waterpark

1455 East Thirteen Mile Road, Madison Heights
313-585-6990

Location: Between John R and Dequindre
Hours: 11 a.m.-7 p.m., Memorial Day-Labor Day
Admission: $6 Oakland County residents, $7 non-residents, $3.50 seniors, $3.50 twilight (after 5 p.m.). Under 43 inches free.
Ages: All ages. Supervise small children closely.
Plan: Half day-full day visit
Parking: Free on site
Lunch: Concessions, picnic areas, and grills
Facilities: Bathrooms, beach house, carpeted pool deck, raft and lounge chair rental at admission window

Red Oaks offers the largest wave-action pool in Michigan. Be sure to arrive early to rent a raft. It's more fun to ride the waves on a raft. The 360-foot water slides splash down into a separate pool and are the longest in the Midwest. What a wild way to beat the summer's heat.

Rolling Hills Water Park

7660 Stony Creek, Ypsilanti
313-482-FUNN

Location: Rolling Hills County Park, Textile and Stony Creek Roads
Hours: 11 a.m.-8 p.m. daily, Memorial Day-Labor Day
Admission: $3 weekdays, $4 weekends and holidays. Children under 36 inches are free.
Ages: Must be 36 inches or taller to use water slide. Small children should be carefully supervised in wave pool.
Plan: Half day-full day visit
Parking: $2.50 vehicle entry fee for Ypsilanti Township residents; $5 non-residents.
Lunch: Concessions, picnic tables and picnic pavillion in county park

Facilities: Water park offers a wave pool, three water slides—a body slide, tube slide, and kiddie slide—and an activity pool for small children. Rolling Hills County Park offers hiking trails, sand volleyball, play area, and disc golf (frisbee golf) course.

Wile away the dog days of summer at Rolling Hills Water Park, where small children can play in their own activity pool and whoosh down their own miniature water slide.

Veterans Park Water Slide

2150 Jackson Road, Ann Arbor
313-761-7240

Location: At the juncture of Jackson and Maple Roads
Hours: 1-7 p.m. Monday-Friday. Noon-7 p.m. Saturday, Sunday and holidays, Memorial Day—mid-June. 1-5 p.m. and 6:30-8 p.m. Monday-Friday. Noon-5 p.m. and 6:30-8 p.m. Saturday, Sunday and holidays, mid-June–mid-September.
Admission: Swim: $2 adults, $1.25 children. Water slide: $4 adults, $2.50 children 17 and under and seniors.
Ages: For water slide, children must be at least 42 inches tall.
Plan: Half day-full day visit
Parking: Free on site
Lunch: Concessions
Facilities: Bathrooms, showers, lockers, skateboard ramp, tennis courts, baseball diamond, TJ's batting cages

Veterans Park offers a full range of water and summer fun. Bring your swim suits, skateboards, and tennis rackets.

Waterford Oaks Wave Pool and Water Slide

1700 Scott Lake Road, Pontiac
313-858-0918

Location: Waterford Oaks County Park, Dixie Highway and Telegraph Road
Hours: 11 a.m.-7 p.m., daily, Memorial Day-Labor Day
Admission: $6 Oakland County residents, $7 non-residents, $3.50 seniors, $3.50 twilight (after 5 p.m.). Under 43 inches free.

Ages: All ages. Supervise small children carefully.
Plan: Half day-full day visit
Parking: Free on site
Lunch: Snack bar, grills, and picnic areas
Facilities: Bathrooms, inflatable rafts available for purchase, beach house. Also in park—tennis, shuffleboard, and volleyball courts.

Take the plunge from Waterford Oaks' dual flume, 340-foot long "Slidewinder" water slide. Or body surf in the three-foot waves that alternate with calm periods in the large wave-action pool.

10
BEST RIDES IN TOWN

Motion and excitement. That's what this chapter is all about. Here are all the best rides in town—on land, sea and air. There are urban trolleys, miniature trains, old-fashioned stern-wheelers, country hay wagons, sleighs, and Detroit's own People Mover. Even when the planes and cars are anchored to the ground in a museum setting, your child will be soaring in his mind's eye.

Abbreviations: SP—site offers school programs; T—site offers group tours; H—wheelchair accessible.

SP	Train

Adrian and Blissfield Railroad
US-223 and Depot Street, Blissfield
517-265-3626

Location: Approximately 60 miles southwest of Detroit
Hours: 12:01 and 2 p.m. Saturday; 12:01 Sunday, April-June and September-October. 12:01, 2 and 4 p.m. Saturday; 12:01 Sunday; 12:01, and 2 p.m. Tuesday and Thursday, July and August. 12:01, 2 and 4 p.m. Saturday and 12:01 Sunday, Thanksgiving Weekend and the first three weekends in December.
Admission: $7.50 adults, $6.50 seniors, $4.50 children 3-12, under 3 free. Group rates and birth-

day party rates available. Dinner train rides are also available at additional charge.

Parking: Free adjacent to train depot

All aboard for a 1½-hour round trip on Michigan's oldest rail line. Relive the golden age of train travel, then disembark and explore Blissfield's quaint country craft and antique shops. Enjoy a meal at the nearby historic Hathaway House Restaurant, which offers young diners a special menu. For Hathaway House Restaurant reservations, call 517-486-2141.

Hot-Air Balloon

Adventures Aloft

Kerr Hardware, 222 South Cedar, Mason
517-676-3740

Location: South of Lansing, off US 127
Hours: Several hours before sunset, Monday-Friday; sunrise and sunset Saturday and Sunday, weather permitting, year-round.
Admission: $140/person, $250/two people, with $110 for an additional person
Parking: Free at Kerr Hardware

The 2½-hour adventure begins at Kerr Hardware. Participants ride out to the fairgrounds or park, enjoy an hour balloon ride, and celebrate afterwards with grape juice or champagne. Flight certificates are awarded to all fliers.

SP T   Hay & Sleigh Rides

Belle River Farms Hay and Sleigh Rides

Masters Road, Memphis
313-392-2000

Location: 20 miles southwest of Port Huron; three miles west of M-19.
Hours: 10 a.m.-3 p.m. Saturday and Sunday, October-February. Groups should call to schedule time.
Admission: For 2-4 people: $50. For groups of 5-10 people: $10 adults, $7 children 11 and younger. For groups of 11 or more people: $100 minimum, $8 adult, $5 children. Discounted rates for youth groups and organizations.

Parking: Free on site

Learn about Percherons in a guided tour of the Percheron horse barn and then take a 45-minute hay or sleigh ride (depending on the snow conditions) through the farm.

Train

Bluewater Michigan Chapter of the National Railway Historical Society
Royal Oak
313-399-7963
313-272-5848

The Bluewater Chapter offers a variety of historic tours and fall color excursions May-October in Southern Lower Michigan and Southwestern Ontario. Call for brochure and dates.

SP H   Passenger Steamship

Boblo Boat
313-284-6116, 519-252-4444

Location: There are two docks. Gibraltar dock —I-75 to exit 29A; 45-minute boat ride. Amherstburg, Ontario, dock—Off Kings Highway 18; 7-minute boat ride.
Hours: Hours vary, May-September
Admission: Tickets cover both boat ride and admission to the Island Theme Park. They vary in price depending on dock and day.
Parking: Each dock charges nominal parking fee
Facilities: Snacks, drinks, and sandwiches are available on the boat as well as on the island

Sure, there are lots of rides, shows, and excitement on Boblo Island, but for some, the main attraction is the windy 45-minute steamship ride from the Gibraltar dock across the Detroit River on the *L.R. Beattie* and *The Friendship.*

Hot-Air Balloon

Capt. Phogg

2084 Thompson Road, Fenton
313-629-3676

Location: 1¼ mile east of US 23 north, off exit 84
Hours: Flying times: Sunrise and two hours prior to sunset, daily, year-round, weather permitting.
Admission: $175/person. Not suggested for small children; older children must be at least 4-feet tall.
Parking: Free in lot

The three-hour program includes pre-flight briefing in the balloon showroom, watching the inflation process, a 45-minute to 1 hour fight, and afterwards, a champagne ceremony in which each participant is awarded a flight certificate and balloon pin.

T   Trolley

Classic Trolley Company

6700 Chase Road, Dearborn
313-945-6100

Location: Ford Road & Warren, 1½ miles east of Southfield
Hours: 9:30 a.m.-5:30 p.m., Monday-Saturday; Noon-5 p.m. Sunday, runs every 50 minutes.
Admission: $1 adults, 75 cents children 3 to 12 and seniors, children 2 and under free.

The Classic Trolley's route includes major Dearborn hotels, the downtown shopping and Village Antiques district, Fairland Shopping Center, Henry Ford Museum and Greenfield Village, and Henry Ford Estate-Fairlane. Take the entire loop around Dearborn or use the trolley to conveniently go from one place to the next. Tours of Metro Detroit are also available, as well as group charters for special occasions.

SP T   Historic Steam Engine

Coe Rail

840 North Pontiac Trail, Walled Lake
313-960-9440

Location: On Pontiac Trail, just north of Maple
Road
Hours: 1 and 2:30 p.m., Sunday, mid-April-
October.
Admission: $6 adults, $5 children 2 to 10 and
seniors. Group rates and group charters avail-
able.
Parking: Free on site
Facilities: Beverages and snacks for sale on
board train.

All aboard for a one-hour ride on a restored 1917
Erie Lakawanna passenger train, with narration
and magic show. School groups and birthday
parties welcome.

Coach Ride

Crown Coach, Inc.

Birmingham
313-360-1373

Location: Coach rides begin in front of Max &
Erma's Restaurant, 250 Merrill Street, Birmingham.
Hours: 7 p.m.-1 a.m., Friday and Saturday, May
1-January 1.
Admisson: $30 for half-hour ride; $55 for one-
hour ride, with four people. $5/each additional
person (coach seats a maximum of 6 people).
Parking: Adjacent lots and metered street parking

Ride in an old-fashioned carriage through downtown and residential Birmingham. Pack a picnic
or sparkling cider and celebrate a family mile-
stone.

Paddlewheel

The Detroiter

300 River Place, Detroit
313-567-1400

Location: At the foot of Jos. Campau at Stroh River Place, on the Detroit River
Hours: Lunch cruise: Noon-2 p.m., daily. Dinner cruise: 7-10 p.m., daily. Moonlight cruise: 11 p.m.-1 a.m. Friday and Saturday, spring-fall. Groups of 25 or more can charter the boat on off-hours.
Admission: Lunch: $19.95 adults, $10 children 12 and under. Dinner Sunday-Thursday: $27.95 adults, $15 children 12 and under. Dinner Friday and Saturday: $30.95 adults, $15 children 12 and under. Moonlight cruise: $14.95.
Parking: Free on site

Cruise the Detroit River while enjoying a deluxe multi-course meal and music. The Detroiter is a 110-foot Mississippi-style paddlewheel.

SP T H   Downtown Transit System

Detroit People Mover
313-962-7245

Location: There are 13 stations along the 2.9 mile route around downtown Detroit
Hours: 7 a.m.-11 p.m., Monday-Thursday. 7 a.m.-midnight, Friday. 9 a.m.-midnight, Saturday. Noon-8 p.m., Sunday. Round-trip rides are approximately 15 minutes long.
Admission: 50 cents, children 5 and under free. Exact change is needed, and token machines selling 50-cent coupons for dollar bills are located in all but the Greektown station.
Parking: Many people find it convenient to park in Greektown and use the station on the third floor of Trapper's Alley, or park in RenCen lots off Jefferson and use the station on the second level of the Millender Center

There's nothing that will make you feel more like a tourist than sailing above the street level and catching a brilliant view of the Detroit River. The People Mover is one of Detroit's best thrills. For a mere 50 cents, you can ride as much as you want, peek into office buildings, view each station's wonderful public art, and feel on top of the world.

Detroit Trolley
1301 East Warren, Detroit
313-933-1300

Location: The trolley runs from Washington and Grand Circus Park to the RenCen and along Jefferson
Hours: Every 12-15 minutes, 7:10 a.m.-5:40 p.m., Monday-Friday. 10 a.m.-5:40 p.m., Saturday, Sunday and holidays. Doesn't run Christmas or New Year's Day.
Admission: 45 cents, exact change
Parking: Best bet—park in RenCen lots and catch the trolley in front of the Visitor's Center at Jefferson, east of Beaubien

Ride the red trolleys and experience downtown Detroit by land after cruising by air on the People Mover. Kids will especially enjoy the old-fashioned pace and the bells.

Detroit Zoo Train
8450 West Ten Mile Road, Royal Oak
313-398-0903

Pay zoo admission and you can ride the train for free, all day. There are two stations, one at the entrance, the other at the back of the zoo, near the Log Cabin Learning Center. *For complete information, see* Science and Nature.

Dossin Great Lakes Museum
100 Strand
Belle Isle Park, Detroit
313-267-6440

Pretend you're on the hull of a great liner or in the cabin of a Detroit River barge. Experience shipping without getting sea sick. *For complete information, see* Museums.

`Paddlewheel`

Frankenmuth Riverboat Tours

445 South Main Street, Frankenmuth
517-652-8844

Location: Behind the Riverview Cafe Restaurant

Hours: 12:30, 2:30, 4:30 and 6 p.m. May, September and October. 12:30, 2:30, 4:30 and 7 p.m. June-Labor Day.

Admisson: $5 adults, $2.50 chidren 3-12, 2 and under are free

Parking: Free

Lean back and enjoy a 45-minute tour on the Cass River in an authentic paddlewheel riverboat, complete with lighthearted music and Cass River folklore.

`SP T`   `Antique Vehicle Rides`

Greenfield Village

20900 Oakwood Boulevard, Dearborn
313-271-1976 (24-hour information)
313-271-1620

During the season (April-Labor Day), visitors can choose a variety of old-fashioned rides, each at an additional fee above admission. There are narrated carriage tours, 30-minute steam engine train rides (the train is open through October), antique car rides, and a 15-minute ride on a old-fashioned sternwheeler, the *Suwanee*. I would recommend the train ride. For $1.50, you can ride back and forth through the village all day. During the winter (January-mid-March), there are sleigh rides, weather permitting, through the closed village. *For complete information, see* Historic Sites.

`SP T H`   `Historic Vehicles`

Henry Ford Museum

20900 Oakwood Boulevard, Dearborn
313-271-1976 (24-hour information)
313-271-1620

Where else can you learn about the automobile in

American life and see such popular culture items as the first McDonald's sign, Texaco service station original pumps, and a 1940s diner? There are also impressive steam trains, motorcycles, airplanes, bicycles, coaches and buggies, as well as antique autos. *For complete information, see* Museums.

SP T   Old-fashioned Train

Huckleberry Railroad

Crossroads Village
G-5055 Branch Road, Flint
313-736-7100

Lean out the windows and catch a breeze. The Huckleberry Railroad is a delightful 45-minute ride on an old-fashioned steam engine. *For complete information, see* Historic Sites.

T   Lightship

Huron Lightship Museum

Pine Grove Park, Port Huron
313-982-0891

Tour the last lightship to operate on the Great Lakes. *For complete information, see* Historic Sites.

SP   Steamboat

Island Queen
Kensington Metropark

2240 West Buno Road, Milford
313-685-1561
1-800-47-PARKS

Location: Kensington Boat Rental
Hours: Noon-6 p.m., daily, June-Labor Day. Weekends only, mid-May-June, and Labor Day-Early October. Group charters available at other times.
Admission: $2 adults, $1.50 children, 12 and under
Parking: Free on site

Step back into history on the 66-passenger, diesel-powered paddlewheel. The 45-minute ride on Kent Lake is a refreshing and relaxing change of pace during summer's dog days.

Old-fashioned Train

Junction Valley Railroad

7065 Dixie Highway, Bridgeport
517-777-3480

Location: Five miles west of Frankenmuth
Hours: 10 a.m.-6 p.m., Monday-Saturday; 1-6 p.m., Sunday, Memorial Day-Labor Day. 1-5 p.m., weekends only, September and October.
Admission: $3.25 adults, $2.75 children, $3 seniors
Parking: Free on site

Kids will love riding 22 feet down a steep grade into a valley on this quarter-size train as lights flash and bells clang. In the valley, there is a railroad-inspired playground.

SP   Hay & Sleigh Rides

Kensington Farm Center's Hay and Sleigh Rides

2240 West Buno Road, Milford
1-800-47-PARKS

Location: Farm Center
Hours: Every 30 minutes, 12:30 p.m.-4:30 p.m., weekends. Group charters available at other times.
Admission: $1.50 adults, $1 children
Parking: Free on site

Ride through Kensington's fields, ripe with shimmering corn during the fall, the bare skeletal corn shucks silhouetted against the white sky in winter. Kids love the sturdy horses, the old-fashioned hay wagon, and red sleigh. Each ride is approximately 20-minutes long. Warm up and have a snack at the Country Store.

`SP T`   Hay Ride

Langenderfer Farm
11844 Strasburg Road, Erie
313-856-4283

Enjoy a hayride and special activities during the spring. Groups of 12 or more can request an evening hayride and bonfire during the fall. *For complete information, see* Michigan at Work.

`SP`   Hot-Air Balloon

Michigan Balloon Corporation
1380 Friel Street, Burton
1-800-882-6456

Location: Flights leave from Seven Lakes Vineyard, Holly
Hours: Sunrise and two hours before sunset, April-September
Admission: $160/person, group rates available. Prefer children to be at least 12 and 4-feet fall.
Parking: Free at vineyard

Three-hour adventure includes briefing, inflation, one-hour balloon ride and a champagne reception at the vineyard with Seven Lakes champagne and appetizers. All participants are awarded a cloisonne pin and full-color balloon poster.

`SP`   Train

Mount Clemens Train Ride
Gratiot Avenue, Mount Clemens
313-466-5035

Location: Gratiot Avenue and Joy Boulevard
Hours: 1, 2, 3, and 4 p.m., every Sunday, mid-May-third Sunday in September
Admission: Train ride only: $4 adults, $2 children 4 to 12. Train ride and Selfridge Military Air Museum: $4.50 adults, $2.25 children, under 4 free.
Parking: Free on site

Take a 45-minute ride back into time on the 1924 diesel locomotive. Banjo and harmonica music crackles over the loudspeaker; inside the train car are faded ads: "Lux soap flakes—only 10 cents a box." The train goes through the Selfridge Military Base and stops at the Selfridge Military Air Museum for those who want to get off. Passengers are picked up one hour later.

Boat

Pelee Island Cruises
Pelee Island, Ontario, Canada
519-724-2115

Location: Docks are located in Kingsville and Leamington
Hours: Boats leave several times a day, spring-fall. Call for specific times and location.
Admission: $8 adults, $4 child, under 6 free
Parking: Free on site

Take a 2½ hour round trip cruise across Lake Erie from Kingsville or Leamington to Pt. Pelee Island and back. Or take a ride along with your car and spend some time exploring Pt. Pelee by car. Vehicle reservations must be made in advance.

SP T H   **Antique Autos**

R.E. Olds Transportation Museum
240 Museum Drive, Lansing
517-372-0422

Automobile lovers will enjoy all the antique cars.
For complete information, see Museums.

SP   **Hay & Sleigh Rides**

Romeo Horse Drawn Hayrides
64040 Mount Road, Romeo
313-752-6328

Location: Mound Road, just north of Twenty-Nine Mile Road, just northeast of Stony Creek Nature Center.
Hours: Call to reserve group ride (minimum: 13 people)
Admission: $5 per person
Parking: Free on site

Facilities: Bathrooms

Two strapping Belgian horses pull the straw-filled wagon on a scenic back-roads route. Evening rides are also available. During October, take the Howling Halloween ride, Friday-Sunday. $8 adults, $5 children, includes cider.

T	Airplanes

Selfridge Military Air Museum
Selfridge Air Base, Mt. Clemens
313-466-5035

Airplanes are everywhere, majestically grounded in the museum's field and roaring through the sky on Sunday maneuvers. *For complete information, see* Museums.

	Train

Shiawassee Valley Railroad Company
Owosso
517-723-5797

The Shaiwassee Valley Railroad connects Owosso, Chesaning, and St. Charles. Call to schedule an excursion during June-October.

SP	Hay & Sleigh Rides

Silver Saddle Hay and Sleigh Rides
2991 Oakwood, Ortonville
313-627-2826

Location: 6 miles west of M-24 on Oakwood
Hours: 9 a.m.-7:30 p.m., daily, year-round. Groups of 15 or more should call ahead.
Admission: $4 for an hour ride before 5 p.m.; $8 after 5 p.m. $12 Saturday and Sunday, $11 Monday-Friday, $9 Tuesday
Parking: Free on site

Take an hour ride through the country on Silver Saddle's 150 acres. Kids will also enjoy seeing the farm animals and several unusual animals—buffalo, llama, and ostrich.

Train

Southern Michigan Railroad

320 South Division Street, Clinton
517-423-7230 (Tecumseh information)

Location: Three blocks south of US-12
Hours: Trains leave Clinton at 11 a.m., 1, and 3
p.m. and leave Tecumseh at noon and 2 p.m.,
Saturday, Sunday, and holidays, May-October.
Group rides may be scheduled at other times.
Color tours offered in October.
Admission: Varies with ride. Yearly member-
ship available
Parking: Free on site

The Southern Michigan Railroad takes you on a
one-hour-and-20-minute ride between Clinton
and Tecumseh, two charming small towns. It is a
wonderful way to introduce your children to train
travel, enjoy fall scenery, and browse through
Tecumseh's restored shopping disrict.

SP T H   Transportation Museum

Southwestern Ontario
Heritage Village

Essex County Road 23
Essex, Ontario, Canada
519-776-6909

A transportation museum that documents the
progress from foot power to modern-day vehicles. *For complete information, see* Historic
Sites.

Miniature Train

Starr-Jaycee Park Train

Thirteen Mile Road, east of Crooks
Royal Oak

Free train rides are offered noon-5 p.m. on the
first full weekend of every month, April-Novem-
ber, weather permitting.

Yankee Air Force Museum

Willow Run Airport, Ypsilanti
313-483-4030

Kids with a passion for planes will love this hangar full of World War II planes and colorful aviation memorabilia. *For complete information, see* Museums.

11
THAT'S
ENTERTAINMENT

Children love live performances. Whether it's a folk concert, puppet show, holiday classic, or outdoor concert, the Detroit area has it all. For first time theater-goers, check the local library or parks and recreation department for a children's theater series. These shows are especially geared for preschoolers and usually last less than an hour. The Summer Children's Concert Series at Pine Knob Music Theatre, which offers a variety of nationally known children's entertainers, is a wonderful experience for youngsters.

The biggest children's show in town is Youtheatre at Music Hall, offering Saturday and Sunday, October-May performances of the best in mime, drama, dance, music, and puppetry from around the country. The Youtheatre's Wiggle Club is a series designed for three to five year olds. Older children find plenty of interest in the remaining lineup.

Children of all ages enjoy Paper Bag Productions, and Lunch Bunch Players, troupes of professional child actors who serve lunch and then perform Saturdays and Sundays during the school year. For older children, watch for matinee concerts, dances, and shows at Detroit's legitimate theaters. Children will never forget their first trip to Detroit's grand theaters—the Fisher, Fox, Masonic Temple, Music Hall, or Orchestra Hall.

Afternoon Tea at The Ritz-Carlton

Dearborn
313-441-2000

Location: On the southwest corner of Southfield Road and Hubbard Drive
Showtime: 2:30-4:30 p.m. Monday-Thursday. 2-4:30 p.m. Friday-Sunday. Call for advance reservations. Special Spring Teddy Bear children's teas.
Tickets: $10.75
Ages: Older elementary school and up
Parking: Free in adjacent lot

Dress up and enjoy an elegant afternoon at The Ritz. This outing is a perfect opportunity to share wih Grandma and Grandpa.

Afternoon Tea at The Townsend Hotel

Birmingham
313-642-7900, ext. 7159

Location: Downtown Birmingham
Showtime: 3-5 p.m. Tuesday-Saturday. Call for advance reservations. Special Monday Teas are offered throughout the year and include a January Japanese Tea, April Mad Hatter's Tea and Christmas Tea.
Tickets: $12.50. Special Theme Teas may have higher price. Birthday party packages are available.
Ages: Older elementary school and up
Parking: Metered lot just west of the hotel

It's time to introduce your children to the rewards of good manners. Surround yourself with plush furniture, fine china, silver, and gentle music. Enjoy scones, tea sandwiches, and sinfully rich confections. Raise your pinkies and drink soothing tea. Believe it or not, your children will rise to the occasion.

Ann Arbor Community Education and Recreation Junior Theatre

2765 Boardwalk, Ann Arbor
313-994-2300, ext. 23
(Parks and Recreation number)

Location: Ann Arbor School theaters
Showtime: 7:30 p.m., Friday. 1 and 3:30 p.m., Saturday and Sunday. There are usually two productions a year, November and April.
Tickets: $5 adults, $4 children. $3 groups 10 or more.
Ages: Elementary school children
Parking: Free on site

Classic fairy tales and children's literature are brought to the stage by talented Ann Arbor-area school children.

Ann Arbor Community Education and Recreation Mini-Matinee Club

2765 Boardwalk, Ann Arbor
313-994-2300 ext. 23

Location: Ann Arbor school auditorium
Showtime: 2 p.m., Sunday. Four performances during the fall.
Tickets: $5 adults, $4 children. $3 groups 10 or more.
Ages: 4 and up
Parking: Free on site

Each Sunday performance, geared to families with young elementary-aged children, includes a short play or puppet show plus an additional entertainer—either magic, music, dance, mime, or juggling.

Ann Arbor Symphony Orchestra

Michigan Theatre
603 East Liberty, Ann Arbor
313-668-8397 (for tickets by phone)

Location: Liberty and State Streets
Showtime: Once a month, selected weekend evenings, September-April. December family matinee.
Tickets: $12-$18 adult, $4 off ticket price for children. $2 off for seniors.
Ages: 5 and up
Parking: Street parking, nearby lots

Children will especially enjoy the early December concert, "Caroling by Candlelight," a lively sing-along with refreshment and a visit with Santa.

Music

The Ark

637½ South Main, Ann Arbor
313-761-1451

Location: Between Hill Street and Madison. Entrance is on Moseley. The Ark is above the South Main Market.
Showtime: Matinee performances, Sunday afternoons for children's concerts. Adult folk, pop and jazz performances are offered selected weekdays and weekend evenings.
Tickets: $5 adults, $3 children (children's concerts)
Ages: Preschool and up
Parking: Free on site

Peter "Madcat" Ruth, the Song Sisters, the Chenille Sisters, Gemini, and other Ann Arbor and national folk notables make annual appearances at this small, intimate folk club, which offers children's concerts almost once-a-month.

Fun & Games

The Art Castle

1061 East Long Lake Road, Troy
313-680-1127

Location: Long Lake Plaza, east of Rochester Road
Showtime: During the school year: Noon-6 p.m., Monday-Friday. 10 a.m.-6 p.m., Saturday. Noon-5 p.m., Sunday. During the summer: 10 a.m.-6 p.m., Monday-Saturday. Noon-4 p.m., Sunday.

Tickets: Molds are $3.75 and up; magnets and pins are also available
Ages: All ages from preschool through adult
Parking: Free on site

Children of all ages will enjoy painting a plaster mold or splatter-painting a t-shirt or sweatshirt. The Art Castle also offers birthday party and group discounts.

Theater

Attic-Strand Theatre
10 North Saginaw, Pontiac
313-335-8100

Attic Theatre's satellite theater also offers series shows.

Theater

Attic Theatre
2990 West Grand Boulevard, Detroit
313-875-8285

Location: Third and West Grand Boulevard
Showtime: Evening and matinee performances.
Tickets: $10-$24; $2 senior and student discount.
Ages: Most plays are geared for an adult audience; occasionally there are family plays and plays that will greatly appeal to middle school and high school students.
Parking: Use street parking or the Fisher Building lot

Dinner Theater

Baldwin Public Library
300 West Merrill, Birmingham
313-647-1700

Location: Downtown Birmingham
Showtime: 7-8 p.m., selected Thursdays
Tickets: Free
Ages: 6 and up
Parking: Use metered adjacent lots or street parking

Advance registration is necessary for this free family dinner theater. Bring a picnic supper; the library provides punch and an hour's worth of fun from local performers.

Music

Birmingham-Bloomfield Symphony Orchestra
313-645-2276

Location: Temple Beth El, 7400 Telegraph Road, Birmingham. "Nutcracker Ballet" at West Bloomfield High School, Orchard Lake Road, West Bloomfield, and additional locations.
Showtime: Weekend evenings and matinees, October-May
Tickets: $15
Ages: Children will enjoy the Nutcracker in December.
Parking: Free

Family Shows

Birmingham Community House
380 South Bates, Birmingham
313-644-5832

Location: Woodward and Maple Roads
Showtime: Several Saturday performances throughout the year
Tickets: $5
Ages: Preschool and up. Children under 5 must have adult chaperones.
Parking: Use street parking or nearby lots

The Community House offers families a variety of mime, music, magic, dance, storytelling, and drama performed by traveling troupes and local entertainers.

Theater

Birmingham Theatre
211 South Woodward, Birmingham
313-644-1096

Location: ½ block south of Maple on South Woodward
Showtime: 8 p.m., Tuesday-Saturday. 2 p.m., Wednesday and Sunday. 7 p.m., Sunday.
Tickets: $15-$32.50
Ages: Most plays are geared for an adult audience; occasionally a family show will play during the holiday season
Parking: There is a lot north of the theater on South Woodward and a structure immediately behind the theater on Brownlee Street.

Family Shows

Boarshead Theatre

425 South Grand Avenue, Lansing
517-484-7800

Location: Downtown Lansing, off I-496
Showtime: Evening and matinee performances
Tickets: $15-$24 Main Stage productions; $6-$7 Family shows
Ages: Ages vary depending on shows.
Parking: Free

Professional theater offering a wide variety of productions. During the Christmas season and spring, the theater offers plays for families with small children.

SP   Theater

Bonstelle Theatre

3424 Woodward Avenue, Detroit
313-577-2960

Location: Woodward and Mt. Elliott, one block south of Mack
Showtime: 8 p.m., Friday and Saturday. 2 p.m., Sunday
Tickets: $6-$8
Ages: Generally, shows for adult audience with a family show each holiday season. Every few years *A Christmas Carol* is performed.
Parking: Lot adjacent to theater on Mt. Elliott

Chrysler Theatre
Cleary International Centre
201 Riverside Drive West, Windsor, Ontario
519-252-8311
519-252-6579 (box office)

Location: Riverside Drive West and Ferry Street, one block west of Ouellette Avenue
Showtime: Evenings and matinees, weekdays and weekend, depending on show.
Tickets: $7-$10
Ages: Preschool and elementary school
Parking: Metered street parking, lots across the street near the river, also in back of the auditorium

Several children's shows are offered each season as part of the Cleary Presents Series, appealing to families with young children. The Windsor Symphony Orchestra also offers a family concert series at Chrysler Theatre.

Clawson Parks and Recreation
Children's Series
509 Fisher Court, Clawson
313-435-4500

Location: Hunter Community Center
Showtime: 2 p.m. Saturday
Tickets: $2
Ages: Preschool-early elementary
Parking: Free on site

A children's concert series offering families a variety of classic tales and performances by local magicians, musicians, and comedians.

Cobo Arena
600 Civic Center Drive, Detroit
313-396-7600

The Detroit Rockers, the area's only professional soccer team, plays here.

Special Events

Cobo Hall
1 Washington Boulevard, Detroit
313-224-1010

Cobo Hall hosts the annual Autoshow in January, Home Furniture and Flower Show in March, and the Christmas Carnival in December.

Family Shows

The Community Center of Farmington and Farmington Hills
24705 Farmington Road, Farmington Hills
313-477-8404

Location: Farmington Road, just north of Ten Mile Road
Showtime: Selected evenings throughout the year.
Tickets: Usually under $5
Ages: All ages
Parking: Free on site

The whole family will enjoy an evening of children's theater, puppet shows, or family entertainment, and also a series of family holiday events followed by desserts.

Family Shows

Concerts For Kids
Grosse Pointe War Memorial
32 Lakeshore Drive, Grosse Pointe Farms
313-881-7511

Location: William Fries Auditorium, Grosse Pointe War Memorial, Lakeshore Drive near Fisher Road
Showtime: 11 a.m., Saturday. Selected Saturdays during the school year.
Tickets: $5 adults, $4 children. Series ticket discounts.
Ages: Preschool-upper elementary

Parking: Free on site

Local children's entertainers perform one-hour concerts and puppet shows in an intimate setting.

Family Shows

Cranbrook Summer Children's Theatre
313-645-3678

Location: Cranbrook Education Community, 500 Lone Pine Road, Bloomfield Hills
Showtime: Public performances held at the end of summer classes in late July, early August. One set of performances involve students in third through fifth grades, the other grades nine-college.
Tickets: Moderate prices
Ages: Preschool and up
Parking: Free on site

Your children will enjoy watching their peers perform folk and fairy tales or modern musicals.

T   Theater

Croswell Opera House
129 East Maumee Street, Adrian
517-264-7469

Location: M-52 and Business US-223
Showtime: 8 p.m., Friday and Saturday. 3 p.m., Sunday. Winter and summer theater. April Grand Opera.
Tickets: Winter: $10-$18. Summer: $12-$14.
Ages: While most shows are geared for an adult audience, a family holiday musical is always offered at the end of November and beginning of December
Parking: Metered street parking, large metered lot behind the theater

The Croswell Opera House, the oldest continuously operating theater in Michigan, is a historic site worth seeing. Drive out for the holiday musical or a light musical during the summer. Call ahead to arrange a tour of the building.

Detroit Center for the Performing Arts

Eastown Theatre
8041 Harper Avenue, Detroit
313-925-9292
313-884-5741 (office)

Location: Two blocks north of I-94 at the Van Dyke exit
Showtime: 10 a.m., Wednesday-Friday. Selected evenings vary with production—call to verify.
Tickets: $4 children. $8-12 evening. Group rates available.
Ages: Preschool and up
Parking: Free parking in three lighted, secure lots within a block of the theater

Detroit Center for the Performing Arts offers six children's theater touring productions, performed at weekday matinees at the Eastown, open to school groups and the public.

Omnimax Theater

Detroit Science Center

5020 John R, Detroit
313-577-8400

The Omnimax Theater's 360° domed ceiling draws you into the movie, creating a sense that you are moving with the motion on the screen. Children will enjoy this excitement. *For more information, see* Museums *and* Science and Nature.

Music

Detroit Symphony Orchestra Young People's Concerts

Orchestra Hall
3711 Woodward Avenue, Detroit
313-833-3700

Location: Between Warren and Mack, one mile south of the DIA

Showtime: 11:30 and 2 p.m., Saturday. Usually four concerts each season.
Tickets: $6-$17
Ages: All ages, but 4 to 8 would derive the greatest enjoyment
Parking: $3, lots on Parsons and on Woodward.

These light classical concerts are designed to familiarize children with serious music in a fun way. The Detroit Symphony plays along with dance, mime, puppets, and guest conductors.

Special Event

Disney's Magic Kingdom on Ice

Mickey and his friends fill the ice in Joe Louis Arena for a week of matinee and evening performances.

Theater

Fisher Theatre

West Grand Boulevard at Second, Detroit
313-872-1000 (information)
313-871-1132 (group sales)

Location: West Grand Boulevard and Second Avenue
Showtime: 8 p.m., Tuesday-Saturday. 2 p.m., Saturday and Sunday. 7:30 p.m., Sunday.
Tickets: $25-$50
Ages: Most plays are geared for an adult audience; occasionally there are plays and musicals appropriate for a young audience.
Parking: Use lots adjacent to the theatre, $3-$5.

The Fisher Theatre is housed in a landmark building (See Historic Sites) and is Detroit's major "Broadway" playhouse.

Family Shows

Flint Youth Theatre

at Bowers Theatre
1220 East Kearlsey, Flint
313-760-1018

Location: Flint's Cultural Center
Showtime: Weekday and weekend performances, November, March, and July.
Tickets: $3.50. Group rates available.
Ages: Preschool and up
Parking: Free on site

Three shows a year with local children and guest performers.

Theater

Flint Youth Theatre
at Whiting Auditorium
924 East 6th Street, Flint
313-760-1018

Location: Downtown Flint
Showtime: 4:30 and 7 p.m. Weekday performances
Tickets: $3.50
Ages: Preschool and up
Parking: Free on site

A series of four touring shows offers puppets, plays and musical tales.

Theater

Fox Theatre
2211 Woodward, Detroit
313-396-7600 (information)
313-645-6666 (tickets by phone)

Location: On Woodward, two blocks south of I-75
Showtime: Evening and matinee performances
Tickets: Prices vary with performances
Ages: While most shows are geared for an adult audience, family holiday concerts are scheduled for December and *Sesame Street Live!* for January.
Parking: Lot across the street between John R and Woodward, Fox parking tower on north side of theater, underground lot at Grand Circus Park. Discounted parking voucher available.

The Fox is an opulently beautiful, landmark Detroit theater you won't want to miss. *See also* Historic Sites.

Freedom Hill

15000 Metroparkway, Sterling Heights
313-979-8750

Location: On Metroparkway (Sixteen Mile) between Utica and Schoenherr Roads
Showtime: Concerts are scheduled May-September
Tickets: Price varies with concert
Ages: Varies depending on type of concert
Parking: $3-$5 on site

Freedom Hill books concerts throughout the summer and offers families a chance to sit up on a hill and enjoy an outdoor concert. Ethnic festivals are also held here during the summer.

The Fun Factory

U of M Dearborn, Dearborn
313-593-5390

Location: U of M Dearborn campus
Showtime: 7:30 p.m. Tuesday, September-April
Tickets: Free
Ages: All ages
Parking: Free on site

This family entertainment series brings to the stage Michigan jugglers, ventriloquists, and musicians.

Fun with Plaster

6718 Orchard Lake Road, West Bloomfield
313-932-5210

Location: Just south of Maple Road
Showtime: Noon-6 p.m. Monday. 11 a.m.-9:30 p.m. Tuesday. 11 a.m.-6 p.m. Wednesday-Saturday. Noon-5 p.m. Sunday.
Tickets: Average plaster mold is $3.50, plus $1 for paint. Group and birthday party rates available.

Ages: Preschool-adult
Parking: Free

Try your hand at painting plaster molds; leave the mess behind you and take home a finished masterpiece.

Gem Theatre

58 East Columbia, Detroit
313-396-7600 (information)
313-963-9800 (box office)
313-645-6666 (tickets by phone)
Location: Across Woodward Avenue, east of the Fox Theatre
Showtime: Evening and matinee performances
Tickets: Prices vary with performances
Ages: While most shows are geared for an adult audience, older children will enjoy the cabaret atmosphere.
Parking: Lots adjacent to theater

Take a trip back to an ornate 1920s movie house in this authentically restored, intimate theater, now offering a variety of musical plays and revues. *See also* Historic Sites.

The George Burns Theatre for the Performing Arts

33330 Plymouth Road, Livonia
313-422-8200
1-800-589-8000 (theater hotline)

Location: Corner of Farmington and Plymouth Roads
Showtime: Evening and matinee performances
Tickets: Prices vary with performances
Ages: Most shows are geared for adult audiences
Parking: Free in front of theater

This newly renovated, former movie theater opened October 1992 and plans to bring Broadway theater to the Detroit suburbs.

Greenfield Village Theatre Company

Henry Ford Museum, Dearborn
313-271-1620

Location: Henry Ford Museum
Showtime: Matinee and evening performances throughout the year. Most plays are geared for an adult audience, but children are welcome. During December, a special children's classic is usually performed.
Tickets: December show: $6. Other shows: $9. Dinner and show: $27.
Ages: 6 and up
Parking: Free on site

Greenfield Village Theatre Company's holiday performances are adaptations of classic children's stories. Older children who enjoy live performances will enjoy the costumes, scenery, and meeting the performers up close after the show.

Grosse Pointe Children's Theatre

Grosse Pointe War Memorial
32 Lakeshore Drive, Grosse Pointe Farms
313-881-7511, 313-885-6219

Location: William Fries Auditorium, Grosse Pointe War Memorial, Lakeshore Drive near Fisher Road
Showtime: Matinees and evenings, selected Saturdays and Sundays
Tickets: $6.50 adults, $5 children and seniors
Ages: All ages
Parking: Free on site

The Grosse Pointe Children's Theatre, made up of school-aged children, performs several energetic shows throughout the year, including one for the December holidays. Birthday parties and groups receive special recognition before the performance.

Theater

Hilberry Theatre
Corner of Cass and Hancock, Detroit
313-577-2972

Location: Cass is one block west of Woodward; Hancock is one block south of Warren.
Showtime: The Hilberry offers first rate adult shows in evening and matinee performances, October-May. A children's show is performed 10:30 a.m., Monday-Saturday for approximately two weeks, end of June-early July.
Tickets: $10-$15 for regular series; $2.50 for July's children's show. Group rates available.
Ages: 3 to 13 years for the children's show
Parking: Two lots across Cass from the theater, $2.50 fee

Children will enjoy summer's special children's play, performed in the Hilberry's intimate Studio Theatre. After the performances, cast members are on hand to give autographs.

Special Event

Ice Capades
During March, Olympic gold medalists and other outstanding skaters perform their annual extravaganza of skill and beauty at the Palace.

Family Shows

Independence Oaks Nature Center Amphitheatre
9501 Sashabaw Road, Clarkston
313-858-0906

Location: 2½ miles north of I-75, on Sashabaw Road
Showtime: Matinees and evening performances throughout the year
Tickets: Varies according to program
Ages: All ages
Parking: Vehicle entry fee: $3.50 weekdays, $4.50 weekends and holidays

The Independence Oaks Amphitheatre offers a variety of entertaining and educational family shows that focus on Michigan history and Michigan's natural resources.

Jewish Community Center

Aaron DeRoy Theatre
6600 West Maple, West Bloomfield
313-661-1000, ext. 34

Location: Maple Road, just west of Drake Road
Showtime: Evening and Sunday matinee performances, depending on show
Tickets: $4
Ages: Preschool and up
Parking: Free on site

Family shows and concerts are offered throughout the year. During November's Jewish Book Fair week, there are children's programs held on Sunday afternoon. In addition, JET, a Jewish repertory theater, offers a series of adult plays (313-788-2900).

Jewish Community Center

15110 West Ten Mile Road, Oak Park
313-967-4030

Location: Ten Mile Road, just east of Greenfield Road
Showtime: Selected Sunday matinees, year-round
Tickets: $4
Ages: Preschool to 7
Parking: Free on site

Throughout the year, the center offers afternoon performances of local storytellers, children's theater, and puppetry.

Joe Louis Arena

600 Civic Center Drive, Detroit
313-396-7600

The arena hosts Ringling Bros. and Barnum & Bailey Circus, Walt Disney's Magic Kingdom On Ice, and a host of rock concerts. Parents who want to take their children to a rock concert, but let the children enjoy the concert without them, can wait in the "Parents' Room."

Karaoke
Wing Hong's Tokyo Japanese Steak House
31431 West Fourteen Mile Road,
Farmington Hills
313-851-8600

Location: At the corner of Fourteen Mile and Orchard Lake Roads.
Showtime: 9:30 p.m.-2 a.m. daily. Call ahead for an earlier starting time or if bringing a group.
Tickets: $5/person includes hors d'oevres, munchies, soft drinks, or menu items.
Ages: All ages
Parking: Free on site

Part sing-along, part follow-the-bouncing ball, part human jukebox, karaoke is a Japanese import you and your kids will find hard to resist. While most karaoke takes place in smoke-filled bars, Wing Hong offers families a spacious dining room and, if you arrive early, you might have the place to yourself. Get ready to sing your favorite 50's or Motown, or one of the hundreds of songs listed in the karaoke songbook.

Kids Koncerts
Southfield Parks and Recreation
26000 Evergreen Road, Southfield
313-354-4717

Location: Room 115, Parks and Recreation Building, Evergreen Road, just north of Ten Mile Road
Showtime: 1:30-2:15, once-a-month on Saturday
Tickets: $3.50. Group rates available.
Ages: 4 to 10
Parking: Free on site

Once-a-month, throughout the year, Southfield Parks and Recreation brings to the stage a series of clowns, mimes, musicians, and magicians to entertain area families.

```
Toy Lending Library/Disabilities
```

Lekotek
12121 Hemingway, Redford
313-937-2777

Location: Inside the Redford Township Community Center, Hemingway and Capitol Avenue
Showtime: Call for appointment; available daytime and evenings
Tickets: $100/year family membership; $75/year with coupon; scholarships available
Ages: 6 weeks-21 years
Parking: Free on site

Lekotek is a non-profit, toy lending library offering positive play experiences for families whose children are mentally or physically disabled. All family members are encouraged to come to the play appointment and with the help of a trained play leader, learn how best to use the toys with their mentally or physically impaired youngster. Up to six toys can be borrowed each visit.

```
Family Shows
```

Lunch Bunch Players
313-277-6669
313-326-7042

Location: Area theaters; varies each season
Showtime: 1 p.m. Saturday; 3 p.m. Sunday, October-May. Special weekday matinees are available for groups
Tickets: $7 adult, $5 child. $2 additional for pizza lunch. Snacks and drinks are often available before the show.
Ages: Preschool-middle school
Parking: Call to verify; depends on site

Producer/director Mary F. Bremer and her troupe of charming and talented child performers present two musical shows a year in area theaters. If ordered ahead, families can come early for a pizza lunch before the show.

MacKenzie Hall
Children's Concert Series—
"The Peanut Gallery"

3277 Sandwich Street
Sandwich, Ontario, Canada
519-255-7600

Location: From the bridge, take Riverside Drive west until it becomes Sandwich Street. MacKenzie Hall is located at Sandwich and Brock.
Showtime: 2 p.m., Sunday, October-February
Tickets: $7.50 (Canadian funds)
Ages: Preschool-11
Parking: Free on site

Mimes, musicians, puppeteers, and dancers entertain children, who are sitting informally on the floor in a bright and modern gallery.

McMorran Place Theatre

701 McMorran Boulevard, Port Huron
313-985-6166

Location: Downtown Port Huron, McMorran Boulevard and Huron Avenue
Showtime: Evening and matinee performances
Ages: Depends on specific show.
Tickets: Prices vary with performances
Parking: On site

McMorran Place Theatre offers a variety of family entertainment year-round, including concerts, dance, and theater.

Macomb Center for
the Performing Arts

44575 Garfield Road, Mount Clemens
313-286-2222
313-286-2268 (group rates)

Location: Garfield and Hall (M-59) Roads, near Lakeside Mall

Showtime: 10 a.m. and 1 p.m., usually one Saturday a month, September-April
Tickets: $4-$20
Ages: Preschool-adult
Parking: Free on site

The Sunshine Series brings national and local children's theater troupes to the Macomb Center stage, performing classic fairy tales and magic. In addition, there are a family series of shows and many December holiday shows, including *A Christmas Carol.*

Theater, Movies

Magic Bag Theatre

22918 Woodward Avenue, Ferndale
313-544-3030

Location: North of Nine Mile Road, on the east side of Woodward
Showtime: Matinee and evening performances and movies.
Tickets: Varies depending on event
Ages: Varies depending on event
Parking: Metered parking along Woodward

This renovated movie theater offers a cozy setting for full schedule of art movies, and concerts.

Dinner Theater

Maplewood Family Theatre

31735 Maplewood, Garden City
313-525-8846

Location: Maplewood Community Center
Showtime: 6 p.m., once a month on Tuesdays, throughout the year
Tickets: $6 includes dinner and show
Ages: All ages
Parking: Free on site

Enjoy a light meal and a performance by a local children's theater troupe.

Marquis Theatre

135 East Main, Northville
313-349-8110

Location: Downtown Northville
Showtime: Selected matinee and evening performances for the public and school groups throughout the year
Tickets: $5 adults, $4 children
Ages: Preschool and up
Parking: Metered parking on street or in municipal lots

Come to the Marquis Theatre, a national historic landmark in Northville, sink into plush red velvet seats and munch on buttery popcorn as you watch a lively rendition of a children's classic, or a popular musical. All shows are suitable for families; three are geared specifically to children and performed during spring, summer, and winter.

Marvin's Marvelous Mechanical Museum and Emporium

Hunter's Square Shopping Plaza
31005 Orchard Lake Road, Farmington Hills
313-626-5020

Location: On Orchard Lake Road, just south of Fourteen Mile Road
Showtime: 10 a.m.-10 p.m., Monday-Saturday. Noon-8 p.m. Sunday.
Tickets: 25 cents for most machines and rides. A dollar bill changer is located near the rides.
Ages: Preschool and up
Parking: Free lot on site

Line your pockets with quarters and come to Detroit's only indoor ride emporium. Over 300 mechanical games, kiddie rides, and authentic old-fashioned pinball machines make this a child's dream come true. Toddlers will love the variety of rides, the circus atmosphere, and the continuous bells and bleeps. Older children will want to try to outwit the "metal grabbers" and snag a special prize, or shoot ducks and enemies on beautifully restored machines, many built in the early part of the century. There's plenty of room for birthday parties.

Masonic Temple

500 Temple, Detroit
313-832-2232 (information)
313-871-1132 (group sales)

Location: Temple and Second
Showtime: Matinee and evening performances
depending on show
Tickets: Vary, depending on show
Ages: Generally geared to an adult audience, al-
though many shows are of interest to children of
all ages
Parking: Use area lots, $3-$5

The Masonic Temple Theatre, a designated historic building with a seating capacity of over
4,000 seats, is one of the area's most beautiful
and largest theatrical houses. It hosts the Michigan Opera Theatre, dance concerts, and touring
shows, including musicals with spectacular sets.

Meadow Brook Music Festival

Oakland University, Rochester
313-396-7600 (information)
313-645-6666 (Ticket orders)

Location: Walton Boulevard, between Adams
and Squirrel Roads
Showtime: Weekday and weekend evening
concerts for families and adults.
Tickets: $22.50-$30 pavilion; $12.50-$17.50
lawn.
Ages: All ages
Parking: $5 parking on site

From June to September the Music Festival also
offers a full season of classical, jazz, and pops,
evening performances. Families are welcome;
they may picnic on the lawn before and after the
concert. Children 12 and under are admitted free
on the lawn when accompanied by paying adults.

Meadow Brook Theatre

Oakland University, Rochester
313-377-3300 (box office)
313-370-3316 (group sales)

Location: Walton Boulevard between Adams
and Squirrel Roads, on the campus of Oakland
University
Showtime: Matinee and evening performances
depending on play. Student discounts, Wednes-
day and Saturday matinees, Tuesday and
Wednesday evenings.
Tickets: $16-29. Student tickets are discounted.
Ages: Generally an adult audience, but many
plays are appropriate for 11 and up
Parking: Free on site

Seven plays are offered each season; each offers
special school matinees. The annual December
favorite, *A Christmas Carol*, is fun for the entire
family.

Puppet Shows

Meadowbrook Village Mall
Puppet Theatre

82 North Adams Road, Rochester
313-375-9451

Location: The puppet theater is located in a
storefront space inside the mall.
Showtime: 7 p.m. Monday-Friday, 1, 2, and 3
p.m. Saturday and Sunday
Tickets: Free
Ages: Preschool-early elementary
Parking: Free in adjacent lot

Each month, a new classic fairy tale adaptation is
presented, offering parents and their small children a 25-minute respite from shopping. Children
sit on miniature bleachers, riveted to the small
puppet stage. Narration, dialogue, and music are
taped, but the puppet manipulation is live.

Michigan Opera Theatre
Detroit
313-874-SING (information)
313-874-7889 (group sales)

Location: The season is split between Masonic Temple (500 Temple Avenue) and the Fisher Theatre (West Grand Boulevard). Fall 1994 the season will move to Grand Circus Theatre, 1526 Broadway.
Showtime: 1 p.m. matinees and 8 p.m. evenings for selected shows. Some 6:30 p.m. Sunday performances. Usually 5-6 productions a season.
Tickets: $14.50-$63.50. 50 percent discount for students and seniors one hour before show. Group rates available.
Ages: 7 and up
Parking: $3.75, lots adjacent to theater

Each season, the Michigan Opera Theatre offers a special student matinee for one of its shows with great appeal for children. A question-and-answer session follows the performance. The MOT also provides a traveling "Community Programs" for performances in the schools and special American Sign Language performances for the hearing-impaired.

Michigan Renaissance Festival
Holly
313-645-9640 (office)

Location: One mile north of Mt. Holly, Inc., on Dixie Highway (US 10) between Pontiac and Flint
Showtime: 10 a.m.-7 p.m., weekends, mid-August-late September
Tickets: $10.95 adult, $5.95 children (5-12), under 5 free. Group prices available.
Ages: All ages
Parking: Free on site

Enter a sixteenth-century village dell and take part in the merrymaking. Children will enjoy old-fashioned rides and entertainment—puppet shows, dance, juggling, jousting, and more.

Michigan Theater

"Not Just For Kids"
603 East Liberty, Ann Arbor
313-668-8397

Location: West of State Street, just off the U of
M campus
Showtime: Weekend afternoons
Tickets: $8.50
Ages: Preschool and up
Parking: Use parking lot on Maynard and East
Liberty

The "Not Just For Kids" series offers children an
introduction to the performing arts by bringing to
the stage nationally prominent singers, dancers,
actors and puppeteers.

Movie Matinees

Boomer parents who remember spending every
Saturday at the movies munching on milk duds
will be happy to know that several area theaters
offer special children's movies—those rated G
and PG—at discounted prices year-round or as a
summer series.

Year-round discounted children's matinees are
offered at the Loeks-Star Theatres: Star Gratiot,
35705 Gratiot Avenue, Clinton Township, 313-
791-5428; Star John R, 32289 John R Road,
Madison Heights, 313-585-4477; Star Lincoln
Park, Southfield and Dix, Lincoln Park, 313-382-
9647; Star Taylor, 22265 Eureka Road, Taylor,
313-287-8040; Star Winchester, 1136 South
Rochester Road, Rochester, 313-656-1160.

Summer movie matinees are offered at the
Novi Town Center Cinema, Novi Road and I-96,
Novi, 313-344-0077, and the Farmington Civic
Theatre, 33332 Grand River, Farmington, 313-
474-1951.

Muppet Babies Live!

The Fox Theatre hosts the Saturday morning cartoon crew during its annual visit in April.

Music Hall

350 Madison Avenue, Detroit
313-963-7680
313-963-7622 (group sales)

Location: Madison Avenue exit off I-75
Showtime: 2 or 8 p.m., depending on performance. Youtheatre at Music Hall: 11 a.m. and 2 p.m. Saturday; Some 2 p.m. Sunday performances, October-May.
Tickets: Varies depending on performance. $4-$6 Youtheatre.
Ages: 3 and up
Parking: Lighted parking on all four sides of theater

Music Hall offers Detroiters a first-rate dance concert series, including legendary modern dance and classical dance companies. Throughout the year, it also hosts a music series, theater series, and well-known entertainers. It has also become the new home of Youtheatre.

Oakland University Department of Music, Theater and Dance

231 Varner Hall, Rochester
313-370-3018 (information)
313-370-3013 (box office)

Location: I-75 and University Drive, Oakland University campus
Showtime: A variety of performances, September-April
Tickets: Minimal fee depending on show
Ages: 6 to 12 years
Parking: Free on site

The Department of Music, Theater and Dance includes children's shows and activities, and a family holiday show in December.

Oak Park Family Entertainment Series

14300 Oak Park Boulevard, Oak Park
313-545-6400

Location: Community Center, Oak Park Boulevard, just west of Coolidge
Showtime: 2 p.m., selected Sundays throughout the year
Tickets: Minimal fee
Ages: 12 and under
Parking: Free on site

The Oak Park Department of Recreation has put together a series of Sunday concerts with well-known local musicians, puppeteers, and magicians, perfect for a family afternoon.

Orchestra Hall

3711 Woodward Avenue, Detroit
313-833-3700

Location: Between Warren and Mack, one mile south of the DIA
Showtime: 8 p.m.
Tickets: Varies depending on show
Ages: All ages
Parking: $3, lots on Parsons and on Woodward

Historic Orchestra Hall is once again the proud home of the Detroit Symphony Orchestra.

The Palace

Two Championship Drive, Auburn Hills
313-377-8600,
313-377-0100 (group sales)

Nationally known rock groups and entertainers, plus dazzling special events, take center stage at the Palace. During selected rock concerts, parents without tickets may stay and relax in the "Quiet Room," a banquet room equipped with refreshments. For easiest access to the room, parents should park in the lot north of the auditorium, entrance 3 off Lapeer Road, then bring the kids through the East Foyer, the place to meet them after the concert.

Lunch Theater

Paper Bag Productions

Players Club
3321 Jefferson Avenue East, Detroit
1-800-824-8314

Location: 2½ miles east of the Renaissance Center
Showtime: Lunch at noon, show at 1 p.m., Saturday; lunch at 1 p.m., show at 2 p.m., Sunday, September-May
Tickets: $6.50 includes lunch. Group admissions and birthday packages available.
Ages: Preschool and up
Parking: Free, behind the club

This talented troupe of children, ages 9 to 17, first act as servers, bringing the audience their hot dog, chips, beverage and apple lunch. Then they change into costumes and engergetically burst forth with song and dance. Paper Bag Productions offers two musical productions during the school year. Producer/Director C.J. Nodus also sponsors the West Bloomfield Youtheatre for aspiring children during the summer.

Theater/Children's Theater

The Performance Network

"Kidding Around?" Series
408 West Washington, Ann Arbor
313-663-0681

Location: 2½ blocks west of Main Street
Showtime: Times vary; children's matinees are offered Saturday and Sunday afternoon.
Tickets: Prices vary with each show but are generally moderate
Ages: Preschool-adult, depending on show
Parking: Free on site

The Performance Network is a 150-seat "black box" theater, nestled in among artists' studios in a converted factory building. It hosts a variety of performances by area talent, including dance, and experimental theater. In addition, the "Kidding Around?" is a Saturday matinee series for young children.

Music/Children's Series

Pine Knob Music Theatre

Clarkston
313-645-6666 (Ticketmaster)
313-377-0100 (group sales)
313-377-8600 (information)

Location: Sashabaw Road, off I-75
Showtime: Children's series 1 and 5 p.m. Saturday or Sunday. Concert series, evenings, late May-early September
Tickets: Both pavilion and lawn tickets are available
Ages: Children's concert series geared to preschool and elementary ages. Family shows and concerts for all ages.
Parking: $5 on site

Pine Knob offers outdoor music and entertainment throughout the summer. Plus, a children's concert series offering the best in nationally known entertainers. Relax on the lawn with a picnic or sit in the pavilion. Parents can drop off children at concerts and wait in the "Parents' Park."

Fun & Games

Plaster Playhouse

43063 Hayes, Sterling Heights
313-566-0666

Location: Lakeshore Plaza at Hayes and Nineteen Mile Road
Showtime: 1-8 p.m. Monday-Friday. 10 a.m.-8 p.m. Saturday. Noon-5 p.m. Sunday.
Tickets: Average plaster mold is $3.50. $1 additional for paint.
Ages: Preschool-adult
Parking: Free

One of the many plaster workshops that have sprung up throughout metro Detroit. Plaster Playhouse offers children a chance to become artists and enjoy taking home their painted creation.

Fun & Games

Plaster Playhouse

3050 Union Lake Road, Union Lake
313-360-9920

Location: Corner of Union Lake and Commerce Lake Roads, in Commerce Town Center
Showtime: 10 a.m.-9 p.m., Monday. 10 a.m.-6 p.m., Wednesday-Friday and Sunday. 10 a.m.-8 p.m., Saturday.
Tickets: $1 for the paint. $3.50 and up for the plaster molds. Group rates and birthday party packages available.
Ages: Preschool-adult
Parking: Free on site

At the Plaster Playhouse, kids of all ages can choose a modern plaster mold and in less than an hour, turn it into a colorful work of art. The atmosphere is informal, and the adult supervision encouraging.

Music, Special Events

Pontiac Silverdome

1200 Featherstone, Pontiac
313-456-1600

A variety of concerts and special events play throughout the year in addition to the Detroit Lions.

Theater, Dance

Power Center

121 Fletcher, Ann Arbor
313-763-3333

Ann Arbor's modern facility hosts concerts, dance, theater, and music series. The kids will love the reflecting glass windows.

Puppets in the Park

Bloomer Park
7581 Richardson Road, West Bloomfield
313-334-5660

Location: Richardson Road, ½ mile east of Haggerty Road
Showtime: 1-2 p.m., one weekday in July and August
Tickets: Free
Ages: Preschool and early elementary
Parking: Free on site

Enjoy a balmy summer day, watch a puppet show, and eat a picnic lunch.

Quirk Theatre

124 Quirk, Ypsilanti
313-487-1221

Location: On the Eastern Michigan University campus
Showtime: Evenings and matinees
Tickets: Varies with show
Ages: While most shows are geared for an adult audience, there are several children's shows offered throughout the year.
Parking: On site

The EMU Players perform a holiday play in December and several adaptations of children's classics throughout the year.

Ringling Bros. and Barnum & Bailey Circus

The beginning of October is the time the "Greatest Show On Earth" comes to the Joe Louis Arena.

Royal Hanneford Circus

This circus comes to The Palace in March with lots of animal acts plus death-defying stunts, clowns, and glitter.

Saturday Fun for Kids

Meadow Brook Theatre
Oakland University, Rochester
313-370-3300

Location: Walton Boulevard between Adams and Squirrel Roads, on the campus of Oakland University
Showtime: 11 a.m. Saturdays
Tickets: $6, group discounts available
Ages: 3 and up
Parking: Free on site

Meadow Brook Theatre offers a series of nationally known children's entertainers puppet theater, storytellers, and singers.

September Productions

1212 Josephine Court, Monroe
313-242-8556

Location: Performances are held on stages throughout metro Detroit
Showtime: Saturday and Sunday matinees; evenings during vacations
Tickets: $4 adults, $2 children
Ages: Preschool-elementary
Parking: Varies with site

September Productions, a professional touring company based in Monroe, performs classic children's stories several times a year.

Sesame Street Live!

The Sesame Street gang takes the stage at the Fox Theatre for a wild and noisy show, held for almost two weeks during the end of January.

Shaine Park Concerts

Shaine Park
Martin and Henrietta, Birmingham
313-644-1807 (Public Services)

Location: Two blocks west of Woodward, one block south of Maple
Showtime: 7:30 p.m., every Thursday, June-August
Tickets: Free
Ages: All ages
Parking: Use metered lots and street parking

Pull up a patch of earth and settle in for a lively outdoor concert in the middle of downtown Birmingham. Kids can play on the climbers and swings in the park while you listen to the music.

Showtime at the Playhouse

Edsel and Eleanor Ford House
100 Lake Shore Road, Grosse Pointe Shores
313-884-4222

Location: Off I-94, Vernier Road Exit. Go east to Lake Shore Drive (Jefferson).
Showtime: Early weekday evening performances
Tickets: $4
Ages: Preschool-eighth grade
Parking: Free on site

The Edsel and Eleanor Ford House offers a summer series of lively local musical story-theater, plus special family holiday shows throughout the year.

Special Event

Shrine Circus

The State Fairgrounds Coliseum hosts the colorful and noisy annual Shrine Circus in March.

Family Shows

Stagecrafters Youth Theatre

Baldwin Theatre
415 South Lafayette, Royal Oak
313-541-6430

Location: Between Ten and Eleven Mile Roads
Showtime: Matinee and evening
Tickets: $4
Ages: Preschool and up
Parking: Free on site

Young children will enjoy watching their favorite fairy tales and children's musicals performed by drama students ages 8 to 17, during the Youth Theatre's winter and summer productions. The Stagecrafters also offer an adult season of drama and musicals, September-April. Older children would enjoy many of these productions.

Family Shows, Special Events

State Fairgrounds

1120 West State Fair Avenue, Detroit
313-368-1000

The State Fairgrounds hosts children's theater performances and dog and horse shows throughout the year, the Shrine Circus in March, and the annual Michigan State Fair at the end of August.

Family Shows

Summer Fun Series

Downtown Farmington
313-473-7276

Location: Under the tent on Grand River east of Farmington Road

Showtime: Generally 10:30 and 11:30 a.m. and 1 p.m. Wednesday, mid-June–mid-August
Tickets: Free or minimal workshop fee
Ages: Preschool-elementary
Parking: Use downtown store lots

Series highlights Michigan entertainers and offers a lineup of storytelling, puppetry, songs, comedy, magic, and playlets.

Studio Audience

Television Studio Audiences

You don't need to travel to Los Angeles or New York to be part of a television studio audience. Channels 2, 4, and 7 offer families a chance to sit in on the taping of local shows and see what goes on behind the camera. Just call at least a month ahead of time; spaces are limited and go quickly. Usually the hardest part of the experience is sustaining several minutes of clapping and screaming at the show's beginning and end, but for children, it's a once-in-a-lifetime experience.

Kelly & Co., WXYZ-Channel 7, 20777 West Ten Mile Road, Southfield. 313-827-7777, 313-827-9336

Michigan Lottery Megabucks Giveaway, WDIV-Channel 4, 550 West Lafayette Boulevard, Detroit. 313-222-0444.

Eli and Denny Show, Straight Talk with Rich Fisher, WJBK-Channel 2, 16550 West Nine Mile Road, Southfield. 313-557-2000.

Family Shows

Temple Beth El

Fisher Concert Series
7400 Telegraph Road, Birmingham
313-851-1100

Location: Telegraph, just south of Maple Road
Showtime: 1 p.m. Sunday. Several concerts each year.
Tickets: Free
Ages: Preschool-upper elementary
Parking: Free on site

The Loren B. Fisher Cultural Art Series offers three free performances for families during the year, offering local singers, magicians, clowns, children's opera, and theater.

Family Shows

Troy Parks and Recreation Family Playhouse

Troy Community Center
520 West Big Beaver, Troy
313-524-3484

Location: Between Livernois and Crooks on Big Beaver
Showtime: 2 p.m., Saturday
Tickets: Minimal fee
Ages: Preschool-12
Parking: Free on site

Throughout the year, Troy Parks and Recreation brings to the stage a series of clowns, mime, musicians, and magicians to entertain area families.

Music

West Bloomfield Parks and Recreation Concerts

Marshbank Park
Hiller Road, West Bloomfield
313-334-5660

Location: Hiller Road, north of Commerce Road
Showtime: 7 p.m., several Sundays during the summer
Tickets: Free
Ages: For the entire family
Parking: Free on site

Bring blankets, lawn chairs, and picnic hampers and enjoy outdoor concerts with the entire family.

Summer Theater

West Bloomfield Youtheater

1-800-824-8314

Location: Rehearsals at Ealy Elementary, West Maple Road, West Bloomfield. Performances at West Bloomfield High School, Orchard Lake Road, West Bloomfield.
Showtime: Rehearsals begin mid-June; performances are the end of July and open to the public.
Tickets: Moderate prices
Ages: Preschool and up
Parking: Free on site

Paper Bag Productions' director/producer C. J. Nodus leads this enthusiastic troupe of children ages 5-18 who audition the first weekend in June for a part in the summer's performance of a children's musical.

Music

Windsor Symphony Orchestra
201 Riverside Drive
Windsor, Ontario, Canada
519-252-6579

Location: Chrysler Theatre, Clearly International Centre, Riverside Drive West and Ferry Street, one block west of Ouellette Avenue
Showtime: 2 p.m. and 7 p.m. Saturday. A three-concert family series is offered.
Tickets: Approximately $8 adults, $5 students (Canadian funds)
Ages: 2 and up
Parking: Metered street parking, lots across the street near the river and in back of the auditorium

The emphasis is on fun as classical music is brought to life with art, mime, and humorous conducting.

Family Shows

Young People's Theater
313-996-3888 (ticket information tape)

Location: Performances held in different Ann Arbor auditoriums.
Showtime: Four or five family shows a year, evening and weekend matinee performances. YPT also offers year-round acting classes.
Tickets: Minimal fees

Ages: Shows are geared to an audience of all ages. Children 5 and up perform and act as stagehands.
Parking: Depends on location

Young People's Theater offers talented children a chance to perform in a variety of shows, from folk and fairy tales to modern musicals. Performances are energetic and creative and perfect for the entire family.

Fun & Games

Your Creation!

37144 Six Mile Road, Livonia
313-462-1470

Location: In the Laurel Commons Plaza
Showtime: 11 a.m.-6 p.m., Tuesday-Thursday. 11 a.m.-7 p.m., Friday. 10 a.m.-6 p.m., Saturday. Noon-5 p.m., Sunday.
Tickets: Average plaster mold is $7.
Ages: Preschool-adult
Parking: Free

Just choose a plaster sculpture, put on a smock and start to paint. Your Creation! offers kids of all ages a chance to create.

Family Shows

Youtheatre

Music Hall
350 Madison Avenue, Detroit
313-963-7680

Location: Public performances at Music Hall. Three school field trip locations: Music Hall; Macomb Center for the Performing Arts, 44575 Garfield Road, Mount Clemens; Mercy High School auditorium, 29300 Eleven Mile Road, Farmington Hills. "Puppets at the DIA" at the Detroit Institute of Arts lecture hall.
Showtime: 11 a.m. and 2 p.m. Saturday, October-May. Wiggle Club Shows: 11 a.m. and 2 p.m. Saturday and 2 p.m. Sunday. Additional matinees scheduled during vacation weeks. School field trip matinees 10 a.m. and 12:30 p.m. weekdays. "Puppets at the DIA": 11:30 a.m. and 2 p.m. Saturday.

Tickets: $6 for 1-9 tickets; $5 for 10-29 tickets; $4 for over 30 tickets.

Ages: Special Wiggle Club shows are geared for age 3. The majority of shows are geared for ages 5-12.

Parking: Music Hall has lots on all four sides: fee. Macomb Center for the Performing Arts and Mercy High School: free parking in lot.

For the past 30 years, Youtheatre has offered the finest and largest children's theater season in the Detroit area, bringing us the best in mime, dance, puppetry, performance arts, and theater from around the country. Now Youtheatre offers families performances every Saturday from October to May in the beautifully restored Music Hall. Plan to hold your next scout or civic group outing or birthday party at Youtheatre. Teachers should call to receive a brochure of field trip performances.

12
CHEERING FOR
THE HOME TEAM

The Detroit area abounds with spectator sports. Tigers in the summer; Lions, Spartans and Wolverines in the fall; Red Wings and Pistons in the winter. Sports fans are loyal and tenacious, and they train their children early.

To avoid disappointing your children, send away for tickets early, or ask your friends with season tickets if they'll sell you a few. And when you go, be ready to part with a lot of cash. Most children go to sporting events as much for the food as for the game.

Don't forget to check the team schedules for special promotions. Many sponsors offer free gifts to the first several thousand patrons at a certain game. Your children will be thrilled to leave with a free calendar, mug, t-shirt, visor, cap, ball, or notebook.

Detroit Compuware Ambassadors

Joe Louis Arena
600 Civic Center Drive, Detroit
313-737-7373

Location: Civic Center at the Riverfront, downtown Detroit
Season: September-March
Tickets: $4 students, $8 adults. Ample supply available at door
Lunch: Concessions
Parking: $6 Joe Louis parking structure

Pro Arena Football

Detroit Drive

Joe Louis Arena
600 Civic Center, Detroit
313-396-7600 (information)
396-7575 (season tickets)
396-7910 (group rates)
645-6666 (Ticketmaster to charge tickets by phone)

Location: Civic Center at the Riverfront, Downtown Detroit
Season: May-August
Tickets: $8-$17.50
Lunch: Lots of food concessions, including Little Caesar's Pizza. Our family's favorite is the large soft ice cream cone with chocolate and nutty topping for $1.75.
Parking: Use Joe Louis parking lot, adjacent to arena on Atwater Street. $6 fee.

Pro Football

Detroit Lions

Pontiac Silverdome
1200 Featherstone Road, Pontiac
313-335-4151
313-645-6666 (Ticketmaster to charge tickets by phone)

Location: M-59 and Opdyke Road
Season: August-December

Tickets: $10-$25
Lunch: The Main Event, a full service restaurant, plus lots of concessions.
Parking: Lot on site. $7 fee.
Highlights: Occasional promotions offer free calendars, posters, or growl towels

Training Camp

Detroit Lions Training Camp

Pontiac Silverdome
1200 Featherstone Road, Pontiac
313-335-4131

Location: M-59 and Opdyke Road
Season: 9-11:15 a.m., 3-5 p.m., daily mid-July-mid-August. No morning practice on Sunday.
Tickets: Free
Lunch: Restaurants are located along Walton Blvd.
Highlights: Visitors are allowed to watch the Lions practice. Arrive a half-hour early, and you might be able to catch a few autographs as the players come out to practice.

Pro Basketball

Detroit Pistons

The Palace
Two Championship Drive, Auburn Hills
313-377-0100 (information)
313-645-6666 (Ticketmaster
to charge tickets by phone)

Location: I-75 and M-24
Season: November-April
Tickets: $10.50-$49
Lunch: Lots of choices including Pizza Hut, and Best kosher hot dogs
Parking: Lot on site. $5 fee.
Highlights: There are special promotions throughout the season when fans 14 and younger receive Pistons t-shirts, basketballs, mugs, wristbands, baseball caps, gym bags, or pennants. We took three boys to one game and came home with three new basketballs. Try to attend one of these games!

Detroit Red Wings

Joe Louis Arena
600 Civic Center Drive, Detroit
313-396-7600 (information)
313-396-7575 (season tickets)
313-396-7910 (group rates)
313-645-6666 (Ticketmaster
to charge tickets by phone)

Location: Civic Center at the Riverfront, downtown Detroit
Season: October-March
Tickets: $14-$36
Lunch: Lots of concessions, including Little Caesar's Pizza
Parking: Use Joe Louis parking lot, adjacent to arena on Atwater Street. $6 fee.
Highlights: There are several special games when fans are given calendars or pucks

Detroit Rockers

Cobo Arena
600 Civic Center Drive, Detroit
313-473-0440

Location: Downtown Detroit
Season: November-March
Tickets: $6 and up
Lunch: Concessions include Little Caesar's Pizza
Parking: Cobo roof, Cobo underground, and Joe Louis parking structure

Detroit Tigers

Tiger Stadium, Detroit
313-962-4000 (information)
313-963-7300 (charge by phone)
313-963-9944 (hotline)

Location: Michigan and Trumbull
Season: April-October

Tickets: $4-$12.50. To mail-order tickets, send money order or check with self-addressed envelope, plus specific information regarding number of tickets, game, etc., to: Ticket Dept., P.O. Box 77322, Detroit, MI 48277.
Lunch: Lots of food choices, including the gotta-have ballpark frank!
Parking: Use lots surrounding stadium. $4-$8 fee.
Highlights: The Tigers also have a schedule of special games when gifts of t-shirts, mugs, tote bags, notebooks, and baseball cards are given out.

Pro Baseball Farm Team

Detroit Tiger Triple-A Farm Team Toledo Mud Hens

Ned Skeldon Stadium
2901 Key Street, Maumee, Ohio
419-893-9483

Location: On Key Street, between Heather-downs and Anthony Wayne Trail
Season: April-September.
Tickets: $5 box, $4 reserved, $3 general
Lunch: Concessions
Parking: Free

Pro Indoor Lacrosse

Detroit Turbos

Joe Louis Arena
600 Civic Center Drive, Detroit
313-396-7600 (information)
313-396-7575 (season tickets)
313-396-7910 (group rates)
313-645-6666 (Ticketmaster to charge tickets by phone)

Location: Civic Center at the Riverfront, downtown Detroit
Season: January-March
Tickets: $8-$17.50
Lunch: Many concessions including Little Caesar's Pizza
Parking: Use Joe Louis parking lot, adjacent to arena on Atwater Street. $6 fee.

Auto Racing

Flat Rock Speedway

14041 South Telegraph Road, Flat Rock
313-782-2480, 313-847-6726

Location: One mile south of Flat Rock on Telegraph Road
Season: 5:30 p.m. qualifying, Saturday; 1:30-7 p.m. race, Sunday. May–mid-September.
Tickets: $8 adults, $3 children 6 to 12, under 6 free
Lunch: Concessions
Parking: Free on site

Basketball

Harlem Globetrotters

Both the Joe Louis Arena and The Palace host the hilarious hoopsters in their annual Motown visit. Dates vary each season.

Harness Racing

Hazel Park Raceway

1650 East Ten Mile Road, Hazel Park
313-398-1000

Location: Ten Mile, between Dequindre Road and Couzens
Season: 7:30 p.m., Monday-Saturday, early April–mid-October
Tickets: $3.50 clubhouse, $2.50 grandstand.
Lunch: Two clubhouse restaurants, grandstand concessions
Parking: Use lots surrounding raceway. $1.50 and up fees.

Harness Racing

Jackson Harness Raceway

200 West Ganson, Jackson
517-788-4500

Location: Jackson and Ganson Roads
Season: 7:30 p.m. Wednesday, Friday, and Saturday. 3 p.m. Sunday. April-June and August-October.

Tickets: Free on Wednesday, $2 Friday, Saturday and Sunday
Lunch: Concessions, clubhouse restaurant
Parking: $1

Thoroughbred Racing

Ladbroke Detroit Race Course
28001 Schoolcraft Road, Livonia
313-525-7300, 313-525-7312

Location: Schoolcraft and Middlebelt Roads
Season: 2:30 p.m., Wednesday-Friday. 1 p.m., Saturday. 5 p.m., Sunday. Late March-late November
Tickets: $4 clubhouse, $2.50 grandstand.
Lunch: Clubhouse restaurants, grandstand concessions
Parking: On site. $2.

Rodeo

Longhorn World Championship Rodeo
Saddle up the gang and bring them to The Palace for the annual rodeo every February.

Auto Racing

Michigan International Speedway
12626 US-12, Brooklyn
517-592-6671, 517-592-6666

Location: M-50 and US-12
Season: Special event races are held on weekends, June-August
Tickets: $20-$65 depending on event. Discounts for children 12 and under.
Lunch: Elias Brothers Big Boy concession.
Parking: Free on site

Michigan State University Spartans—Go Spartans!
220 Jenison Field House, East Lansing
517-355-1610

Location: MSU Campus: Football—Spartan Stadium. Basketball—Jack Breslin Student Events Center. Hockey—Munn Arena.
Season: Football—September-November. Basketball—November-March. Hockey—October-March.
Tickets: Football $20, basketball $12 and $10, hockey $9 and $8
Lunch: Concessions
Parking: Most lots around the Football Stadium and Jennison Field House charge $4-$5

Northville Downs
301 South Center, Northville
313-349-1000

Location: Seven Mile and Sheldon Roads
Season: Hours vary with season; call ahead for specific times. Generally, nightly 7:30 p.m. post times and 1:30 p.m. Saturday matinees.
Tickets: $3.50 clubhouse, $2.50 grandstand. Children must be 12 years or older.
Lunch: Clubhouse restaurant, grandstand concessions
Parking: Use lots surrounding site.

University of Detroit Titans
4001 West McNichols Road, Detroit
313-993-1700

Location: On Fairfield between Puritan and McNichols (Six Mile Road), Calihan Hall
Season: December-March (Basketball)
Tickets: $9.75
Lunch: Concessions
Parking: Use adjacent lot.

University of Michigan Wolverines — Go Blue!

1000 South State Street, Ann Arbor
313-764-0247

Location: UofM Campus: Football—UofM Stadium. Basketball—Crisler Arena. Hockey—Yost Field House.
Season: Football—September-November, Basketball—November-March. Hockey—October-March.
Tickets: Football $22, basketball $12-$15, hockey $5-$8
Lunch: Concessions
Parking: Use lots surrounding sites or park on campus and walk

Waterford Hills Road Racing

Waterford Road, Waterford
Independence Township
313-623-0070

Location: Six miles north of Pontiac and ¼-mile east of Dixie Highway (U.S. 10)
Season: 10 a.m. Saturday; 11 a.m. Sunday, May-September.
Tickets: $4 Saturday, $6 Sunday, under 12 free. $5 additional for Pit Pass.
Lunch: Concessions
Parking: Free in lot

Wayne State University Tartars

5101 John C. Lodge Detroit
313-577-4280

Location: Lodge Expressway (M-10) and Warren: Football—WSU Stadium. Basketball—Matthaei Building
Season: Football—September-November. Basketball—November-March.
Tickets: Tickets are available at box office on day of game. Football: $5 adults, $3 students, $1

children 12 and under. Basketball: $3 adults, $2 students, $1 children 12 and under.
Lunch: Concessions
Parking: Use street along Lodge Service Drive or adjacent to sports facilities

Windsor Raceway
Windsor, Ontario, Canada
313-961-9545 or 519-969-8311

Location: Highway 18 and Sprucewood, about three miles from the Ambassador Bridge
Season: 7:30 p.m., Tuesday-Sunday, October-April.
Tickets: $3.50 clubhouse, $2.50 grandstand, children under 12 free
Lunch: Concessions and restaurant
Parking: Lot on site, $1.50.

World Wrestling Federation
The Palace, 3777 Lapeer Road, Auburn Hills
313-377-0100 (information)
313-645-6666 (Ticketmaster)

Location: I-75 and M-24
Season: Hulk Hogan and his gang of comic wrestlers invade The Palace
Tickets: $10-$16
Lunch: Lots of choices, including Pizza Hut, and Best kosher hot dogs
Parking: Lot on site. $5 fee.

13
BURNING
OFF ENERGY
A Sampling of
Participant Sports

If your kids are like mine, they are always full of energy and raring to play. Here's a sampling of sites where they can burn off one or two hours of energy, without signing up for costly lessons. There are places for Little Leaguers' batting and fielding practice, a friendly fishing hole where kids are assured of a catch, area municipal pools, and ice-skating rinks. You have your pick of places that rent canoes and offer bumper bowling, sledding, horseback riding, go-karts, and miniature golf.

Many unusual sports—croquet, archery, frisbee golf, laser tag and splat ball—are also listed. In addition, I've added Michigan's dude ranches, and ski resorts that cater to families, to help you plan your family vacations.

To help your selection, sports are listed alphabetically. I have intentionally omitted specific hours and prices because they fluctuate so rapidly. Please call for directions, hours, and fees.

Archery

It's okay for Jason to play William Tell, just don't fall for the apple-on-the-head trick. You can rent equipment and play for one hour during open shooting.

Detroit Archers Club
5795 Drake Road, West Bloomfield
313-661-9610
313-661-2550

Starlight Archery Co.
3001 Rochester Road, Royal Oak
313-585-1818

Starlight Archery Co.
21570 Groesbeck, Warren
313-771-1580

Batting Cages

Here's your chance to be MVP (Most Valuable Parent) and indulge your child in a Tiger fantasy. Most area batting cages are open April to October and offer slow-pitch and fast-pitch in both softball and hardball. The sites provide bats and batting helmets; bring mitts if there are fielding cages.

Canton Softball Center Complex
4655 West Michigan Avenue, Canton
313-483-9440
313-483-5624

Features: Batting cages (April-October), indoor soccer fields (October-April), restaurant, concessions, softball diamonds

C.J. Barrymore's Sports Center
21750 Hall Road, Mount Clemens
313-469-2800

Features: Batting cages, softball diamonds, go-carts, kiddie karts, miniature golf, video arcade, driving range, pro shop, family restaurant, indoor/outdoor concessions

Four Bears Water Park

3000 Auburn Road, Utica
313-739-5863

Features: Batting cages, miniature golf, water slides, bumper boats, go-carts, petting zoo, restaurant. *For full information, see* Parks.

Grand Slam Baseball
Training Center

3530 Coolidge Highway, Royal Oak
313-549-7100

Features: Batting cages, fielding cages, pro shop, snack bar

Grand Slam U.S.A.

42930 West Ten Mile Road, Novi
313-348-8338

Features: Indoor batting cages, small basketball court, concessions, and birthday party rooms

Home Plate Sports Center

32909 Harper, St. Clair Shores
313-296-5655

Features: Batting cages

Marino Sports Center, Inc.

38951 Jefferson, Mount Clemens
313-465-6177

Features: Batting cages, miniature golf, driving range, pro shop

Midway Golf Range

22381 Van Born, Taylor
313-277-9156

Features: Batting cages, go-carts, miniature golf, driving range

Oasis Golf/Tru Pitch Batting Cages

39500 Five Mile Road, Plymouth
313-420-4653

Features: Batting cages, miniature golf

Red Oaks Golf Dome and
Sports Village

29601 John R, Madison Heights
313-548-1857

Features: Batting cages, go-carts, miniature golf, indoor and outdoor driving range, playscape and snack bar

Sport-Way
38520 Ford Road, Westland
313-728-7222

Features: Batting cages, go-carts, miniature golf

T.J.'s Cages
2150 Jackson Road, Ann Arbor
313-996-1884

Features: Batting cages

T.J.'s Sportsworld
630 Phoenix, Ann Arbor
313-973-0943

Features: Indoor batting cages, basketball courts, volleyball, floor hockey, soccer, frisbee or arena football gym

Van Dyke Sport Center
32501 Van Dyke, Warren
313-979-2626

Features: Batting cages, go-carts, miniature golf, indoor/outdoor driving range, video arcade, restaurant, concessions, pro shop

Bicycling

Rent bicycles-built-for-two or single seaters and take a spin with the kids, April-October

Gallup Park Livery
3000 Fuller Road, Ann Arbor
313-662-9319

Kensington Metropark
2240 West Buno Road, Milford
313-685-1561
For full information, see Parks

Stony Creek Metropark
4300 Main Park Road, Washington
313-781-4242
For full information, see Parks

Waterford Oaks

2800 Watkins Lake Road, Pontiac
313-858-0915

Features: Bicycle motocross (BMX) track, weekly practices and races, and BMX rentals, May-August

Boating

Take your children out to sea every summer on a wild boat ride. Paddle under bridges, talk to the fish, spin some yarns, have a picnic. Surrounded by lakes and rivers, Metro Detroit offers a variety of boat rentals.

Addison Oaks

1480 West Romeo Road, Leonard
313-693-2432

Features: Rowboat and paddleboat rental on Buhl Lake and Adams Lake. *For full information, see* Parks.

Argo Park Livery

1055 Longshore Drive, Ann Arbor
313-662-9319

Features: Canoe and rowboat rental, snacks, and fishing supplies

Delhi Metropark

8801 North Territorial Road, Dexter
313-426-8211

Features: Canoe rental on Huron River. *For full information, see* Parks.

Dodge Park No. 4

4250 Parkway, Pontiac
313-666-1020

Features: Rowboat, paddleboat, and canoe rental on Cass Lake. *For full information, see* Parks.

Gallup Canoe Livery

3000 Fuller Road, Ann Arbor
313-662-9319

Features: Canoe, paddleboat, rowboat and bicycle rental, snacks, fishing supplies, and live bait

Great Lakes Yachts

24400 East Jefferson, St. Clair Shores
313-778-7030

Features: Yacht rental on Lake St. Clair

Groveland Oaks

5990 Grange Hall Road, Holly
313-634-9811

Features: Paddleboat, canoe, rowboat, and
one-person "waterbug" rental on Stewart Lake.
For full information, see Parks.

Heavner's Canoe and Cross
Country Ski Rentals

2775 Garden Road, Milford
313-685-2379

Features: Canoe rental on the Huron River

Independence Oaks

9501 Sashabaw Road, Clarkston
313-625-0877

Features: Rowboat, paddleboat, waterbug,
canoe rental on Crooked Lake. *For full information, see* Parks.

Kensington Metropark

2240 West Buno Road, Milford
313-685-1561

Features: Canoe, paddleboat, and rowboat
rental on Kent Lake. *For full information, see*
Parks.

Orchard Lake Boats
and Windsurfing

3840 Orchard Lake Road, Orchard Lake
313-682-1990

Features: Rowboat, windsurfer rental on Orchard Lake

Pine Lake Marina

3599 Orchard Lake Road, Orchard Lake
313-682-2180

Features: Pontoon boat, motorboat, and rowboat rental on Pine Lake

Stony Creek Metropark
4300 Main Road, Washington
313-781-4242

Features: Paddleboat, sailboat, rowboat, and canoe rental on Stony Creek Lake. *For full information, see* Parks.

Sun and Ski Marina
3981 Cass Elizabeth Road, Pontiac
313-681-7100

Features: Pontoon boat rental on Cass Lake

Bumper Bowling

For preschoolers, bumper bowling is the greatest invention since Sesame Street. Children are protected against bowling gutter balls by plastic tubing that sits in the gutters. Throw the ball any which way, and it's bound to bounce off the bumper, careen down the lane and knock off a few pins. Here is a sampling of area lanes offering bumper bowling on a regular basis. For more information, call the Bowling Proprietors Association of Greater Detroit, 559-5207.

Allen Park Bowling
7226 Allen Road, Allen Park
313-381-6922

Astro Lanes
32388 John R, Madison Heights
313-585-3131

Bel Aire Lanes
24001 Orchard Lake Road, Farmington
313-476-1550

Belmar II
3351 West Road, Trenton
313-675-8319

Bowl One
1639 East Fourteen Mile, Troy
313-588-4850

Cherry Hill Lanes North
6697 Dixie Highway, Clarkston
313-625-5011

Cherry Hill Lanes

300 North Inkster Road
Dearborn Heights
313-278-0400

Colonial Lanes

1950 South Industrial Highway, Ann Arbor
313-665-4474

Drakeshire Lanes

35000 Grand River, Farmington Hills
313-478-2230

East Warren Lanes

17225 East Warren, Detroit
313-885-0060

Friendly Ark Sterling Lanes

33200 Schoenherr, Sterling Heights
313-979-5200

Friendly Bonanza Lanes

24600 Hoover, Warren
313-756-3000

Friendly Bronco Lanes

22323 Ryan Road, Warren
313-756-8200

Friendly Frontier Lanes

37370 Gratiot, Mount Clemens
313-465-1958

Friendly Merri-Bowl Lanes

30950 Five Mile Road, Livonia
313-427-2900

Garden Bowl

4120 Woodward Avenue, Detroit
313-833-9850

Harbor Lanes

25419 Jefferson, St. Clair Shores
313-772-1200

Hartfield Lanes

3490 West Twelve Mile Road, Berkley
313-543-9338

Langans Northwest Lanes

32905 Northwestern Highway, Farmington Hills
313-626-2422

Liberty Bowl
17580 Frazho, Fraser
313-778-6390

Mayflower Lanes
26600 Plymouth Road, Redford
313-937-8420

Novi Bowl
21700 Novi Road, Novi
313-348-9120

Oakwood Blue Jackets Bowl
850 South Oakwood Boulevard, Detroit
313-841-1351
313-841-1352

Pampa Lanes
31925 Van Dyke, Warren
313-264-8877

Plum Hollow Lanes
21900 West Nine Mile Road, Southfield
313-353-6540

Recreation Bowl
40 Crocker Boulevard, Mount Clemens
313-468-7746

Redford Bowl
22150 Grand River, Detroit
313-531-2271

Regal Lanes
27663 Mound Road, Warren
313-751-4770

Rose Bowl Lanes
28001 Groesbeck, Roseville
313-771-4140

Universal Lanes
2101 East Twelve Mile, Warren
313-751-2828

West Bloomfield Lanes
6800 Orchard Lake Road, West Bloomfield
313-855-9555

Woodland Lanes
33775 Plymouth Road, Livonia
313-522-4515

Ypsi-Arbor Lanes

2985 Washtenaw, Ypsilanti
313-434-1110

Rock 'N Bowl

This new bowling alley trend combines bowling with dancing. Music is provided by a live band or dee jay. Often there are contests and prizes. West Bloomfield lanes offers summer Rock 'N Bowl evenings for ages 10-15 that are alcohol free; Detroit's Garden Bowl features live bands or dee jays on Friday and Saturday nights and attracts an older crowd.

Croquet

Put on your best manners and shoot the wickets at the area's only indoor croquet club. The court is available for an hour of supervised play; all equipment is provided. Indoor croquet is offered year-round; an outdoor court is available beginning mid-May.

River Place Athletic and Croquet Club

1400 River Place, Detroit
313-259-1106

Cross-Country Skiing

It's possible to cross-country ski almost everywhere in metro Detroit, from city, county, state, and national parks, to golf courses, ski resorts, and nature preserves. Many area ski shops and resorts rent equipment on a daily basis. Here is a sampling of sites that rent equipment and offer scenic trails.

Addison Oaks

1480 West Romeo Road, Leonard
313-693-0220
For full information, see Parks

Glen Oaks

30500 Thirteen Mile Road
Farmington Hills
313-851-8356
For full information, see Parks

Heavner's Canoe and Cross Country Ski Rental

2775 Garden Road, Milford
313-685-2379

Howell Nature Center

1005 Triangle Lake Road, Howell
517-546-0249
For full information, see Science and Nature

Hudson Mills Metropark

8801 North Territorial Road, Dexter
313-426-8211
For full information, see Parks

Huron Hills Ski Center

3465 East Huron River Drive, Ann Arbor
313-971-6840

Huron Meadows Metropark

8765 Hammel Road, Brighton
231-4084
For full information, see Parks

Independence Oaks

9501 Sashabaw Road, Clarkston
313-625-0877
For full information, see Parks

Indian Springs Metropark

5200 Indian Trail, Clarkston
313-625-7870
For full information, see Parks

Kensington Metropark

2240 West Buno Road, Milford
313-685-1561
For full information, see Parks

Lake Erie Metropark

32481 West Jefferson, Rockwood
313-379-5020
For full information, see Parks

Maybury State Park

20145 Beck Road, Northville
313-349-8390
For full information, see Parks

Metro Beach Metropark

Metropolian Parkway, Mount Clemens
313-463-4581
For full information, see Parks

Stony Creek Metropark

4300 Main Park Road, Washington
313-781-4242
For full information, see Parks

White Lake Oaks

991 South Williams Lake Road, White Lake Twp.
313-698-2700
For full information, see Parks

Willow Metropark

South Huron, Huron Township
313-697-9181
For full information, see Parks

Downhill Skiing

Five area ski resorts offer southeastern Michiganians an easy escape to the slopes. Generally open from November to March, they offer rental, instruction, ski shop, and restaurant. See also Ski Resorts for outstate resorts.

Alpine Valley

6775 East Highland, Milford
313-887-4183

Mt. Brighton Ski Area

4141 Bauer Road, Brighton
313-229-9581

Mt. Holly, Inc.

13536 South Dixie Highway, Holly
313-634-8260
582-7256 (snowline)

Pine Knob Ski Resort

Sashabaw Road and I-75, Clarkston
313-625-0800

Riverview Highlands Ski Area

15015 Sibley Road, Riverview
313-479-2080

Dude Ranches

If you or the kids like horseback riding, here's a chance to become cowboys or cowgirls during your summer vacation. The following sites offer accommodations ranging from motel to campground. All offer horseback riding and trails; some offer riding lessons and canoe rental. Call ahead to find out about package prices. In general, the season runs May–November.

Double JJ Ranch/Resort

6886 Water Road, Rothbury
616-894-4444

Accommodations: Resort. For ages 18 and over.

Double R Ranch

4424 White Spruce Road, Smyrna
616-794-0520

Accommodations: Family campground

El Rancho Stevens

East Dixon Lake Road, Gaylord
517-732-5090

Accommodations: Resort

Hell Creek Ranch

10866 Cedar Lake Road, Pinckney
313-878-3632

Accommodations: Family campground

Ranch Rudolf

6841 Brownbridge Road, Traverse City
616-947-9529

Accommodations: Motel and campground

Wolf Lake Ranch
M-37, Baldwin
616-745-3890

Accommodations: Cabins

Fishing

Sure you can rent a rowboat and take along all your fishing gear. But if you want a hassle-free fishing trip, head over to the Spring Valley Trout Farm in Dexter (*see* Science and Nature), where fishing is fun, quick, and everyone is guaranteed a catch.

Frisbee Golf

If you like throwing Frisbees and want a new challenge, try Frisbee golf. On a 9- or 18-hole course, participants throw frisbees or Frisbee-like discs into a raised basket, trying to play or beat the par on each hole. Like golf, Frisbee golf courses offer hazards and other challenging obstacles. Children five and up, who are able to throw a Frisbee, will enjoy the game. Here are a sampling of courses located at public parks. Some offer equipment and free score cards for use. Others ask you to bring your own trusty Frisbee.

Addison Oaks County Park
1480 West Romeo Road, Leonard
313-693-2432

Firefighters' Park
On the north side of Square Lake Road,
between Crooks and Coolidge, Troy
313-524-3484 (Parks and Recreation)

Rolling Hills County Park
7660 Stony Creek Road, Ypsilanti
313-484-3871

Starr-Jaycee Park
On the south side of Thirteen Mile Road,
east of Crooks Road, Royal Oak
544-6680 (Parks and Recreation)

Stony Creek Metropark

Lakeview Picnic Area
Enter on Twenty-Six Mile Road,
west of M-53 (Van Dyke), Washington
313-781-4242

Wagner Park

On Detroit Avenue, between
Rochester and Main (Livernois), Royal Oak
313-544-6680 (Parks and Recreation)

Go-Carting

Treat your little daredevils to a fast ride around
the go-cart track. Children under 51 inches can
ride around only on an adult's lap.

C.J. Barrymore's Sports Center

21750 Hall Road, Mount Clemens
313-469-2800

Features: Batting cages, softball diamonds, go-
carts, kiddie karts, miniature golf, video arcade,
driving range, pro shop, family restaurant, in-
door/outdoor concessions

Four Bears Water Park

3000 Auburn Road, Utica
313-739-5863

Features: Batting cages, miniature golf, water
slides, bumper boats, go-carts, petting zoo, restaurant. *For full information, see* Parks.

Midway Golf Range

22381 Van Born, Taylor
313-277-9156

Features: Batting cages, go-carts, miniature
golf, driving range, trampolines.

Red Oaks Golf Dome and Sports Village

29601 John R, Madison Heights
313-548-1857

Features: Batting cages, go-carts, miniature
golf, indoor and outdoor driving range, playscape
and snack bar.

Sport-Way

38520 Ford Road, Westland
313-728-7222

Features: Batting cages, go-carts, miniature golf

Van Dyke Sport Center

32501 Van Dyke, Warren
313-979-2626

Features: Batting cages, go-carts, miniature golf, indoor/outdoor driving range, video arcade, restaurant, concessions, pro shop

Hiking

The area's many arboretums, parks, and nature centers offer a variety of self-guided hiking trails. *See* Science and Nature *and* Parks.

Horseback Riding

Get along little doggies, time for some horsing around. Here is a sampling of area ranches that offer riding by the hour. Many are open year-round, weather permitting.

Fenton Riding Academy

7335 Old U.S. 23, Fenton
313-750-9971

Finley Stables

7684 Twenty-Five Mile Road, Washington
313-781-5151

Great Western Riding Stable

5444 Bates, Mount Clemens
313-749-3780

Hell Creek Ranch

10866 Cedar Lake Road, Pinckney
313-878-3632

Hidden Ridge Stables

9005 Maceday, White Lake Township
313-625-3410

Lucy's Livery
6386 Shea Road, Marine City
313-765-9910

Maybury State Park
20145 Beck Road, Northville
313-349-8390
For full information, see Parks

Oakland County 4-H Horseback Riding for Handicappers
313-858-0889

Pontiac Lake Recreation Area
7800 Gale Road, Pontiac
313-666-1020
For full information, see Parks

Silver Saddle Riding Stable
2991 Oakwood, Ortonville
313-627-2826
For full information, see Best Rides in Town

Tollgate 4-H Center
Exceptional Equestrian Program
(Horseback riding for the handicapped)
28115 Meadowbrook Road, Novi
313-347-3860

Ice-Skating

Celebrate winter by taking a twirl on the area's many indoor rinks during family open skating. Or enjoy the real thing—bundle up and skate out in the open, with snowflakes falling all around you. Here is a sampling of the area's indoor and outdoor rinks. Skate rental is noted.

Adams Ice-Skating Area
10500 Lyndon, Detroit
313-935-4510

Features: Indoor rink, skate rental

Addison Oaks

1480 West Romeo Road, Leonard
313-693-2432

Features: Outdoor rink. *For full information, see* Parks

Adray Ice Arena

14900 Ford Road, Dearborn
313-943-4098

Features: Indoor rink

Allen Park Arena

15800 White Street, Allen Park
313-928-8303

Features: Indoor rink

Bald Mountain Recreation Area

1330 Greenshield, Lake Orion
313-693-6767

Features: Outdoor rink. *For full information, see* Parks

Berkley Ice Arena

2300 Robina, Berkley
313-546-2460

Features: Indoor rink, skate rental

Birmingham Ice Sports Arena

2300 East Lincoln, Birmingham
313-645-0730
313-645-0731

Features: Indoor rink

Buhr Park Ice Rink

2751 Packard Road, Ann Arbor
313-971-3228

Features: Outdoor rink, skate rental

Canfield Ice Arena

2100 Kinloch, Dearborn Heights
313-563-9700

Features: Indoor rink

Clark Park

1400 Scotten, Detroit
313-297-9328

Features: Outdoor rink, skate rental

Compuware-Oak Park Arena
13950 Oak Park Boulevard, Oak Park
313-543-2338
313-543-2339

Features: Indoor rink, skate rental

Devon-Aire Arena
9510 Sunset, Livonia
313-425-9790

Features: Indoor rink

Eddie Edgar Arena
33841 Lyndon, Livonia
313-427-1280

Features: Indoor rink

Ella Mae Power Park
45175 West Ten Mile Road, Novi
313-347-0400

Features: Outdoor rink

Fraser Hockeyland
34400 Utica Road, Fraser
313-294-2400

Features: Indoor rink

Garden City Ice Arena
200 Long Cabin Drive, Garden City
313-261-3490
Features: Indoor rink

Hart Plaza
Jefferson at Woodward, Detroit
313-224-1184

Features: Outdoor rink, skate rental

Highland Recreation Area
M-59 east of US-23, Milford
313-887-5136

Features: Outdoor rink. *For full information, see* Parks

Holly State Park
8100 Grange Hall Road, Holly
313-634-8811

Features: Outdoor rink

Independence Oaks
9501 Sashabaw Road, Clarkston
313-625-0877

Features: Outdoor rink. *For full information, see* Parks

Inkster Civic Arena
20277 South River Park, Inkster
313-277-1001

Features: Indoor rink, skate rental

John Lindell Ice Arena
1403 Lexington, Royal Oak
313-544-6690

Features: Indoor rink

Kennedy Ice Rink
3131 West Road, Trenton
313-676-7172

Features: Outdoor rink

Kensington Metropark
2240 West Buno Road, Milford
313-685-1561

Features: Outdoor rink. *For full information, see* Parks

Lake Erie Metropark
32481 West Jefferson, Rockwood
313-379-5020

Features: Outdoor rinks. *For full information, see* Parks

Lakeland Ice Arena
7730 Highland (M-59), Pontiac
313-666-2090

Features: Indoor rink, skate rental

Lincoln Park Community Center
3525 Dix, Lincoln Park
313-386-4075

Features: Indoor rink, skate rental

Lower Huron Metropark
17845 Savage Road, Belleville
313-697-9181

Features: 3 outdoor rinks. *For full information, see* Parks

McMorran Place Complex
701 McMorran Boulevard, Port Huron
313-985-6166

Features: Two indoor rinks

Melvindale Ice Arena
4300 South Dearborn, Melvindale
313-928-1200

Features: Indoor rink

Metro Beach Metropark
Metro Parkway at Jefferson
Mount Clemens
313-463-4581

Features: 2 outdoor rinks. *For full information, see* Parks

Palmer Park
Third Avenue and Merrill Plaisance, Detroit
313-935-3800

Features: Outdoor rink

Plymouth Ice Rink
525 Farmer, Plymouth
313-455-6623

Features: Indoor rink, skate rental

Redford Arena
12400 Beech Daly, Redford
313-937-2757

Features: Indoor rink, skate rental

River Rouge Arena
141 East Great Lakes, River Rouge
313-842-0670

Features: Indoor rink

St. Clair Shores Civic Arena
20000 Stephens, St. Clair Shores
313-445-5350

Features: Indoor rinks

Southfield Sports Arena

26000 Evergreen Road, Southfield
313-354-9357

Features: Indoor rink, skate rental

Southgate Ice Arena

14700 Reaume Parkway, Southgate
313-246-1342

Features: Indoor rink

Stony Creek Metropark

4300 Main Park Road, Washington
313-781-4242

Features: Outdoor rink. *For full information, see* Parks

University of Michigan-Dearborn Arena

4901 Evergreen Road, Dearborn
313-593-5670

Features: Indoor rink, skate rental

Veterans Ice Arena

2150 Jackson Road, Ann Arbor
313-761-7240

Features: Indoor rink, skate rental

Wayne Ice Arena

4635 Howe Road, Wayne
313-721-7400

Features: Indoor rink, skate rental

Westland Multi-Purpose Arena

6210 North Wildwood, Westland
313-729-4560

Features: Indoor rink, skate rental

Yack Arena

3131 Second, Wyandotte
313-246-4515

Features: Indoor rink

Yost Ice Arena
State and Hoover, Ann Arbor
313-763-0064

Features: Indoor rink

Laser Tag

Jump into a Nintendo-esque game where you can "take out" the enemy with a trusty laser gun. First, suit up with a Star Trek-inspired metal headpiece, battery pack, and laser gun. Then, enter the dark and foggy game room, where "danger" lurks behind neon-outlined city buildings.

Phazer Land
31166 Grand River, Farmington
313-442-7880

Miniature Golfing

Test your putting skills against green hills, blue lagoons, colorful windmills, or wishing wells. Time to show the kids the difference between a bogey and a boogie. Here is a sampling of area miniature golf sites. Most are open seasonally during the summer and early fall. At Recreation Bowl you won't have to worry about the weather; the summer-only golf course is indoors.

Captain's Cove Adventure Golf
3409 Edgar Street, Royal Oak
313-549-7676

C.J. Barrymore's Sports Center
21750 Hall Road, Mount Clemens
313-469-2800

Emerald Greens
31900 Little Mack, Roseville
313-293-6780

Ford Road Miniature Golf
29060 Ford Road, Garden City
313-425-9816

Four Bears Water Park

3000 Auburn Road, Utica
313-739-5863
For full information, see Parks

Hock Acres

54300 Ten Mile Road, South Lyon
313-437-2850

Marino Sports Center, Inc.

38951 Jefferson, Mount Clemens
313-465-6177

Mauro's Miniature Golf

600 East Nine Mile Road, Hazel Park
313-547-2331

Metro Beach Putt-Putt

Metro Parkway at Jefferson, Mount Clemens
313-963-3022
For full information, see Parks

Midway Golf Range

22381 Van Born, Taylor
313-277-9156

Oak Park Mini-Golf

14300 Oak Park Boulevard, Oak Park
313-545-6400

Oasis Golf/Tru-Pitch Batting Cages

39500 Five Mile Road, Plymouth
313-420-4653

Putt-Putt Golf and Games

30749 Grand River, Farmington Hills
313-471-4700

Red Oaks Golf Dome and Sports Village

29601 John R, Madison Heights
313-548-1857

Sport-Way

38520 Ford Road, Westland
313-728-7222

Ted's Southgate Golf Center

11125 Reeck Road, Southgate
313-374-2211

Van Dyke Sport Center
32501 Van Dyke, Warren
313-979-2626

Vinson's Golf Range
12101 Telegraph Road, Taylor
313-287-9870

Willow Creek
"Walk in the Woods" Miniature Golf
3120 South Lapeer Road, Lake Orion
313-391-1230

Ypsilanti Putt-Putt
2675 Washtenaw, Ypsilanti
313-434-2838

Paintball

This game, popular in North and South America, Europe, and Australia, has just begun to catch on in Metro Detroit. Teams play against each other on an indoor or outdoor playing field, using paint pellets and guns. Not recommended for children younger than twelve.

Hell Survivors, Inc.
D-19, Pinckney
313-878-5656

Splat Ball City Playing Field
1580 East Grand Boulevard, Detroit
313-925-2489 (on site)
313-875-7549 (office)

Rollerblading

Pull on your spandex, helmet, knee and elbow pads and get ready for indoor in-line skating. In addition to Joe Louis and the Silverdome, several Metro Detroit roller-skate arenas now allow skaters to bring their own rollerblades, but reserve the right to inspect them at the door. Several area arenas also rent rollerblades. Call ahead.

Roll at the Dome

Pontiac Silverdome
1200 Featherstone, Pontiac
313-646-7655 (hotline)
313-775-4880 (information)

The Rink, Inc.

50625 Van Dyke, Utica
313-731-5006

Rolladium

4475 Highland, Waterford Township
313-674-0808

Shores Skateland

35020 Klix, Clinton Township
313-792-0901

Skateworld of Troy

2825 East Maple Road, Troy
313-689-4100

The Wellness Roll at the Joe

Joe Louis Arena
600 Civic Center Drive, Detroit
313-824-0011 (hotline)

Roller-Skating

The music's on, the lights are blinking. Put the kids into continuous motion at the roller rink. Here is a sampling.

Ambassador Roller Rink

96 West Fourteen Mile, Clawson
313-435-6525

Ann Arbor Skate Company

3815 Plaza Drive, Ann Arbor
313-663-6767

Bonaventure Roller Skating Center

24505 Halstead Road, Farmington Hills
313-476-2201

Dearborn Rollerdome

21655 West Warren, Dearborn
313-561-1370

The Great Skate
29100 Hayes, Roseville
313-777-4300

Northland Roller Rink
22311 West Eight Mile Road, Detroit
313-535-1443

The Rink, Inc.
50625 Van Dyke, Utica
313-731-5006

Riverside Roller Arena
36635 Plymouth, Livonia
313-421-3542

Rolladium
4475 Highland, Waterford Township
313-674-0808

Roller-Cade
2130 Schaefer, Detroit
313-386-5710

Shores Skateland
35020 Klix, Clinton Township
313-792-0901

Skateland West
37550 Cherry Hill, Westland
313-326-2800

Skateworld of Troy
2825 East Maple Road, Troy
313-689-4100

Skateworld of Woodhaven
23911 Allen Road, Woodhaven
313-671-0220

Skatin' Station
8611 Ronda Drive, Canton
313-459-6400

Skateboarding

Bring your skateboard and required safety equipment—helmet, knee pads, elbow pads, and shoes. Try your skill on the area's newest skateboarding ramps. All participants (parental signatures required for minors) must register and sign a waiver form before using the skateboard ramps.

Sports Afield 2

216 Patilla Road, Hwy. 2
Tecumseh, Ontario, Canada
519-727-3967, 519-727-6604

A large, year-round, indoor complex with a variety of half-pipe, mini, wall-ride, fly and rail-slide ramps, just 10 miles outside of Windsor.

Veterans Park

2150 Jackson Road, Ann Arbor
313-761-7240

A large outdoor ramp open April-October.

Ski Resorts

If you're looking for the perfect winter family vacation, consider one of Michigan's many ski resorts. Each of the resorts listed below caters to families and offers both child care for small children and a children's ski school, plus children and family activities. And talk about incentives. How about a pizza party at the lodge after a day on the slopes? Or special coloring books and ski jacket patches? The following Michigan ski resorts offer a variety of amenities, including winter sports, ski rental, lessons, and indoor family activities. Call to find out about package prices. The season generally runs from mid-October through April, depending on the weather.

Big Powderhorn Mountain Ski Corporation

N11375 Powderhorn Road, Bessemer
1-800-222-3131
906-932-3100

Blackjack Ski Resort

Blackjack Road, Bessemer
906-229-5115
906-229-5157

Boyne Highlands

Hedrick Road, Harbor Springs
1-800-GO-BOYNE
616-526-2171

Boyne Mountain

Boyne Falls
1-800-GO-BOYNE
616-549-2441

Caberfae Ski Resort
Caberfae Road, Cadillac
616-862-3301

Crystal Mountain Resort
M-115, Thompsonville
1-800-968-7686
616-378-2911

The Homestead
Wood Ridge Road, Glen Arbor
616-334-5000

Indianhead Mountain Resort
Indianhead Road, Wakefield
906-229-5181

Michaywe Slopes
1535 Opal Lake Road, Gaylord
517-939-8919

Nub's Nob Ski Area
4021 Nub's Nob Road, Harbor Springs
1-800-878-NUBS
616-526-2131

Pine Mountain Lodge
N3332 Pine Mountain Road, Iron Mountain
1-800-321-6298
906-774-2747

Shanty Creek/Schuss Mountain
Route 3, Bellaire
1-800-748-0249
616-587-9162

Ski Brule/Ski Homestead
397 Brule Mountain Road, Iron River
1-800-338-7174
906-265-4957

Sugar Loaf Resort
4500 Sugarloaf Mountain Road, Cedar
1-800-748-0117
616-228-5461

Treetops Sylvan Resort
3962 Wilkinson Road, Gaylord
1-800-444-6711
517-732-6711

Tyrolean Ski Resort
Route 1, Gaylord
517-732-2743

Sledding

Many city and country parks, nature preserves, arboretum and golf courses offer toboggan runs and sledding sites. (*For full information, see* Parks *and* Science and Nature). Here is a sampling.

Addison Oaks
1480 West Romeo Road, Leonard
313-693-2432

Bald Mountain Recreation Area
1330 Greenshield, Lake Orion
313-693-6767

Beverly Hills Village Park
Beverly (13½ Mile Road)
west of Southfield Road, Beverly Hills
313-646-6404 (City office)

Bloomer State Park
John R at Bloomer Road, Rochester
313-739-1600

David Shepherd Park
Oak Park Boulevard, west of Coolidge, Oak Park
313-545-6400 (Recreation Department)

Highland Recreation Area
M-59 east of US-23, Milford
313-887-5135

Holly State Park
8100 Grange Hall Road, Holly
313-634-8811

Kensington Metropark
2240 West Buno Road, Milford
313-685-1561

Madison Heights Civic Center
Thirteen Mile Road, Madison Heights
313-588-1200 (City Hall)

Middle Rouge Parkway (Edward Hines Parkway)
Cass-Benton area between Six and
Seven Mile Roads, Northville
313-224-7733
313-224-7734

Muskegon Sports Complex

Muskegon State Park
3560 Memorial Drive, North Muskegon
616-744-9629

Features: Luge track

Pontiac Lake Recreation Area

7800 Gale Road, Pontiac
313-666-1020

Southfield Civic Center— Evergreen Hills

26000 Evergreen Road, Southfield
313-354-9603

Stony Creek Metropark

4300 Main Park Road, Washington
313-781-4242

Willow Metropark

I-275 at South Huron Road, Flat Rock
313-697-9181

Swimming

Municipal pools, recreation centers, and area YMCAs—for a small fee you can beat the heat in both indoor and outdoor pools. Even with lifeguards on duty, be sure to supervise your kids. (*See* Parks for a listing of water parks). Here is a sampling of area pools.

Beech Woods Recreation Center

22200 Beech Road, Southfield
313-354-9510

Features: Outdoor pool. Non-resident must be accompanied by a Southfield resident.

Detroit Recreation Department Pools

313-224-1184

There are 13 locations.

Brewer Recreation Center

4535 Fairview, Detroit
313-267-7152
Features: Indoor pool

Butzel Family Center
7737 Kercheval, Detroit
313-267-7125
Features: Indoor pool

Butzel-Adams Recreation Center
10536 Lyndon, Detroit
313-935-3319
Features: Indoor pool

Heilmann Recreation Center
19601 Crusade, Detroit
313-267-7153
Features: Indoor/Outdoor pool

Johnson Recreation Center
8640 Chippewa, Detroit
313-935-3121
Features: Indoor pool

Kemeny Recreation Center
2260 South Fort, Detroit
313-297-9332
Features: Indoor pool

Kronk Recreation Center
5555 McGraw, Detroit
313-898-6359
Features: Indoor pool

Maheras Recreation Center
12550 Avondale, Detroit
313-267-7155
Features: Outdoor pool

Palmer Park
313-876-0428
Features: Outdoor pool

Patton Recreation Center
2301 Woodmere, Detroit
313-297-9337
Features: Indoor/Outdoor pool

Rouge Park
313-935-3761
Features: Outdoor pool

Williams Recreation Center
8431 Rosa Parks Boulevard, Detroit
313-898-6584
Features: Indoor pool

Young Recreation Center
2751 Robert Bradby Drive, Detroit
313-224-0530
Features: Indoor pool

Jewish Community Center Pool

6600 West Maple Road, West Bloomfield
313-661-1000

Features: Indoor/Outdoor pool. Non-member must be accompanied by member and pay a fee.

Mercy Center Pool

28600 Eleven Mile Road, Farmington Hills
313-476-8010

Features: Indoor pool

Metro Beach Metropark Pool

Metro Parkway at Jefferson, Mount Clemens
313-463-4581

Features: Indoor pool. *For full information, see* Parks.

YMCA Pools

Seventeen area YMCAs have indoor pools. Non-members pay a fee.

Birmingham
400 East Lincoln, Birmingham
313-644-9036

Downriver (YWCA)
3211 Fort Street, Wyandotte
313-281-2600

Downtown
2020 Witherell Street, Detroit
313-962-6126

Eastside
10100 Harper, Detroit
313-921-0770

Fairlane
19500 Ford Road, Dearborn
313-271-3400

Farmington
28100 Farmington Road, Farmington Hills
313-553-4020

Lakeshore Family
23401 East Jefferson, St. Clair Shores
313-778-5811

Livonia Family
14255 Stark Road, Livonia
313-261-2161

Macomb
10 North River Road, Mount Clemens
313-468-1411

Northside
13220 Woodward, Detroit
313-868-1946

North Oakland County
116 Terry, Rochester
313-651-9622

Northwestern
2175 West Seven Mile Road, Detroit
313-533-3700

Plymouth Community Family
248 Union Street, Plymouth
313-453-2904

South Oakland
1016 West Eleven Mile Road, Royal Oak
313-547-0030

Warren Area Family
8777 Common Road, Warren
313-751-1050

Wayne/Westland
827 South Wayne Road, Westland
313-721-7044

Western
1601 Clark Street, Detroit
313-554-2136

Trampoline

Children four years and older can flip, leap, or bound on their choice of eight trampolines.

M.V. Tampoline Center
22381 Van Born, Taylor
313-277-9156

Tubing

Take a slow-moving, relaxing ride lounging inside an inner tube down the Rifle River.

Russell Canoes and Campgrounds
146 Carrington, Omer
517-653-2644

Sturgeon and Pigeon River Outfitters, Inc.
4271 South Straits Highway, Indian River
616-238-8181

Whirly Ball

This new sport is a combination bumper car, basketball, and jai-alai. Kids age ten and up can participate. Prices run about $120/hour (ten people share the court and the cost).

Whirly Ball of Michigan
19781 Fifteen Mile Road, Mount Clemens
313-792-4190

Whirly Ball West
5700 Drake Road, West Bloomfield
313-788-8900

Whirly Ball Ann Arbor
3820 Plaza Drive, Ann Arbor
313-769-7555

14
MICHIGAN
AT WORK
Tours

Everyone enjoys peeking behind the scenes. Children especially benefit from seeing people at work and watching made-in-Michigan products being born. Unfortunately, the rising insurance costs of the last few years have forced many companies to discontinue their tours. This chapter lists Michigan companies and cottage industries that still welcome families and groups with a regularly scheduled tour. While most of the tours are within a two-hour drive from Detroit, I have also included tours farther away to help you plan your overnight adventures.

There are also many community sites that will take small groups on a tour, provided you call first and arrange a mutually convenient time. Try police and fire stations, courthouses, hospitals, theaters, fast-food restaurants, grocery stores, butcher shops, radio and TV stations, even your own job site. You are limied only by your imagination. Many of the museums, historic and science and nature sites listed in this book offer tours to school and civic groups; several theaters offer school field trips. Be sure to look carefully for the "T" or "SP" symbol in chapter 5, 6, 7, and 10.

Industry

AC Spark Plug Tour

1300 North Dort Highway, Flint
313-257-3900

Location: Take Robert T. Longway Boulevard exit 2 miles east of I-475 to North Dort Highway
Hours: One-hour tour. 1 p.m., Monday-Friday. Call for reservation.
Admission: Free
Ages: Minimum age 12 years
Parking: Free on site

Walk right into the parts assembly room and watch cruise control "brains" being made, presses clinking, furnaces roaring, and people boxing row upon row of spark plugs. Children will love the sights and sounds.

Transportation

Amigo Mobility, Inc.

6693 Dixie Highway, Bridgeport
517-777-0910

Location: Approximately ¼ mile toward Frankenmuth, from Dixie Highway exit off I-75 north.
Hours: 8 a.m.-5 p.m., Monday-Friday. Call ahead to reserve. Maximum is 30 people.
Admission: Free
Ages: Preschool-adult
Parking: Free on site
Freebies: Logo pins

Tours are customized to the age of participants and primarily teach disability awareness and the reasons for the Amigo mobility aid. Children are also brought through the sales and marketing offices and the manufacturing assembly plant. Amigo produces a platform mobility aid that is similar to a wheelchair with a steering handle.

Farming

Amon Orchard Tours
7404 North US-31, Traverse City
616-938-1644, 616-938-9160

Location: 1½ miles north of Acme on US-31
Hours: Call for tour reservation, May-October
Admission: $1
Ages: All ages
Parking: Free on site

Tour the cherry orchard, watch the mechanical harvesting of cherries, and learn why Traverse City is the Cherry Capital of the World. After the tour, you can purchase a wide selection of specialty cherry foods and freshly picked fruits in the farm market.

Industry

Amway Corporation
7575 East Fulton Road, Ada
616-676-6701

Location: M-21 (Fulton Road), 12 miles east of downtown Grand Rapids and 11 miles west of the I-96 Lowell exit
Hours: One-hour tour. 9 and 11 a.m., 1 and 3 p.m., Monday-Friday. Closed holidays and mid-June. Two-week advance reservations are required for groups of ten or more. Tours for the handicapped are available upon advance request.
Admission: Free
Ages: Minimum age 6 years
Parking: Free on site
Freebies: Amway product for adults, and Amway coloring book and crayons for children

Tour the extensive Amway World Headquarters and learn all about the growth, products, and markets of one of the world's largest direct-selling companies. The tour includes a slide presentation, product showcase room, bus trip of the grounds, and guided tour of printing department, computer area, and administration building. Kids will enjoy the printing room, bus tour, and slide show.

Mining

Arcadian Copper Mine Tours, Inc.

M-26, Hancock
906-482-7502

Location: Turn right off Potage Lake Lift Bridge to Ripley
Hours: 9 a.m.-6 p.m., daily, Memorial Day-Labor Day. After Labor Day: 9 a.m.-5 p.m., daily. Last tour is always 40 minutes before closing.
Admission: $4 adults, $2 children ages 6-12, under 6 free
Ages: All ages. Can bring stroller on tour
Parking: Free on site

A guided tour ¼-mile into an old copper mine. You'll learn about mining operations and equipment.

Arts and Crafts

Arts & Scraps

12110 Morang, Detroit
313-527-2727

Location: One mile north of the I-94 Cadieux exit.
Hours: 11 a.m.-2 p.m., Tuesday. 3-6 p.m., Thursday. 10 a.m.-2 p.m., Saturday. Also by appointment. Adult workshop teacher training, and group field trips are available.
Admission: Free. Children can stuff a bag full of artistic scraps for a very modest price.
Ages: Preschool and up
Parking: Free

Arts & Scraps offers parents and early elementary teachers a rainy day treasure trove of scraps and odds and ends—everything that children need for creative expression. Kids will enjoy peeking into barrels and looking through boxes, "shopping" for items they can paint, color, glue, and cut into special projects.

Besser Company

801 Johnson Street, Alpena
517-354-4111

Location: North of Alpena, Johnson Street and
US 23 north
Hours: 10 a.m.-3 p.m., Thursday. Call one day
ahead.
Admission: Free
Ages: Only Middle School age and up can go
through the factory. Younger children are wel-
come to visit the offices.
Parking: Free on site
Freebies: Pencils with logo and industry litera-
ture

One-hour tour of offices and factory offers a historical display about the Besser Company, a walk
through the computer design offices, and the
steel assembly line where concrete block-making
machinery mixers are made.

Food

Big Boy Warehouse

4199 Marcy, Warren
313-759-6000

Location: Off Ryan Road, south of Ten mile
Road
Hours: One-hour tour. 10 a.m. and 12:30 p.m.,
Tuesday and Wednesday. Call ahead to reserve
time.
Admission: Free
Ages: Minimum age 6 years
Parking: Free on site
Freebies: Before the tour, everyone is treated
to juice and homemade sweet rolls. After the
tour, everyone receives a gift.

After a slide show and treat, the tour starts in the
bakery distribution center where sweet rolls,
buns, pie crusts, and breads are sliced, frosted,
and packaged. Walk through the cool ice cream
room, marvel at the spice bins in the pungent
seasonings room, continue through the stocked
warehouse, meat and vegetable processing
rooms, and end up in the bakery—a warm, won-
derful-smelling room. This is a tour that makes
your nose come alive.

Bissel, Inc.

2345 Walker NW, Grand Rapids
616-453-4451

Location: Take I-96 west past Grand Rapids to
exit 28. Turn left on Walker.
Hours: 1 hour tour offered morning and afternoon, weekdays, September-April. Schedule
three weeks ahead
Admission: Free
Ages: Recommended 12 and up
Parking: Free on site
Freebies: After the tour, visitors can go to the
adjacent factory outlet store and receive a discount on their purchases

Tour the factory that manufactures home care
products. Watch shampoo bottles blown, metal
parts pressed, and sweeper motors assembled.

Brooks Beverages Plant

777 Brooks Avenue, Holland
616-396-1281

Location: 32nd Street and US-31
Hours: For small groups, 10 to 30 minute self-
guided tour. 8:30 a.m.-5 p.m., Monday-Friday. For
groups of 20 or more, call to schedule a guided
tour
Admission: Free
Ages: All ages
Parking: Free on site
Freebies: Free sample of pop

Tour a soft-drink bottling factory and watch production of various soft drink brands from the syrup
room to the finished product.

Buick City Tour

902 East Hamilton, Flint
313-236-4494

Location: North side of Flint, Broadway-Stever
exit off I-475

Hours: 1½ hour tour, 9:30 a.m. or noon, Tuesday and Thursday. Call to reserve a space.
Admission: Free
Ages: Minimum ages 6 years
Parking: Free on site
Freebies: Children can keep their Mickey Mouse "safety" sunglasses

Watching a car being born is a hometown treat. Kids will be amazed at the hi-los, levers, robots, sparks, noises, and conveyor belts. You will too. This is one tour that shouldn't be missed.

Farming

Calder Brothers Dairy Farm
9334 Finzel Road, Carleton
313-654-2622

Location: South Stoney Creek and Finzel Roads. Carleton is about 70 minutes south of downtown Detroit, off I-75 south.
Hours: 10 a.m.-8 p.m., Monday-Saturday. 11 a.m.-8 p.m., Sunday. Closes at 9 p.m. during the summer. Call ahead to schedule tours.
Admission: $4.25
Ages: All ages
Parking: Free on site
Freebies: Ice cream cone

Milk a cow by hand, bottle feed a calf, watch a cow being machine milked, and see how milk is stored for transport to the Calder Bros. processing plant. Kids will also enjoy petting the other animals—peacocks, dogs, burros, and geese.

Arts & Crafts

The Candle Factory
301 Grand View Parkway
Traverse City
616-946-2280, 616-946-2850

Location: South side of Grandview Parkway, one block west of downtown
Hours: Generally 10 a.m.-6 p.m., Monday-Saturday; noon-5 p.m., Sunday, year-round. Extended hours seasonally. To view candle making, call ahead; production hours fluctuate.
Admission: Free

Ages: All ages
Parking: Free on site

Surround yourself with candles and their heavenly fragrance. Kids will enjoy peeking into the candlemaking area to see how candles are hand-carved and hand-dipped. The Candle Factory sells a wide variety of hand-made candles.

Ecology

Candy Cane Christmas Tree Farm

4780 Seymour Lake Road, Oxford
313-628-8899

Location: Sashabaw and Seymour Lake Roads
Hours: Weekdays, April-first week in May. Call for appointments.
Admission: $2.50
Ages: Preschool-early elementary
Parking: Free. Park along driveway
Freebies: One small tree with planting instructions

Enjoy an ecological talk explaining why trees are important to the earth, then walk through the tree farm and listen to the spring birds, busy in the farm's bird houses. Each child receives a 18-24-inch tree to take home to replant. Groups can bring their own snack and use a picnic table on the grounds.

Media

Channel 50 WKBD

26905 West Eleven Mile Road, Southfield
313-350-5050

Location: Between Inkster and Telegraph
Hours: 9 a.m.–5 p.m., Monday-Friday. Call several weeks in advance to arrange an appointment
Admission: Free
Ages: All ages
Parking: Free on site
Freebie: Items with Channel 50 logo

Walk through the TV station, peeking into sales and business offices, engineering and news rooms. See the news set and weather board up close, and sit in on a taping if your tour corresponds to show time.

Food

Chocolate Vault, Ice Cream Parlour and Candy Shoppe

110 West Chicago, Tecumseh
517-423-7602

Location: Downtown Tecumseh
Hours: 10 a.m.-10 p.m., Monday-Saturday. Noon-10 p.m., Sunday
Admission: Free
Ages: All ages
Parking: Metered lots and street parking

Kids will enjoy watching employees hand dip a variety of centers and other goodies into an 80-pound chocolate melter.

Food

Cook's Farm Dairy

2950 Seymour Lake Road, Ortonville
313-627-3329

Location: Take I-75 north to M-15 north. Go one mile east on Seymour Lake Road
Hours: One-hour tour. Summer: 9 a.m.-10 p.m., Monday-Saturday. 2-10 p.m., Sunday. Winter: 9 a.m.-8 p.m., Monday-Saturday. 2-8 p.m., Sunday. Call to schedule tours for groups of ten or more.
Admission: $2
Ages: All ages
Parking: Free on site
Freebies: Ice cream cone and glass of Cook's chocolate milk

Tours start in the cow barn. After meeting newborn calves, you are taken into the production plant for a dry run of the process that turns cows' milk into ice cream and chocolate milk. The tour ends in the ice cream parlor/farm store.

Arts & Crafts

Davisburg Candle Factory

634 Davisburg Road, Davisburg
313-634-4214

Location: I-75 north to exit 93 (Dixie Highway), downtown Davisburg

Hours: May-December 25: 10 a.m.-4:30 p.m., Monday-Saturday. Noon- 4 p.m., Sunday. January-May: 10 a.m.-4:30 p.m., Monday-Saturday. For groups of ten or more, schedule in advance. Also call in advance to be sure the taper line is running.
Admission: Free
Ages: All ages
Parking: Free on street

Watch tapers being dipped into hot wax colors and suspended to dry. This is done courtesy of a wonderful home-made taper line contraption. Kids will enjoy watching it run. You'll love the sweet musky, cinnamon smell of the candles. A candle shop with a variety of candles and accessories is located upstairs.

Mining

Delaware Copper Mine

On The Keweenaw Penisula, Kearsage
906-289-4688

Location: 12 miles south of Copper Harbor, in Kearsage.
Hours: 10 a.m.-5 p.m. daily, mid-May–mid-June and after Labor Day-October, self-guided tours only. 10 a.m.-6 p.m., daily, mid-June–Labor Day, guided tours.
Admission: $5 ages 13 and up, $3 ages 6-12, 5 and under free. Self-guided tour: $4 adults, $2.50 children.
Ages: All ages
Parking: Free on site

Go deep into the bowels of the earth and take a guided 35-45 minute underground tour of a former copper mine.
Above ground, see a mining museum, prehistoric mining pits, and the ruins of nineteenth century mining buildings. Afterwards, shop in the gift shop.

Transportation

Detroit People Mover

Classroom in the Sky
313-224-2160

Location: Maintenance Control Facility, 1250 Park Place, Detroit. Adjacent to Time Square Station.

Hours: 10 a.m. and 1 p.m. Monday-Friday. Call ahead to schedule tours. Minimum group is 15; maximum is 60.

Admission: $1

Ages: 1st grade and up

Parking: School buses park free on street; cars should use nearby parking lots.

Freebies: Buttons, bags, or coloring books with the People Mover logo. Children also receive free membership in the "Riders in the Sky" Club.

Take a behind-the-scenes tour of the transit system; watch a control officer control the train; learn how the communication system works; take a ride on the People Mover; and stop at several stations to learn about the public art.

Police

Detroit Police Horse Stables

100 East Bethune, Detroit
313-876-0061

Location: North of East Grand Boulevard and east of Woodward. There are two other police horse stables. One is located on Belle Isle. The other is in Rouge Park on Joy and Southfield Roads, Detroit. Call 876-0061 to schedule a visit to any of the three.

Hours: One-hour tour, 11 a.m., Monday-Friday. Call to schedule tour several weeks ahead.

Admission: Free

Ages: 5 and up. Group maximum is 20 people

Parking: Free on site

Walk through the stables and meet regal police horses. See where they sleep, eat, and exercise. The stable on Bethune also houses blacksmith and leatherworks shops.

Utilities

Detroit Water Department— Springwells Water Plant

8300 West Warren, Detroit
313-224-3834

Location: Warren and Wyoming, just east of Ford Road
Hours: One-hour tour, 9 a.m.-2 p.m., Monday-Friday. Call 2 weeks in advance to schedule tour.
Admission: Free
Ages: Minimum age 12 years. Group maximum is 20 people; minimum is 5 people.
Parking: Free on site

Watch the pumps and cisterns working as they bring in raw water, purify, and filter it and pump it out to metro Detroit households. The plant is an architectural wonder.

Industry

Dow Visitor's Center

500 East Lyon Road, Midland
517-636-8658

Location: East Lyon Road and Bayliss Street
Hours: 2 hour and 15 minute tour, 9:30-11:45 a.m., Monday. Call at least two weeks in advance to schedule tour.
Admission: Free
Ages: Minimum age 12 years
Parking: Free on site
Freebies: A roll of Saran Wrap

Tour one of the world's largest and most diversified specialty chemical production facilities. Watch a slide presentation about Dow's earliest beginnings and learn about the many chemical, plastic, and agricultural products manufactured at this site. Then walk through the Saran Wrap plant and see production and shipping first hand.

Farming

Erie Orchards and Cider Mill

1235 Erie Road, Erie
313-848-4518

Location: Just west of Telegraph Road on Erie Road, south of Monroe
Hours: Call to arrange one-hour tour, Monday-Friday, during the fall.
Admission: $3 per person includes tour, hayride, one pumpkin, glass of cider, and donut
Ages: Preschool and up

Parking: Free on site
Freebies: Children receive coloring books. Adults are given fruit fact sheets and recipes.

Look behind the scenes at an apple orchard, starting with a hayride through the orchard full of 3,500 dwarf trees. Walk into the grading room and cold storage room. Watch how cider and donuts are made, pick apples and pumpkins, and then relax with a complimentary glass of cider and a fresh donut.

Library

Farmington Library Tours

Farmington Hills Branch Library
32737 West Twelve Mile Road
Farmington Hills
313-553-0300

Location: West of Orchard Lake Road
Hours: Call to arrange a tour and program in the Children's Department during library hours. 10 a.m.-9 p.m., Monday-Thursday. 10 a.m.-5 p.m., Friday and Saturday. 1-5 p.m., Sunday. Closed on Sunday during summer.
Admission: Free
Ages: Preschool and up
Parking: Free on site

Hear a story, play on the creative climbers, and explore the children's department resources— computers, puppets, puzzles, hands-on realia collection, and, of course, books.

Utilities

Fermi 2 Power Plant

6400 North Dixie Highway, Newport
313-586-5228

Location: I-75 exit 21 Newport Road to North Dixie
Hours: 9 a.m.-5 p.m., by reservation. Groups should call 3 to 5 weeks in advance. Families are often added on to large groups; please call for appointment.
Admission: Free
Ages: Interest level 2nd grade and older.
Parking: Free on site

Freebies: Free literature on Fermi 2 and nuclear power

Watch a videotape about the future of nuclear power, take a bus tour of the cooling towers, walk through the control room simulator, play energy-related video games, and use a power-generating bicycle.

Fire Safety

Fire Safety House
Southfield Fire Station #1
18400 Nine Mile Road, Southfield
313-827-0608

Location: Nine Mile Road and Northwestern Highway
Hours: 9 a.m.-7 p.m. Monday-Saturday. By prearranged appointments only. For Southfield residents only.
Admission: Free
Ages: K-8
Parking: Limited parking behind station
Freebies: Fliers and helmets when available

Tour the stationhouse and see how firemen live and work. Watch a film on fire safety and watch a demonstration of fire equipment. During spring-late fall, weather permitting, children have a hands-on experience learning how to safely exit a "burning" house—the children's safety house is filled with non-toxic smoke and children practice a fire drill.

Transportation

Four Winns Boat Company
Number 4 Winn Way, Cadillac
616-775-1351

Location: North end of Cadillac in the Cadillac Industrial Park
Hours: 10 a.m.-2 p.m. Monday-Friday. Call ahead to reserve tour time. One-hour tour.
Admission: Free
Ages: Preschool and up, accompanied by an adult.
Parking: Free on site

Walk through the boat factory and watch performance boats and sports boats being made from start to finish.

Industry

Frank Industries, Inc.
3950 Burnsline Road, Brown City
313-346-2771

Location: 65 miles north of Detroit, near I-69.
Hours: 9 a.m.-2 p.m. Monday-Friday. Call ahead to reserve tour time.
Admission: Free
Ages: All ages. Children must be accompanied by an adult
Parking: Free on site
Freebies: Brochures

Walk through the factory, watch conveyor belts and assembly lines as robots and people create recreational vehicles, including vans, campers, and motor homes.

Food

Frankenmuth Brewery, Inc.
425 South Main, Frankenmuth
517-652-2088

Location: Tuscola and South Main
Hours: Noon-6 p.m., Monday-Friday. 11 a.m.-7 p.m., Saturday. Noon-5 p.m., Sunday. Tours offered every hour on the hour. Last tour starts one hour prior to closing. Hours are shortened January-March.
Admission: $1.50/person for full brewery tour
Ages: All ages
Parking: Free on site
Freebies: Free samples of beer for those age 21 and over

After a 15-minute video on the brewing process, walk right into the brewery and see up close how beer is made. You'll marvel at the large copper kettles and fermenting tanks and enjoy watching the fill-er-up process of the bottling line.

Frankenmuth Pretzel Company

333 Heinlein Strasse, Frankenmuth
517-652-2050

Location: On the street behind Bronners, on the south end of town
Hours: Pretzel School is offered daily, year-round for groups of 12 or more. Call ahead for a reservation. Pretzel School and bakery tour is also offered 11 a.m. and 1 p.m. daily, for families and small groups.
Admission: $2 for Pretzel School and tour
Ages: All ages
Parking: Free on site
Freebies: Pretzel School: Hot pretzel, bakery hat, and graduation certificate

Become a Pretzel School student—don a bakery hat, hear the pretzel story, tour the pretzel bakery, roll your own soft pretzel, receive a graduation certificate, and celebrate with a complimentary hot pretzel.

Gerber Products Company

445 State Street, Fremont
616-928-2000

Location: Main Street, Fremont (northeast of Muskegon)
Hours: 9 a.m.-4 p.m., Monday-Friday. Gerber's visitor center offers a video and 3-D movie. Large groups should call ahead to schedule time.
Admission: Free
Ages: All ages
Parking: Free on site

Visit the home of America's most recognized baby food and watch a step-by-step video describing how baby food is made. Next, don 3-D glasses and settle in for a humorous 3-D look at one day in the life of a baby, from the baby's point of view. Afterwards, shop for some Gerber "souvenirs" to take home.

Guernsey Farm Dairy

21300 Novi Road, Northville
313-349-1466

Location: Between Eight and Nine Mile Roads
Hours: 1-5 p.m., the Sunday before St. Patrick's
Day only, held every-other year.
Admission: Free
Ages: All ages
Parking: Free on site

Enjoy a tour of the plant, clowns and balloons for
the kids, and samples of homemade dairy products. Browse in the general store, and stay for a
meal in the restaurant or an ice cream from the
ice cream parlor.

Gypsum Mine Tour
Michigan Natural Storage

1200 Judd SW, Grand Rapids
616-241-1619

Location: Chicago Drive and Burlingame Street
Hours: 1¼-hour tour, 8 a.m.-5 p.m., Tuesday-
Friday, by appointment only
Admission: $2 adults, $1.50 junior high stu-
dents, $1.25 elementary students and seniors.
$30 minimum charge.
Ages: All ages
Parking: Free on site
Freebies: You can keep the rocks you find

Go down into the mine, hear about the history
and geology of gypsum mining, and spend some
time exploring for rocks. The mine is currently
used by local businesses for natural cold storage.

Harvard Clothing Company

411 North Marshall Street, Litchfield
517-542-2986

Location: 30 miles southwest of Jackson

Hours: By appointment; hours vary depending on seson
Admission: Free
Ages: All ages
Parking: Free on site

Harvard Clothing Company creates nylon warm-up athletic jackets, worn by many high school athletes. Visitors can see jackets being made from scratch, how they are cut, sewn, and how the knit trim is made.

Food

Homestead Sugar House Candies

11393 Homestead Road, Beulah
616-882-7712

Location: South of Traverse City
Hours: 9:30 a.m.-5 p.m., Memorial Day-Christmas
Admission: Free
Ages: All ages
Parking: Free

Watch hand-dipped maple cream candies and rum brandy cherries being created by the candy makers at the Homestead Sugar House. Then browse, buy, and try a few new sugar treats.

Mining

Iron Mountain Iron Mine

US-2, Iron Mountain
906-563-8077

Location: 9 miles east of Iron Mountain, on US-2
Hours: 8 a.m.-5 p.m., daily. Memorial Day–mid-September
Admission: $5.50 adults, $4.50 children ages 6-12, under 6 free
Ages: All ages
Parking: Free on site

Don raincoats and hard hats and ride an underground train one quarter-mile through underground drifts and tunnels. Your tour guide will point out geological formations and mining equipment. You'll come away with a first-hand understanding of the dangers of the mining industry. Browse in a gift shop after the tour.

Clothing

Iverson Snowshoe Factory

Box 85, Maple Street, Shingleton
906-452-6370

Location: Off M-28, two blocks past intersection of M-94 and M-28
Hours: 8 a.m.-3:30 p.m., Monday-Friday, April–mid-July. 7 a.m.-3:30 p.m., Monday-Friday, mid-July–Spring
Admission: Free
Ages: All ages
Parking: Free

Ten-minute tours demonstrate how wood is bent and rawhide shoes are laced, as workers create snowshoes. The retail showroom sells trout fishing net, miniature snowshoes for decorations, hats, scarves, mittens, t-shirts, and snowshoes.

Cultural

Japanese Cultural Center and Tea House

315 South Washington Avenue, Saginaw
517-759-1648

Location: Ezra Rust Drive and South Washington Street, across from the Saginaw Zoo
Hours: Spring and summer tours: Noon-4 p.m. Tuesday-Friday. Noon-6 p.m., Saturday and Sunday. Gardens 9 a.m.-6 p.m. daily. Fall and winter tours: Noon-4 p.m., Wednesday-Sunday. Gardens 9 a.m.-6 p.m., Wednesday-Sunday. Formal tea offered second Sunday of every month, year-round. Call ahead to schedule groups of 15 or more.
Admission: Tour of garden and tea house plus informal tea service (green leaf tea and sweets): $3 adults, $1.50 children. School groups should ask about origami craft and video.
Ages: All ages
Parking: Use zoo parking lot across the street

Experience the serenity and simple beauty of the Japanese garden and tea house. Children will especially enjoy creating an origami figure and, if they are adventurous, tasting a sweet gelatin candy and green tea.

Kalamazoo Toy Trains
541 Railroad Street, Bangor
616-427-7927

Location: One block north of M-43 in old restored depot. Bangor is approximately 20 miles west of Kalamazoo.
Hours: 30-minute tour, 10 a.m.-5 p.m., Monday-Sunday, April-Christmas
Admission: Free
Ages: All ages
Parking: Free, across the street from depot

Visitors walk through the restored depot into six rooms full of Kalamazoo trains, arranged on multi-level tracks, chugging along to music and sounds. A Christmas room will inspire even the youngest collector.

Kids on the Air
WUOM-Michigan Public Radio
500 South State, Ann Arbor
313-764-9210

Location: State and South University, next to the Michigan Union
Hours: 1 p.m., Monday-Friday. By reservation only; call at least one month in advance. Maximum of 25 people.
Admission: Free
Ages: School age
Parking: Metered parking on street.
Freebies: Logo pins and one tape/group

Tour the radio station and have a recording session. The station provides a working script, but school groups are encouraged to write their own script. Call for guidelines.

Kilwins Candy Kitchens, Inc.
200 Division Road, Petoskey
616-347-4831

Location: Northeast of the downtown shopping district
Hours: 30-minute tour, offered Monday-Friday. Call ahead for times.
Admission: Free
Ages: All ages
Parking: Free on site
Freebies: A sample chocolate

This is a heavenly tour for chocoholics. Walk through the candy-making rooms and drool over 500-pound chocolate melters, watch the candy conveyor belts merrily chugging along, and then (yum!) taste a special sample. After your tour, you can buy candy in the gift shop.

Farming

Langenderfer Farm

11840 Strasburg Road, Erie
313-856-4283

Location: Take Telegraph Road six miles south of Monroe to Woods Road. Go west one mile to Strasburg Road. Go south ¼ mile to farm.
Hours: March-June: 9 a.m.-5 p.m., Monday-Saturday. Fall hours vary. For a tour, call ahead.
Admission: $3.50
Ages: All ages
Parking: Free on site
Freebies: Beverage and homemade donut. Spring tour: seedling with planting instructions. Fall tour: pumpkin.

In spring, the farm is full of chicks and ducklings. Spring tours teach children about the incubation process, provide a hands-on activity in the greenhouse, and offer a hayride. The farm also offers "Rent-an-Animal" program. Families can take home chicks and ducklings for Easter and then return them to the farm through June, provided they keep their receipts.

Fall tours include a hayride to the pumpkin patch, u-pick pumpkins, fun in the corn-husk maze, and a visit to the Halloween haunted barn, full of G-rated Halloween displays. Groups with a minimum of 15 can call ahead to schedule an evening hayride and bonfire.

Leader Dog for the Blind

1039 South Rochester Road, Rochester
313-651-9011

Location: Adams and Rochester Roads
Hours: Two-hour tour, held one Sunday afternoon each month except June, July. August, and December. Call for exact dates. Tour registration is requested.
Admission: Free
Ages: All ages
Parking: Free on site

This tour offers an in-depth look at the dogs and the training program that creates seeing-eye dogs. Visitors are taken through the kennels, infirmary, training areas, and people dormitories. A 20-minute movie explores the special bond between seeing-eye dogs and their blind owners.

Leah Gold, Ltd.

218 East Grand River, Brighton
313-227-6009
1-800-233-5324

Location: Grand River, 1½ blocks south of Main Street
Hours: Tours offered Monday-Sunday, when kitchen is open. Call ahead to reserve tour.
Admission: Free
Ages: Five and up
Parking: Free on site
Freebies: Candy samples

Watch the "candy elves" in the kitchen cooking, working with chocolate, decorating candies, and packing the candies for sale. A retail store is connected to the kitchen and offers lots of Leah Gold goodies.

Little Dipper Shoppe

415 North Fifth Street, Ann Arbor
313-994-3912

Location: Kerrytown
Hours: 9:30 a.m.-5:30 p.m., Monday-Friday. 9 a.m.-5 p.m., Saturday.
Admission: $1.25 for one pair of dipped candles
Ages: All ages
Parking: Use metered lot adjacent to Kerrytown

Kids will enjoy choosing their own small tapers and then dipping them in the color of their choice. The store's fragrance is a pleasure for the noses in your family.

Industry

Lorann Oils, Inc.
4518 Aurelius, Lansing
517-882-0215

Location: Jolly and Mt. Hope Roads
Hours: Half-hour tour, 9 a.m.-5 p.m., Monday-Friday. Call to schedule. Tours are arranged according to the group's needs and when the production line is running.
Admission: Free
Ages: School-age through adult
Parking: Free on site
Freebies: Visitors receive a small souvenir

Walk through the plant and watch small, one gram bottles being filled, capped, sealed, labeled, and packed. Lorann Oils, Inc. manufactures and bottles food flavoring and pharmaceuticals.

Food

Mary Klever Kreations
"Chocolate Parties"
3177 Dixie Highway, Waterford
313-673-9494

Location: Dixie Highway, between Scott and Watkins Roads
Hours: 10 a.m.-3 p.m. Monday-Friday. Call ahad to reserve times.
Admission: $4/child for a "Chocolate party." Includes created candy and a decorated box. Minimum of 10 children.
Ages: 3 and up
Parking: In lot

During the two-hour, supervised "Chocolate Parties," children make 8-10 different candies, or dip candies, and decorate a box to carry their chocolate.

Mary Maxim, Inc.

2001 Holland Avenue, Port Huron
313-987-2000

Location: Holland and Pine Grove Avenue
Hours: 9:30 a.m.-5:30 p.m., Monday-Saturday. Noon-5 p.m., Sunday. Call at least one week in advance to arrange a tour. A minimum of 12 people are needed for a tour.
Admission: Free
Ages: School-age children through adult
Parking: Free on site
Freebies: Coffee and cookies, a special tour bag with a complimentary gift, and Mary Maxim catalog

Enjoy a snack and watch a demonstration of needlework at this leading manufacturer of needlecraft kits.

Michigan Humane Society— Genesee County

G-3075 Joyce Street, Flint
313-744-0511

Michigan Humane Society-North

3600 Auburn Road, Auburn Heights
313-852-7420

Michigan Humane Society-West

37255 Marquette, Westland
313-721-7300

Each office will take children through the kennels, infirmary and office, 10 a.m.-5 p.m., Monday-Friday. Call to arrange a convenient tour time for your group.

Animals

Michigan State Veterinary School Vet-A-Visit

Veterinary Clinical Center
Michigan State University, East Lansing
517-353-5420

Location: Bogue and Wilson, near Wharton Center
Hours: 9 a.m.-4 p.m., Saturday, usually held the third Saturday in April
Admission: Free
Ages: All ages
Parking: Use Wharton Center lot

Take a peek behind the scenes at MSU's Veterinary School. This is a perfect tour for veterinary-wannabe's and animal lovers.

Food

Morley Candy Makers, Inc.

23770 Hall Road, Mount Clemens
313-468-4300

Location: On Hall Road, between Gratiot and Groesbeck
Hours: One-hour tours, 10 a.m., 1 and 3 p.m., Monday-Friday, September-Mother's Day. Call at least one week ahead for reservations.
Admission: Free
Ages: 1st grade and up. Minimum 25; maximum 50.
Parking: Free in front of office
Freebies: Free candy samples

Watch a slide presentation on the history of chocolate and the history of Morley Candy Makers, a Michigan company since 1919. Then, walking along an observation walkway, peek into the production and packing plant and witness chocolate candies being created, tended and packaged. End up in the retail store for a few free samples and a chance to buy some candy and chocolate topping to take home.

Animals

Oakland County Animal Care Center

1700 Brown, Auburn Hills
313-858-0863

Location: West of M-24 on Brown Road
Hours: ½-hour tour, 10 a.m.-5 p.m., Tuesday-Friday. Call to schedule a tour.
Admission: Free
Ages: All ages
Parking: Free on site

Tour the kennels and meet the dogs who are waiting for adoption.

Media

Observer and Eccentric Newspapers

36251 Schoolcraft, Livonia
313-591-0500

Location: Corner of Schoolcraft and Levan
Hours: 8 a.m.-12:30 p.m., Monday-Thursday. 3:30 p.m. Wednesday. Call several months ahead to reserve tour. Maximum group size is 25. Families should ask to be tacked onto other groups.
Admission: Free
Ages: 9 and up
Parking: Free on site
Freebies: Sample newspaper

See up-close how a modern newspaper is created. The tour takes you through the advertising, composing, and editing offices, through the photo lab and plate room, and from a viewing deck, you can watch the paper actually being printed.

Arts & Crafts

O'Neill Pottery

1841 Crooks Road, Rochester
313-375-0180

Location: Between Avon and M-59

Hours: Call two weeks in advance to schedule a tour or hands-on workshop
Admission: Tour $2. 1½-hour hands-on workshop: $5 per person to create a ceramic work and have it glazed and fired (work is ready two weeks from date of workshop). Minimum 10 people.
Ages: All ages
Parking: Free on site

Children will enjoy visiting this 135-year-old home, now the studio of working potter Helen O'Neill. Learn about clay work, watch her work on the potter's wheel, and then walk around the two-acre grounds and feed the farm animals living in the 130-year-old barn. Older children or adults may choose the hands-on workshop and create their own ceramic work.

Sports

The Palace

Two Championship Drive, Auburn Hills
313-377-8214

Location: Take exit 81, Lapeer Road, off I-75
Hours: 10:30 a.m., noon, and 1 p.m., Tuesdays. Call ahead to arrange a tour. Groups of 10 to 40 can be accommodated. Families can be added on to larger groups.
Admission: Tour prices include guided tour, lunch in the Palace Grille, and a souvenir item (we received a photograph of Isiah Thomas). $5.95 children, $9.75 for adults.
Ages: Preschool and up
Parking: Free on lot

Immerse yourself in Pistons glory, peek behind the scenes into the multimillion dollar Pistons broadcast center, owners' suites, Hall of Fame, press box, dressing rooms, and take a peek at the championship trophies. If you're lucky, you might even catch a glimpse of a player or coach. Your preteen sons will nominate you best parent of the year.

Food

Pelee Island Winery

455 Highway 18, East Kingsville
Ontario, Canada
519-733-6551

Location: Downtown Kingsville. Take Ambassador Bridge over and follow the Huron Line to Highway 3, all the way to Kingsville (about 40 minutes from the bridge).
Hours: One-hour tours. May-December: Noon, 2, and 4 p.m., daily. January-April: Noon, 2 and 4 p.m., Saturday.
Admission: $3 adults, $2 seniors, 18 and under free
Ages: All ages
Parking: Free on site

See a slide presentation of the history of Pelee Island and its winery, walk through the processing plant, see rooms used for bottling, fermentation, and laboratory. After the tour, sample the wines and browse in the gift shop.

Arts & Crafts

Pewabic Pottery

10125 East Jefferson, Detroit
313-822-0954

Location: On East Jefferson between Cadillac and Hurlbut Streets, across from Waterworks Park, 3½ miles east of downtown Detroit
Hours: 10 a.m.-6 p.m., Tuesday-Saturday. Call two weeks in advance to schedule a tour or hands-on workshop. Individuals are welcome to drop in and tour the building, as well as browse in galleries and gift shop.
Admission: Tour: $3.50 adults, $2 students or seniors. 1½ hour hands-on workshop: $5 children for the experience only, $8 children to have work glazed and fired (work is ready four weeks from date of workshop).
Ages: Minimum 6 years for tour or workshop.
Parking: Free on site

Pewabic Pottery is a historic, turn-of-the-century pottery, famous for its contemporary ceramics. Children are allowed to tour the workshops and galleries, but they will benefit more from participating in hands-on workshops that explore clay works.

Phoenix Memorial Laboratory

230 Bonisteel Boulevard, Ann Arbor
313-764-6220

Location: Bonisteel Boulevard and Murfin
Hours: 9 a.m.-4 p.m., Monday-Friday. Last tour
is at 3 p.m. Call to arrange a tour.
Admission: Free
Ages: 1st grade and up
Parking: Free on site

Tour the nuclear reactor plant and laboratory.
Kids will enjoy peering into the azure pool surrounding the nuclear reactor and watching demonstrations that show the radioactivity of various
materials.

Industry

Pontiac West-Division of General Motors

600 South Saginaw, Pontiac
313-456-6965

Location: South Boulevard and South Saginaw
Hours: 9 and 11:30 a.m., Monday-Thursday. Call
to reserve tour date at least one week in ad-
vance.
Admission: Free
Ages: 5 and up. Must be citizen of United States.
No wheelchairs or strollers; must be able to walk
freely.
Parking: Free on site

This 1½-hour tour takes you inside the busy truck
plant to watch Blazers and Typhoons being born.

Utilities

Saginaw Water Works

522 Ezra Rust, Saginaw
517-759-1640

Location: Across from the Saginaw Zoo
Hours: One-hour tour, 12:30-4 p.m., Monday,
Wednesday, Friday. Call two weeks in advance to
reserve tour.

Admission: Free
Ages: Minimum age: second grade
Parking: Free on site

Watch a movie that explains how water is treated and purified, then walk through the treatment plant. Kids will enjoy the sights and sounds of pumps and gushing water.

Food

St. Julian Winery

716 South Kalamazoo, Paw Paw
616-657-5568

Location: ¼ mile north of I-94 on M-40. Paw Paw is about 15 miles west of Kalamazoo.
Hours: 20-minute tour held every half-hour, 9 a.m.-4 p.m., Monday-Saturday. Noon-5 p.m., Sunday. Call to schedule a large tour.
Admission: Free
Ages: All ages
Parking: Free on site
Freebies: Wine tasting for adults, non-alcoholic juice for kids

Walk through the cellars, crushing room, bottling room, and warehouse in this guided tour that shows you how wine is made using both state-of-the-art equipment and old world methods.

Arts & Crafts

Scrap Box

521 State Circle, Ann Arbor
313-994-4420

Location: Off State Street, one block south of I-94
Hours: 10 a.m.-2 p.m., Tuesday. 2-6 p.m., Thursday. 10 a.m.-2 p.m., Saturday. Arrange for group workshops during hours the store is closed to regular business.
Admission: Free
Ages: Preschool and up
Parking: Free on site

At the Scrap Box, junk comes in all sizes and shapes. Children can look through bins and boxes of foam, wood, plastic, paper, cardboard, and cork discards and fill a grocery bag for $2.50.

Creativity and playfulness will turn the scraps into treasures. This is the perfect place to stock up on materials for rainy day projects. Birthday parties and classroom field trips can be scheduled.

Stahl's Bakery

51021 Washington, New Baltimore
313-725-6990

Location: Washington and Main Streets, downtown New Baltimore
Hours: Call several weeks ahead to arrange a Monday-Friday morning tour
Admission: Free
Ages: All ages
Parking: Free on site
Freebies: A "belly button cookie" (chocolate chip butter cookie)

Step into the sweet, humid cloud of Stahl's Bakery and watch bread made the old-fashioned way, by a fraternity of flour-dusted young men wearing white aprons. Kids will enjoy watching large batches of dough kneaded by hand and made into loaves, and watching the bakers take out finished loaves with long bread oars called "peels."

State Capitol

Capitol Avenue, Lansing
517-373-2353 (Monday-Friday)
517-373-2348 (weekends)

Location: Between Allegan and Ottawa Streets
Hours: 9 a.m.-4 p.m., Monday-Friday. 10 a.m.-4 p.m., Saturday. Noon-3 p.m., Sunday. Groups of ten or more should call to schedule a tour several weeks in advance of visit.
Admission: Free
Ages: All ages
Parking: Meters on street, reserved areas for buses behind Capitol on Walnut Street or at Historical Museum

Tour the elegant state capitol, recently restored to its 1879 splendor. Visit Senate and House viewing galleries and committee rooms and take a look at our lawmakers' workplace. Don't forget to notice the portraits of former Michigan governors, located on the second floor rotunda, near the Governor's executive office and reception rooms.

Food

Superior Fish Company

309 East Eleven Mile Road, Royal Oak
313-541-4632

Location: Downtown Royal Oak
Hours: ½–hour tour, 2-5 p.m., Monday and Tuesday
Admission: Free
Ages: All ages. Approximately ten people minimum needed for a tour.
Parking: Free, park behind store
Freebies: Children are often given fish-related gifts and snacks.

Peek into the glass-enclosed cutting room and watch fish being processed. Children are also shown a table of many types of fish to identify and touch.

Food

Tom Walker's Gristmill

8507 Parshallville Road, Fenton
313-629-9079

Location: 2 miles north of M-59
Hours: 10 a.m.-6 p.m., daily, September–mid-November
Admission: Free
Ages: All ages
Parking: Free on site

Walk through the historic grist mill; watch a player piano demonstration; witness the cider-making operation and yum! watch as donuts are freshly created. Don't leave without browsing through the candy shop, gift shop, and country store.

TV 2 WJBK
16550 West Nine Mile Road, Southfield
313-557-2000, ext. 382

Location: Just east of Southfield Road
Hours: Call to arrange a time
Admission: Free
Ages: All ages
Parking: Free on site

Walk into the newsroom, studios, control room, and onto the news set. Kids of all ages will enjoy peeking behind the scenes and talking to a station personality.

United States Olympic Training Center Tours
Meyland Hall
Northern Michigan University, Marquette
906-227-2888

Location: On the corner of Wright and Tracy Streets, on the edge of campus
Hours: 8 a.m.-5 p.m., Monday-Friday, year-round
Admission: Free
Ages: All ages
Parking: Guest parking on campus

Twenty-minute tour of training facility includes a short video, a peek into the weight room, sports medicine room, athletes' housing, and boxing facility.

United States Post Office—General Mail Facility
1401 West Fort, Detroit
313-963-8933

Location: Between Trumbull and Eighth Streets
Hours: Monday-Friday. Schedule tours at least two weeks in advance.
Admission: Free

Ages: All ages
Parking: Free lot just east of the building on Eighth Street.
Freebies: Calendars, ZIP code directory, pamphlets, coloring books, and stamp pins.

Take a behind-the-scenes look at what happens to a letter after it as been flipped into the neighborhood collection box and trucked downtown. Watch envelopes fed into and spit out of state-of-the-art sorting machines.

Art

University of Michigan Museum of Art
CHAMPS
525 South State Street, Ann Arbor
313-764-0395

Location: On the University of Michigan campus, at the corner of State and University
Hours: Saturday programs, workshops and tours
Admission: $10/yearly membership fee per child
Ages: 5-12
Parking: Metered parking on street
Freebies: Membership fee includes souvenir packet, museum shop discount, tours, workshops, and performances

CHAMPS—Children's Art Museum Programs—offers children a chance to look behind the scenes at an art museum and feel at home, hopefully becoming the art patrons of the future.

Food

Warner Champagne Cellars and Bistro
706 South Kalamazoo, Paw Paw
616-657-3165

Location: ¼ mile north of I-94 on M-40. Paw Paw is approximately 15 miles west of Kalamazoo.
Hours: 9 a.m.-6 p.m., daily year-round. Three guided tours daily; call to schedule. Bistro open 11:30 a.m.-9:30 p.m., Monday-Saturday; 11 a.m.-

6 p.m., Sunday. Closed Thanksgiving, Christmas, and New Year's Day.
Admission: Free
Ages: All ages
Parking: Free on site
Freebies: Champagne tasting for adults, non-alcoholic sparkling juices for children

Watch how champagne is made. Travel through the tierage vaults and riddling rooms to the finishing room where champagne is corked and labeled. End the tour with a champagne or sparkling juice-tasting session and then stay for lunch or dinner at the Bistro.

Clothing

Wolverine World Wide, Inc.
9341 Courtland, Rockford
616-866-5500

Location: 15 minutes north of Grand Rapids
Hours: Tours set up at convenience of group; call at least one week in advance
Admission: Free
Ages: Third grade and up
Parking: Free on site

Watch famous Hush Puppy shoes being made in this half-hour tour that includes the heat, steam, and pressure areas, assembly line, and an up-close look at materials used for soles.

Arts & Crafts

Wooden Shoe Factory
447 US-31 at 16th Street, Holland
616-396-6513

Location: Two miles west of I-96 from Grand Rapids
Hours: 8 a.m.-5:30 p.m., Monday-Saturday
Admission: 25 cents, children 5 and under free
Ages: All ages
Parking: Free on site

Kids will enjoy watching serious shoemakers turn blocks of wood into wooden shoes or "klompens" using 100-year-old machinery and old-fashioned hand carving. After the tour, browse around the gift shop, full of Dutch imports, wooden toys, and homemade fudge.

Medical Research

Wright & Filippis, Inc.
2845 Crooks Road, Rochester
313-853-1855

Location: M-59 and Crooks
Hours: 8 a.m.-4:30 p.m., Monday-Friday. Call to schedule tours.
Admission: Free
Ages: Minimum age 6 years
Parking: Free on site

Children acquire a better understanding of the physically challenged when they visit Wright & Filippis, a firm that researches and develops high-tech products for the disabled. Tour groups learn the difference between an orthosis and prosthesis, tour the workshops and try out the wheelchairs.

Last minute addition:

Transportation/Toys

Lionel Trains Visitor Center
26750 Twenty-Three Mile Road, Mount Clemens
313-949-4100, ext. 1211

A 10-minute video offers Lionel Trains history. Visitors are introduced to Lionel's founder, Joshua Lionel Cowen, who invented the first electric car and moveable track in 1900, and then are treated to footage of today's train factory and watch as trains are molded, painted, and decorated. The highlight of the tour is the Visitor Center, where ten miniature trains roar through tunnels, over and around bridges and up and down hills on the detailed 560-square foot village display.

15
REGIONAL ADVENTURES

Michigan is waiting for you. Its waterways and forested trails, historic sites and museums are yours to explore. Pack the car with an overnight case, camera, and treats. Let the kids pile in and you're off. Here are a variety of regional adventures, arranged geographically, that received "thumbs up!" from Jordan, Andrew, and Garrett, the three junior Field travelers. We hope your family has as much fun traveling together and sharing memories as we do.

Along I-75

Turn your next trip "Up North" along I-75 into an adventure by making a few well-chosen stops.

Frankenmuth (Exit 136 off I-75 north)

Children can eat their way along Frankenmuth's Main Street tasting samples of sausage, cheese, or fudge. They can also watch woodcarving, leather-making, and pretzel making demonstrations. Most stores are open 10 a.m.-5 p.m., daily, Labor Day-May, and 10 a.m.-8 p.m., daily, Memorial Day-Labor Day. Here are some highlights.

Antique Auto Village

576 South Main Street, Frankenmuth
517-652-2669

Have some fun in this old-fashioned, mechanized toy museum-store, complete with player piano, Lionel Train City, and juke box.

Bronner's Christmas Wonderland

25 Christmas Lane, Frankenmuth
517-652-9931

Called the world's largest Christmas store, Bronner's is a year-round Christmas paradise of ornaments, nativity sets, animated figures, decorations, holiday trees, garlands, ribbons, gifts, and more. June-Christmas: 9 a.m.-9 p.m., Monday-Friday. 9 a.m.-7 p.m., Saturday. Noon-7 p.m., Sunday. After Christmas: 9 a.m.-5:30 p.m., Monday-Thursday and Saturday. 9 a.m.-9 p.m., Friday. 1-5:30 p.m., Sunday.

Frankenmuth Brewery, Inc.

425 South Main, Frankenmuth
517-652-2088

Tour the factory and, for those age 21 or older, sample the brew. *See* Michigan at Work.

Frankenmuth City Tours

Bavarian Inn, Frankenmuth
517-652-9941

45-minute conducted tours of historic Frankenmuth leave continuously from the Fischer Platz near the covered bridge.

Frankenmuth Flour Mill and General Store

701 Mill Street, Frankenmuth
517-652-8422

The General Store has barrels of penny candy; the Flour Mill offers a self-guided tour. Walk onto the balcony overlooking the Cass River and watch a waterwheel in action.

Frankenmuth Pretzel Company

333 Heinlein Strasse, Frankenmuth
517-652-2050

Tour the factory and shape your own pretzel. *See* Michigan at Work.

Frankenmuth Riverboat Tours

445 South Main Street, Frankenmuth
517-652-8844

Take a 45-minute ride aboard an old-fashioned paddle wheel. *See* Best Rides in Town.

Holz-Brucke and Woodcarvers' Pavilion

Main Street, Frankenmuth

Walk across the Holz-brucke, the wooden covered bridge, spanning the Cass River. Stop for a drinking fountain break at the Woodcarvers' Pavilion, decorated with wooden scenes from Grimm's Fairy Tales.

Michigan's Own Inc. Military and Space Museum

1250 South Weiss Street, Frankenmuth
517-652-8005

The displays, artifacts, and uniforms feature the Michigan men and women who fought for our country from the Spanish-American War of 1898 to Vietnam. Also, exhibits tell the story of Michigan governors and Michigan-born astronauts. 10 a.m.-5 p.m. Monday-Saturday. 11 a.m.-5 p.m., Sunday. Closed January and February.

Gaylord (Exit 282 off I-75 north)

Bavarian Falls Park

820 Wisconsin Avenue, Gaylord
517-732-4336, 517-732-4087

Adventure golf, go-cart track, bumper cars, and kiddie rides. Adjacent to the Call of the Wild. 8:30 a.m.-10:30 p.m, daily. Memorial Day-Labor Day.

Call of the Wild Museum

850 South Wisconsin Avenue, Gaylord
517-732-4336

You'll be surprised at the quality of this museum's wildlife displays. Your kids will be over-whelmed by the sheer number of stuffed, animated, and mounted Michigan animals. The gift shop offers kids a variety of inexpensive items. 8:30 a.m.-9 p.m., daily, June 15-Labor Day. 9:30 a.m.-6 p.m., daily, September-May.

Grayling (Exit 259 off I-75 north)

Civilian Conservation Corps Museum

North Higgins Lake State Park
South of Grayling, on Roscommon Road, off US-27
517-821-6125

Replica CCC barracks and exhibits recall the nine-year Depression era program that offered over 100,000 Michigan men a chance to work. In Michigan, the CCC planted trees, constructed truck trails, bridges and buildings, and revitalized the state park system. 10 a.m.-5 p.m. daily. June-September. By appointment only, October-May.

Hartwick Pines State Park

7 1/2 miles northeast of
Grayling on M-93
517-348-7068

Once a center of Michigan's lumbering industry, this state park offers a 49-acre preserve of white pines and a Lumberman's Museum and Interpretive Center with hands-on displays that tell the lumbering story. 8 a.m.-8 p.m. daily, Memorial Day-November. When winter weather begins, 8 a.m.-4 p.m., daily.

Pinconning (Exit 164 off I-75 north)

Deer Acres Storybook Amusement Park

2346 M-13, Pinconning
517-879-2849

It's a petting zoo, children's playground, amusement park, folk art exhibit, and picnic grounds all rolled into one. Ringing the park are colorful sculptural renditions of popular nursery rhymes, rides for the whole family and a small petting farm. Kids will love the safari train, antique cars, and moon walk. They will also enjoy feeding the deer. 9 a.m.-6 p.m., Monday-Friday; 9 a.m.- 7 p.m., Saturday and Sunday, Memorial Day-Labor Day. 10 a.m.-5 p.m., weekends only, Labor Day-mid-October.

Dunes and Harbors

Explore Michigan's dunes and harbors, its lumbering and pioneer history.

Cadillac

Johnny's Wild Game and Fish Park
Route 2, Cadillac
616-775-3700

The park offers trout fishing and a petting farm of animals—rabbits, lambs, calves, goats, and raccoons, plus more exotic animals like buffalo and llama. 10 a.m.-6 p.m., daily, Memorial Day-Labor Day.

Grand Haven

Harbor Steamer
541 Gidley Drive, Grand Haven
616-842-8950

Take a 1 1/2-hour tour of the Grand Haven waterfront on an old-fashioned sternwheeler. Daily, Memorial Day-Labor Day.

Harbor Trolley
440 North Ferry, Grand Haven
616-842-3200

Take a refreshing ride along Lake Michigan through Grand Haven, Spring Lake, and Ferrysburg. 11 a.m.-10 p.m., daily, Memorial Day-Labor Day.

Tri-Cities Museum

One North Harbor Drive, Grand Haven
616-842-0700

Two levels chock full of tools, memorabilia, clothes, photographs, toys, and household implements tell the stories of Michigan's pioneer, railroad, and fur-trapping days. Hours vary with the seasons.

Waterfront Stadium

Washington at Harbor Drive, Grand Haven
616-842-2550

Home of summer concerts and "the world's largest musical fountain." The fountain provides a nightly sound, light, and water show during the summer.

Ludington

Great Lakes Visitor Center

Ludington State Park
M-116, Ludington
616-843-8671

The Great Lakes come to life in the center's multi-projector slide show and colorful exhibits. 10 a.m.-5 p.m., Monday-Thursday and Sunday; 10 a.m.-8:30 p.m., Friday and Saturday, Memorial Day-Labor Day.

Rose Hawley Museum

115 West Loomis Street, Ludington
616-843-2001

On display are the artifacts of Michigan's first settlers—Native Americans, farmers, and lumbermen—plus Lake Michigan maritime history exhibits. 9:30 a.m.-4:30 p.m. Monday-Saturday, Memorial Day-Labor Day. 9:30 a.m.-4:30 p.m., Monday-Friday, during the rest of the year.

S. S. Badger Ferry Service

between Ludington and Manitowoc, Wisconsin
616-843-2521

Four-hour ferry trips depart once a day and ferry

you and your car across Lake Michigan to Wisconsin. Mid-May–Labor Day.

White Pine Village

1687 South Lakeshore Drive, Ludington
616-843-4808

This historic village houses 20 restored historic buildings, including a general store, trapper's cabin, blacksmith shop, county courthouse, school, and 1880 farmhouse, plus lumbering exhibits and demonstrations by costumed guides. 10 a.m.-5 p.m., Tuesday-Sunday, Memorial Day–Labor Day. By appointment during the rest of the year.

Mears

Mac Wood's Dune Rides

Off US 31, Mears
616-873-2817

Take a wild dune buggy ride over a desert-like sand dune and climb to the summit for a panoramic view of Silver Lake and Lake Michigan. Located 10 miles west of Shelby and Hart, off U.S.-31. Open mid-May–mid-October.

Silver Queen Riverboat Rides

Route 1, Mears
616-873-4741

Take a one-hour cruise on Silver Lake aboard a paddle boat. June-September.

Muskegon

E. Genevieve Gillette Nature Center

Hoffmaster State Park
6585 Lake Harbour, Muskegon
616-798-3573

The Nature Center offers hands-on exhibits, live animals, a slide show, and displays telling the story of the sand dunes. Walk out back and take the trail down to an untouched sandy beach along Lake Michigan. Then climb up the 150-step boardwalk, and you'll find yourself 190-feet above water level on a wonderfully breezy overlook. Nature Center hours: Summer: 9 a.m.-5 p.m., daily. Fall-spring: 1-5 p.m., Tuesday-Sunday. Park is open 8 a.m.-10 p.m., daily, year-round.

Hackley and Hume Historic Site

430 West Clay Avenue, Muskegon
616-722-7578

Take a 40-minute tour through two beautifully ornate homes built in the late 1880s by wealthy lumber barons. Tour guides encourage children's questions. May 15-September: 1-4 p.m., Wednesday, Saturday, Sunday. Victorian Christmas: 1-4 p.m., Sunday, Thanksgiving weekend-Christmas.

Michigan's Adventure Amusement Park

4750 Whitehall Road, Muskegon
616-766-3377

Carnival rides, live shows, refreshment stands, and gift shops. $14 per person (children 2 and under free) includes admission to Wild Water Adventure, a water park. 11 a.m.-8 p.m., daily, Memorial Day-Labor Day. Water Park: Noon-7 p.m., daily, Memorial Day-Labor Day.

Muskegon County Museum

430 West Clay Avenue, Muskegon
616-728-4119

This small museum offers lots of hands-on exhibits and family fun. Kids will enjoy the "Body Works," plus exhibits on Michigan lumbering, Indians, and pre-historic life. 9:30 a.m.-4:30 p.m., Monday-Friday. 12:30-4:30 p.m., Saturday and Sunday.

Muskegon Museum of Art

296 West Webster Avenue, Muskegon
616-722-2600

This ornately constructed museum houses a small permanent collection and a changing collection of interest to children. 10 a.m.-5 p.m., Tuesday-Friday. Noon-5 p.m., Saturday and Sunday.

Muskegon Race Course

616-798-7123

Watch the ponies race early May-late October.

Muskegon Sports Complex

Muskegon State Park
Luge Track
616-744-9629

A quarter-mile outdoor luge track is open to the public for ages 8 and older. Costs include a lesson, helmet, and all the luging you can stand. Wear old clothes and lots of layers to help you bounce off the luge track wall.

Muskegon Trolley Company

Muskegon
616-724-6420

Ride all over Muskegon on an old-fashioned trolley for 25 cents, Memorial Day-Labor Day. Call for hours and routes.

Pleasure Island Water Fun Park

99 East Pontaluna Road, Muskegon
616-798-7857

This water amusement park offers six water slides, bumper boats, miniature golf, water cannons, picnic areas, kiddie water slide, and water play area. 10 a.m.-9 p.m., Memorial Day-Labor Day.

Port City Princess

2411 Lake Avenue, North Muskegon
616-728-8387

A variety of cruises with entertainment and/or meals are offered. Spend several hours relaxing along Muskegon Lake and Lake Michigan. Children under 4 are free; children 12 and under are half price. May-September. Hours and prices vary depending on cruise.

U.S.S. *Silversides*

Off Lakeshore Drive in the Muskegon Channel
616-722-1790

Kids will enjoy climbing deep into the belly of this

famous World War II submarine and seeing the equipment and facilities up close. 10 a.m.-5:30 p.m., daily, June-August.

Waterfront Centre

1050 West Western, Muskegon
616-725-7418

Overlooking a marina, this restored curtain roll factory now houses restaurants and shops.

Saugatuck

Star of Saugatuck Boat Cruises

716 Water Street, Saugatuck
616-857-4261

Take a narrated cruise on the Kalamazoo River and Lake Michigan aboard an authentic stern-wheeler. May-Labor Day.

Saugatuck Dune Rides

Blue Star Highway, Saugatuck
616-857-2253

Take a narrated, scenic and wild drive over the sand dunes between Lake Michigan and Goshorn Lake. May-October.

Magic Journey

Take a magic journey and then stop in "Turkey-ville" for some old-fashioned fun.

Colon

Abbott's Magic Manufacturing Company

124 St. Joseph Street, Colon
(southeast of Kalamazoo
between Three Rivers and Coldwater)
616-432-3235, 616-432-3236

Colon, the Magic Capital of the World, is home to the world's largest mail-order magic supply company. Visit Abbott's and treat your kids to a magic trick; salespeople will gladly demonstrate. The showroom is a magician's paradise, full of magic posters and paraphernalia. 8 a.m.-5 p.m., Monday-Friday. 8 a.m.- 4 p.m., Saturday.

Marshall

American Museum of Magic

107 East Michigan Avenue, Marshall
616-781-7674, 616-781-7666

Owner Robert Lund will arrange private one-hour tours of his magic museum. He suggests children be at least 14 years old before embarking on the journey through his magic memorabilia–hundreds of tricks, books, diaries, posters, photographs, coins, statues, letters, and popular culture items with a magic theme.

Cornwell's Turkey House

18935 15 1/2 Mile Road, Marshall
616-781-4293

If you feel like talking turkey, you'll enjoy "Turkeyville, USA," the site of Cornwell's Turkey House, an ice cream parlor-restaurant-gift shop-antique barn located on a 180-acre turkey farm. Don't expect to hear much gobbling if you visit near Thanksgiving. February-December: 11 a.m.- 8 p.m., Monday-Saturday. 11 a.m.-6 p.m., Sunday.

Out West

Trains, planes, animals, and nature preserves. Western Michigan offers a lot for kids to see and do.

Augusta

Kellogg Bird Sanctuary

12685 East C Avenue, Augusta
616-671-2510

Buy a bucket or two of bird seed and follow the path around the lake. You'll find yourself in the midst of geese, ducks, and swans that make their home in the sanctuary. Scatter your bird seed, stay on the trail, and you'll see caged birds of prey and wild deer. The sanctuary is located halfway between Battle Creek and Kalamazoo, 1 1/4 miles north of M-89. 9 a.m.-8 p.m. daily, year-round, except Winter: 9 a.m.-6 p.m. daily.

Bangor

Kalamazoo Toy Trains

541 Railroad Street, Bangor
(about 20 miles west of Kalamazoo)
616-427-7927

Tour a former train dept, now showcase for Kalamazoo Toy Trains. *See* Michigan at Work.

Battle Creek

Binder Park Zoo

7400 Division Drive, Battle Creek
616-979-1351

Children will love this small zoo. There are exotic animal settings, an area to feed and pet animals, life-sized dinosaur models, and a miniature train. Open mid-April to mid-October: 9 a.m.-5 p.m., Monday-Friday. 9 a.m.-6 p.m., Saturday, 11 a.m.-6 p.m., Sunday. June-August, same hours with additional 11 a.m.-8 p.m., Wednesday.

Kingman Museum of Natural History

175 Limit Street, Battle Creek
616-965-5117

Three floors of natural history, including hands-on dinosaurs, health, animals, and Indian exhibits. There are also planetarium shows. July and August: 9 a.m.- 5 p.m., Monday-Saturday. 1-5 p.m., Sunday. Rest of year: 9 a.m.-5 p.m., Tuesday-Saturday. 1-5 p.m., Sunday. Closed Monday.

McCamly Place

35 West Jackson Street, Battle Creek
616-961-3090

Downtown festival marketplace.

Coloma

Deer Forest

6800 Marquette, Coloma
(north of Benton Harbor on I-196)
616-468-4961

An animal wonderland with over 500 animals to hand feed and pet, a safari train ride to view African animals, nursery rhyme exhibits, playgrounds, and picnic tables. 10 a.m.-6 p.m., daily, Memorial Day-Labor Day.

Hastings

Charleton Park
Historic Village

2545 South Charlton Road, Hastings
(about 30 miles southeast of Grand Rapids)
616-945-3775

Eighteen restored buildings depict life in a midwestern rural village from 1850 to 1900. Children will love the hands-on experience offered to tours and school groups. Village is open 8 a.m.-5 p.m., daily. Park is open 8 a.m.-9 p.m., daily; third weekend May-third weekend in September.

Kalamazoo

Gilmore Classic Car Museum

6865 Hickory Road, Hickory Corners
616-671-5089

Over 110 antique automobiles exhibited in large red barns, trace the history and technological developments of the automobile industry. 9 a.m.-5 p.m. daily, mid-May–mid-October.

Kalamazoo Aviation History Museum

2101 East Milham Road, Kalamazoo
616-382-6555

Children's imaginations will soar when they see the colorfully restored World War II aircraft and airplane exhibits. They can also play inside several aircraft. Call ahead for tours, 10 a.m.-6 p.m., Monday-Saturday. 1-6 p.m., Sunday. 10 a.m.-8 p.m., Wednesday.

Kalamazoo Institute of Arts

314 South Park Street, Kalamazoo
616-349-7775

Children will enjoy this small art gallery with its changing exhibits and wonderful outdoor sculpture. 10 a.m.-5 p.m., Tuesday-Saturday. 1-5 p.m., Sunday. Closed August and Sundays in June and July.

Kalamazoo Nature Center

7000 Westnedge Avenue, Kalamazoo
616-381-1574

Cross a low-slung wooden bridge to enter the interpretive center, a wonderful place for kids. There are live animals, hands-on exhibits, plants, and more. Don't forget to visit the 1858 DeLano Homestead, a living pioneer farm, where children can watch demonstrations of pioneer crafts, rural Michigan history, and domestic animals. 9 a.m.-5 p.m., Monday-Saturday. 1-5 p.m., Sunday.

Kalamazoo Public Museum and Planetarium

315 South Rose Street, Kalamazoo
616-345-7092

Kids will enjoy the Egyptain Tomb Room, planetarium shows, and exhibits of Indian and pioneer implements, as well as hands-on science and technology. 9 a.m.-5 p.m., Tuesday-Saturday. After Labor Day, additional hours: 9 a.m.-9 p.m., Wednesday. 1-5 p.m., Sunday. Planetarium shows: 1:30, 2:30, 3:30 p.m., Wednesday and Saturday (Summer); After Labor Day, Saturday and Sunday, plus 7 and 8 p.m. Wednesday.

Scott's Mill Park
2900 Lake Street, Kalamazoo
616-626-9738

Tour a restored, working 1870 grist mill powered by a waterwheel, and walk along nature trails. 9 a.m.-9 p.m., daily, Memorial Day-Labor Day.

Train Barn
10234 East Shore Drive, Kalamazoo
616-327-4016

The top floor of this large barn is filled to the brim with intricate Lionel train layouts. The main floor is a museum displaying model trains of all varieties from the turn-of-the-century to the present. Top floor: 11 a.m.-4:30 p.m., Saturday only. Main floor: 4-9 p.m., Tuesday-Friday. 10 a.m.-5 p.m., Saturday.

Paw Paw

St. Julian Winery
716 South Kalamazoo, Paw Paw
616-657-5568

Tour a winery. *See* Michigan at Work.

Warner Champagne Cellars and Bistro
706 South Kalamazoo, Paw Paw
616-657-3165

Tour a champagne winery. *See* Michigan at Work.

Southwest Corner

Although the people who live here probably root for the Chicago sports teams, their backyards are still part of the Wolverine State. You'll find spectacular Lake Michigan vistas and sandy dunes.

Sarett Nature Center

2300 Benton Center Road, Benton Harbor
616-927-4832

Interpretive building with Michigan nature displays and gift shop, plus a 40-acre wildlife sanctuary with five miles of hiking trails. 10 a.m.-5 p.m., Tuesday-Saturday. 1-5 p.m., Sunday. Closed Monday, year-round.

Berrien Springs

Historic Courthouse Square

S-31 and Union Street, Berrien Springs
616-471-1202

The Midwest's most complete complex of county government buildings includes a 1939 courthouse with exhibits and gift shop, Victorian sheriff's house, 1830s log cabin built for the county's first lawyer, and a forge with blacksmith demonstrations. 9 a.m.-4 p.m., Tuesday-Friday. 1-5 p.m., Saturday and Sunday, year-round.

Lemon Creek Fruit Farms and Winery

533 East Lemon Creek Road, Berrien Springs
616-471-1321

U-pick cherries, raspberries, and peaches, wine tasting, and farm market. 9 a.m.-6 p.m., Monday-Saturday. Noon-6 p.m., Sunday, April-October.

Love Creek County Park and Nature Center

9228 Huckleberry, Berrien Center
616-471-2617

200-acre county park with nature trails, cross-country ski and snowshoe rental and cozy nature center with reptiles and amphibians and wildlife observation window. Nature Center: 11 a.m.-5 p.m., Tuesday-Friday, 11 a.m.-6 p.m., Saturday and Sunday. Trails open daily.

Michigan Fisheries Interpretive Center

Wolf Lake State Fish Hatchery
Fish Hatchery Road off M-43
34270 Country Road 652, Mattawan
616-668-2696

Learn how hatcheries operate, explore the history of commercial fishing, and see over 100 different kinds of fishing gear. 10 a.m.-8 p.m., Wednesday-Saturday. Noon-8 p.m., Sunday.

Fernwood Nature Center and Botanic Garden

13988 Range Line Road, Niles
616-695-6491

105 acres of gardens and wild land include a conservatory, rock garden, and herb garden, and a 45-acre aboretum. 9 a.m.-5 p.m., Monday-Friday. 9 a.m.-6 p.m., Saturday. Noon-6 p.m., Sunday. After the October time change, the center closes at 5 p.m.

Fort St. Joseph Historical Museum

Fifth and Main Strets (US-31 and SR-51), Niles
616-683-4702

Indian artifacts, hands-on log cabin exhibit, and curious items like a stuffed lamb with two heads! 10 a.m.-4 p.m., Tuesday-Saturday, 1-4 p.m., Sunday.

Curious Kid's Museum

415 Lake Boulevard, St. Joseph
616-983-2543

Two floors of hands-on exhibits include face painting and a let's pretend television news broadcasting station. This is a full-service discovery center where children learn about history, culture, and science while having loads of fun. Memorial Day-Labor Day: 10 a.m.-5 p.m., Tuesday-Saturday. Noon-5 p.m., Sunday. Rest of year: 10 a.m.-5 p.m., Wednesday-Saturday. Noon-5 p.m., Sunday.

Sawyer

Warren Dunes State Park
Red Arrow Highway, Sawyer
616-426-4013

All-season park offers a Lake Michigan beach and spectacular sand dunes to climb. 8 a.m.-10 p.m., daily, year-round.

South Haven

Lake Michigan Maritime Museum
Dyckman Avenue at Bridge, South Haven
616-637-8078

Exhibits including historic Coast Guard boats and Lake Michigan fishing boats tell the story of Great Lakes commerce. Be sure to take a walk along the public boardwalk. 10 a.m.-5 p.m., Tuesday-Sunday. Hours shorten in the fall.

Thumbs Up

Take a drive north on US-25 and explore the sites along Lake Huron. Michigan's thumb offers lighthouses, beaches, and state parks.

Croswell

Croswell Swinging Bridge
Howard & Maple Streets, Croswell
(10 miles north of Lexington)

Croswell city park has a very long, swinging bridge, suspended over a gorge. The bridge leads to a creative children's playground. Kids of all ages will enjoy running back and forth across the bridge. Be sure to snap a photo of Dad under the playground sign: "Be Good to Your Mother-In-Law." At the other end of the playground is more advice: "Be Good to Your Mother."

Lexington

Lexington Marina
On the shores of Lake Huron
about 25 miles north of Port Huron

Walk along an elevated, concrete boardwalk that reaches out into Lake Huron. You'll hear the sounds of sail ropes clinking against boat poles.

Port Austin

Huron City Museum
7930 Huron City Road, Port Austin
(at the tip of the Thumb)
517-428-4123

This restored 1850 lumbering town has authentically furnished original buildings including a country store, log cabin, inn, church, and museum. Tour guides offer commentary. 10 a.m.-5 p.m., daily except Tuesday, July and August. Groups can schedule tours by special appointments in June and September.

Sanilac Petroglyphs
Port Crescent State Park, Port Austin
517-373-6362

Prehistoric people left their markings on a sandstone outcrop that can be found in the Port Crescent State Park. The park also offers picnic sites, playgrounds, swimming, and boat launch. 10 a.m.-5 p.m., Thursday-Monday, mid-May–Labor Day.

Port Sanilac

Sanilac Historical Museum

228 South Ridge Street, Port Sanilac
(about 40 miles north of Port Huron)
313-622-9946

The restored Loop-Harrison home includes authentic 1870s furnishings, medical instruments, and marine, military, and Indian artifacts. On the grounds are a restored pioneer barn, log cabin, and dairy museum. 1-4:30 p.m., Tuesday-Sunday, mid-June-Labor Day.

East Coast

You're on to Huron. Lake that is. Explore the morning side of the state.

Alpena

Jesse Besser Museum

491 Johnson Street, Alpena
517-356-2202

Children will enjoy this natural history museum and planetarium. Be sure to visit the gallery of early man, 1890 avenue of shops and the lumbering exhibit. 10 a.m.-5 p.m., Monday-Friday. Noon-5 p.m., Saturday and Sunday. Summer evening planetarium shows.

Harrisville

Cedarbrook Trout Farm

Lakeshore Drive, off US-23, Harrisville
517-724-5241

You're always assured a catch and a relaxing fishing experience at this spring-fed trout farm. 9 a.m.-6 p.m., daily. Memorial Day-Labor Day. Weekends until November 1.

The Cross in the Woods
7078 M-68, Indian River
616-238-8973

A 55-foot tall crucifix overlooks Burt Lake at this unique Catholic shrine. Grounds always open. Shrine and gift shop: 9 a.m.-6:30 p.m., Sunday-Thursday. 9 a.m.-8 p.m., Friday and Saturday, Easter-November 15.

Sturgeon and Pigeon River Outfitters, Inc.
4271 South Straits Highway, Indian River
616-238-8181

Spend a refreshing and challenging morning or afternoon tubing, kayaking, or canoeing down the Pigeon or Sturgeon River. The outfitters provide the equipment and transportation to and from the trip's starting and ending points. May-November 1. Call ahead for reservations.

Russell Canoes and Campgrounds
146 Carrington, Omer
517-653-2644

Rent a canoe or a tube and spend the day lazily traversing the Rifle River. These outfitters provide equipment and transportation to and from the trip's starting and ending points. May-November, weather permitting. Call ahead for reservations.

Oscoda

Au Sable River Queens
7634 West Wicker Road, Hale
517-739-7351

Enjoy an old-fashioned paddle wheel riverboat on the Au Sable River. Noon and 3 p.m., daily, last week in May-last week in October.

Paul Bunyan Statue
On US-23, Downtown Oscoda
517-739-7322 (Chamber of Commerce)

The statue of Paul Bunyan recognizes and pays tribute to James MacGillivary, author of Paul Bunyan tales and a native of Oscoda.

Ossineke

Dinosaur Gardens Prehistoric Zoo
11160 South US-23, Ossineke
517-471-5477

Incredible, life-size, cement reproductions of 26 prehistoric animals and birds, all set deep in the woods. 9 a.m.-6 p.m., daily, Memorial Day-Labor Day.

Presque Isle

Old Lighthouse and Museum
5295 Grand Lake Road, Presque Isle
517-595-2059

Climb the stairs to the top of the tower and look out onto the Lake Huron shoreline. The restored home of the lighthouse keeper offers artifacts of a seafaring life. 9 a.m.-6 p.m., daily, May-October.

Ocqueoc Falls

M-68, 12 miles west of US-23, Rogers City

The Lower Peninsula's largest falls, "Ocqueoc," is a Native American name meaning "sacred."

Tulips and Fish Ladders

Take a factory tour, explore "Little Holland," or enjoy the many cultural sites of Grand Rapids.

Ada

Amway Corporation

7575 East Fulton Road, Ada
(just east of Grand Rapids)
616-676-6701

Tour Amway Corporation World Headquarters. *See* Michigan at Work.

Coopersville and Marne Railroad Company

616-949-4778

Call for train tours, offered each season.

Fremont

Gerber Products Company

445 State Street, Fremont
(northeast of Muskegon)
616-928-2000

Visit the Gerber baby food plant. *See* Michigan at Work.

Grand Rapids

Bissel, Inc.

2345 Walker NW, Grand Rapids
616-453-4451

Watch home products assembled, *See* Michigan at Work.

Blandford Nature Center

1715 Hillburn Avenue NW, Grand Rapids
616-453-6192

Children will enjoy the pioneer farmstead, one-room schoolhouse and wild animal hospital. Several self-guided trails meander through the nature center's 143 acres, and the Interpretive Center offers many hands-on experiences. 9 a.m.-5 p.m., Monday-Friday. 1-5 p.m., Saturday and Sunday.

Fish Ladder Sculpture

Front and 6th Streets, Grand Rapids

There's a special spectator's area for watching salmon whoosh over the 6th Street dam on their way up the Grand River to spawn.

Gerald Ford Museum

303 Pearl Street NW, Grand Rapids
616-456-2675

Artifacts revealing the life and times of our 38th president are on display in this large, airy museum. Be sure to watch the 28-minute movie when you first come in. 9 a.m.-4:45 p.m., Monday-Saturday. Noon-4:45 p.m., Sunday.

Grand Rapids Art Museum

155 North Division Street, Grand Rapids
616-459-4677

A large permanent collection hangs in the beautiful, turn-of-the-century Federal Building. Children will enjoy the hands-on art and color experiments in the Children's Gallery. 10 a.m.-4 p.m., Tuesday-Saturday. Noon-4 p.m., Sunday.

Grand Rapids Public Museum and Roger B. Chaffee Planetarium

54 Jefferson SE, Grand Rapids
616-456-3977

Kids will find much of interest including the Gaslight Village, a turn-of-the-century city street, Michigan mammals, Indian artifacts, and prehistoric exhibits. 10 a.m.-5 p.m., Monday-Friday. 1-5 p.m., Saturday and Sunday. The planetarium offers sky shows for children 3 and up and laser light shows. Call for schedule.

Grand Rapids Zoological Gardens
West Fulton and Valley NW, Grand Rapids
616-776-2590

This is the second largest zoo in Michigan with over 350 animals, a fresh-water aquarium, and snake house. 10 a.m.-6 p.m., daily, mid-May–Labor Day. 10 a.m.-4 p.m., daily, after Labor Day.

Gypsum Mine Tour
Michigan Natural Storage
1200 Judd SW, Grand Rapids
616-241-1619

Tour an old gypsum mine. *See* Michigan at Work.

Splash—Family Water Park
4441 28th Street SE, Grand Rapids
616-940-3100

Several water slides, water play areas, miniature golf, scooter derby, and picnic sites. 10 a.m.-9 p.m., daily, Memorial Day-Labor Day.

Holland

Brooks Beverages Plant
777 Brooks Avenue, Holland
616-396-1281

Tour the plant. *See* Michigan at Work.

De Graaf Nature Center
600 Graafschap Road, Holland
616-396-2739

Self-guided trails, hummingbird garden, and small prairie, plus interpretive center with Michigan rocks, birds and insects. Center: 12:30-4:30 p.m., Tuesday-Friday. 2-4 p.m., Saturday and Sunday. Trails: Dawn-8:30 p.m., daily.

Deklomp Wooden Shoe and Delftware Factory and Veldheer Tulip Garden

12755 Quincy Street, Holland
616-399-1803

Watch craftspeople make wooden shoes and hand-paint Delftware. During the spring, there are two million tulips on the grounds, nestled in between windmills and drawbridges. May: 8 a.m.-dark, daily. June-December: 8 a.m.-6 p.m., Monday-Friday. 9 a.m.-5 p.m., Saturday and Sunday. Rest of year: 9 a.m.-5 p.m., Monday-Friday.

Dutch Village

US-31 at James Street, Holland
616-396-1475

A quaint village complete with canals, windmills, tulips, Dutch farmhouse and barn, live animals, street organs, wooden shoe carving, folk dances, rides, and merry-go-round. June-August: 9 a.m.-6 p.m., daily. April-June and September-October: 9 a.m.-5 p.m., daily.

Windmill Island

Windmill Island Municipal Park, Holland
616-396-5433

A 36-acre island with canals, drawbridge, miniature Dutch village, tulip gardens, and "De Zwaan," a 200-year-old operating windmill from the Netherlands. Kids will enjoy climbing up to the top of the windmill on a guided tour, browsing through the gift shops of the Dutch village, and watching "Klompen" dancing presentations. May and July-Labor Day: 9 a.m.-6 p.m., Monday-Saturday. 11:30 a.m.-6 p.m., Sunday. June: 10 a.m.-5 p.m., Monday-Saturday. 11:30 a.m.-5 p.m., Sunday. Shortened hours after Labor Day-October.

Wooden Shoe Factory

447 US-31 at 16th Street, Holland
616-396-6513

Tour the shoe factory. *See* Michigan at Work.

Howell's Apple Ranch
811 North State Street, Stanton
517-831-4918

Watch cider and donuts being made, mid-August–Christmas.

Tri-Cities

Paul Bunyan legends could have started in either of these three cities, once bustling lumbertowns.

Bay City

Historical Museum of Bay County
321 Washington, Bay City
517-893-5733

Learn about the area's lumbering and fur trading eras, shipbuilding industry, and Indian heritage. 10 a.m.-5 p.m., Monday-Friday. 1-5 p.m. Sunday, year-round.

Jennison Nature Center
Bay City State Park
3582 State Park Drive, Bay City
517-667-0717

Located in the middle of a wetland and marsh, the park offers tours of the marshes and a chance to watch migrating waterfowl from a 30-foot tower during spring and fall. 10 a.m.-4 p.m., Tuesday-Saturday. Noon-5 p.m., Sunday, year-round.

St. Laurent Brothers
1101 North Water, Bay City
517-893-7522

Candy in bins and freshly made caramel corn will make kids want to stay forever. Browse to your heart's content and take home a big bag of caramel corn. 9 a.m.-9 p.m., Monday-Friday. 11 a.m.-5 p.m., Sunday.

Automotive Hall of Fame

3225 Cook Road, Midland
517-631-5760

The men and women who advanced the automobile industry are immortalized on the walls of this museum. Older children might enjoy a short visit. 9 a.m.-4 p.m., Monday-Friday, year-round.

Chippewa Nature Center

400 South Badour Road, Midland
517-631-0830

One thousand acres of woods with 14 miles of nature trails, museum with hands-on exhibits and discovery room, restored homestead farm, log schoolhouse, maple sugarhouse, and arboretum of Michigan trees. Children can explore the past. 8 a.m.-5 p.m., Monday-Friday. 9 a.m.-5 p.m., Saturday. 1-5 p.m., Sunday, year-round.

Dow Gardens

1018 West Main, Midland
517-631-2677

Sixty acres of streams, trees, flowers, waterfalls. Children will enjoy walking over many small bridges. 10 a.m.-sunset, daily.

Dow Visitor Center

500 East Lyon Road, Midland
517-636-8658

Tour the Saran Wrap production plant. *See* Michigan at Work.

Midland Center for the Arts

1801 West St. Andrews Drive, Midland
517-631-5930

Don't miss the Hall of Ideas, full of hands-on exhibits of science, technology, and health. Children will enjoy learning about Michigan's past from the colorful Indian, fur trading, farming, and lumbering exhibits. 10 a.m.-6 p.m., Monday-Friday. 1-5 p.m., Saturday and Sunday, year-round.

Andersen Water Park

1830 Fordney Road, Saginaw
517-759-1386

Wave-action pool and double water slide. 11
a.m.-7 p.m., daily, Memorial Day-Labor Day.

Bintz Apple Mountain

4535 North River Road, Freeland
517-781-2590

Depending on the season, you can walk through
the apple orchards and admire the apple blos-
soms or pick apples, cross country ski, or take
part in a Civil War encampment. And throughout
the year, you can visit the tiny apple chapel, buy a
country trinket in the gift shop, enjoy apple cider
and donuts, or feast on individually chosen
steaks at the restaurant. Open year-round.

Green Point Nature Center

3010 Maple Street, Saginaw
517-759-1669

Kids will enjoy the spacious Interpretive Center
with its hands-on displays, wildlife feeding stations, beehives, live animals, and aquariums. Nature trails are open dawn to dusk. Interpretive
center's hours vary; call before visiting.

Historical Museum for
Saginaw County

500 Federal Avenue, Saginaw
517-752-2861

Historical artifacts, memorabilia, clothing, and
tools tell the story of Saginaw's pioneer and lum-
ber-rich past. 10 a.m.-4:30 p.m., Tuesday-Saturday. 1-4:30 p.m., Sunday.

Japanese Cultural Center
and Tea House

1315 South Washington Avenue, Saginaw
517-759-1648

Enjoy a cultural experience. *See* Michigan at
Work.

Marshall Fredericks Sculpture Gallery

Saginaw Valley State University
2250 Pierce Road, Saginaw
517-790-4200

200 original plaster casts of Michigan sculptor Marshall Fredericks' most well-known works are housed inside this modern, new gallery on the campus of SVSU. Outside, children can interact with a dozen of Fredericks' bronze sculptures. 1-5 p.m., Tuesday-Sunday.

Saginaw Art Museum

1126 North Michigan Avenue, Saginaw
517-754-2491

This cozy art museum offers kids the "Vision-area," a special hands-on, creative gallery only during the school year. 10 a.m.-5 p.m., Tuesday-Saturday. 1-5 p.m., Sunday.

Saginaw Children's Zoo

1435 South Washington Avenue, Saginaw
517-759-1657

This delightful children's zoo offers a miniature train ride, petting farm, pony rides, and several creative sculptures that house animals, such as a Noah's Ark and whale's mouth. 10 a.m.-5 p.m., Monday-Saturday. 11 a.m.-6 p.m., Sunday and holidays. Mother's Day Weekend–Labor Day.

Saginaw Harness Raceway

2701 East Genesee, Saginaw
517-755-3451

Enjoy harness racing April through August. Post time changes throughout the summer, so call for a schedule.

Saginaw Rose Garden

Rust Avenue (M-46)
west of Washington Avenue, Saginaw
517-760-1670

Over 1,000 rose bushes of 60 varieties burst into vivid bloom beginning the second week in June, and continue through fall.

Saginaw Trolley Company
615 Johnson, Saginaw
517-753-9531

Hop aboard the trolley and take a narrated, historical journey through Saginaw.

Saginaw Water Works
522 Ezra Rust, Saginaw
517-759-1640

Tour a water processing plant. *See* Michigan at Work.

Up North

Michigan's favorite resort area has many attractions in addition to sand, water, and fudge.

Acme

Music House
7377 North US-31, Acme
(northeast of Traverse City
on the East Arm of Grand Traverse Bay)
616-938-9300

You'll find old-fashioned nickelodeons, grand pianos, radios, a 97-key dance organ, and other antique automatic instruments. Kids will enjoy the period music in the turn-of-the-century Hurry Back Saloon, Acme General Store, and Lyric Theatre. May-October: 10 a.m.-4 p.m., Monday-Saturday. 1-5 p.m., Sunday. Weekends in December.

Beulah

Homestead Sugar House Candies
11393 Homestead Road, Beulah
616-882-7712

Watch a variety of candies being made by hand. *See* Michigan at Work.

Chief Blackbird Museum

SR-119, Harbor Springs
616-347-0200 (Chamber of Commerce)

This museum is full of Ottowa crafts, weavings, tools and implements. Children will enjoy the totem pole on the front lawn and the museum's showcases of traditional Indian clothes and arrowheads. July-Labor Day: 10 a.m.-noon and 1-5 p.m., daily.

Interlochen

Fun Country

US-31, Interlochen
616-276-6360

Miniature golf, go-carts, rides, bumper boats, and water slide. Daily, Memorial Day-Labor Day.

Interlochen Center for the Arts

M-137, Interlochen
616-276-9221

This world-class fine arts school and camp for students of dance, music, visual arts, and theater offers frequent summer performances by guest artists and students.

Leland

Good Harbor Vineyards

Route 1, Lake Leelanau
616-256-7165

Self-guided tours of winemaking operations ends with a wine-tasting session. 11 a.m.-6 p.m., Monday-Saturday. Noon-6 p.m., Sunday, end of May-October.

Leelanau Scenic Railway
616-947-6667

Take a 90-minute fall color tour aboard the historic train. Call for times and reservations.

Petoskey

American Spoon Foods Kitchen
411 East Lake Street, Petoskey
616-347-9030

This is one of my children's favorite stores in Petoskey. It's steamy-sweet inside; employees are preserving and canning in the kitchen. There are always free samples of preserves and crackers. Other locations: 309 Bridge Street, Charlevoix, 616-547-5222, and Grand Traverse Resort, Acme, 616-938-5358. Hours fluctuate with the seasons; call first.

Kilwins Candy Kitchens, Inc.
200 Division Road, Petoskey
616-347-4831

Tour the candy factory. *See* Michigan at Work.

Little Traverse Historic Museum
Off Dock Street on US-31, Petoskey
616-347-2620

Children will enjoy the collection of old-fashioned items including a dentist's chair, doctor's table, wheelchair, sewing machine, and baby buggy. 10 a.m.-4 p.m., Monday-Saturday, Memorial Day-Labor Day. 10 a.m.-4 p.m., Tuesday-Saturday, after Labor Day-October. Rest of year: open by appointment.

Pirate's Cove Adventure Golf
1230 US-31 North, Petoskey
616-347-1123

Eighteen-hole adventure miniature golf with waterfalls, bridges, and hills. 10 a.m.-11 p.m., daily. April-October.

Sleeping Bear Dunes

Walking up the sand dunes in the hot summer sun is an experience that's all Michigan. Kids love it! Sleeping Bear Dunes, located approximately one hour west of Traverse City, is a natural wonder. The visitor center is located off SR-72 in Empire, and many dune climbs are in the general area from Empire to Glen Haven. For maps and information, call 616-326-5134. Visitor center hours: 9 a.m.-6 p.m., daily, end of June-Labor Day. Rest of year: 8 a.m.-4:30 p.m., daily. *See* Parks.

Traverse City

Amon Orchard Tours
7404 North US-31, Traverse City
616-938-1644

Tour the cherry orchard. *See* Michigan at Work.

The Candle Factory
301 Grand View Parkway, Traverse City
616-946-2280, 616-946-2850

Watch candles being made. *See* Michigan at Work.

Clinch Park Zoo
400 Boardman Street, Traverse City
616-922-4904 (zoo)

Young children will enjoy this small zoo's Michigan animals and aquarium with Michigan fish. Memorial Day-Labor Day: 9:30 a.m.-7:30 p.m., daily.

Denoss Museum
Northwestern Michigan College
College Drive and Munson Avenue, Traverse City
616-922-1055

This new 40,000-square foot museum houses one of the nation's most extensive collections of Inuit art, a 367-seat auditorium, a permanent discovery hands-on room for children with interactive videos, and three galleries set up for unique traveling exhibitions of art and natural history.

Grand Traverse Balloons
616-947-7433

Two flights a day, at dawn and dusk, weather permitting. Children must be at least nine years old. Call ahead for reservations.

Leelanau Wine Cellars, Ltd.
County Road 626, 1/4 mile west of Omena
616-386-5201

Guided tours of the winery with a wine tasting session at the end. April-Labor Day: 11 a.m.-7 p.m., Monday-Friday. 10 a.m.-7 p.m., Saturday. Noon-7 p.m., Sunday. Shortened hours after Labor Day. January-March, weekends only.

McManus' Southview Orchards
Garfield Road, Traverse City
616-941-5767

U-pick cherries at the end of July, 9 a.m.-5 p.m., daily.

Pirate's Cove Adventure Golf
1710 US-31 North, Traverse City
616-938-9599

Eighteen-hole adventure miniature golf complete with waterfalls, bridges, and hills. 10 a.m.-11 p.m., daily, April-October.

Underwood Orchards and Farm Market
360 McKinley Road, Traverse City
616-947-8799

U-pick cherries and peaches, farm market and bakery. 9 a.m.-6 p.m., daily. June-December.

Upper Peninsula

Drive across the Mackinac Bridge into the ruggedly natural Upper Peninsula. Here you'll see Michigan's national treasures—Pictured Rocks along Lake Superior, and Tahquamenon Falls. Summer turns into autumn earlier here, so bring along with warm clothes. And don't come home without trying pasties, the Upper Peninsula's specialty food, steaming hot dough pockets filled with meat, potatoes, and onion.

Calumet

Coopertown U.S.A. Mining Museum

Red Jacket Road, Calumet
Downtown Calumet
906-337-4354

Exhibits trace the history of mining in the Upper Peninsula and offer a glimpse into a miner's life. 10 a.m.-8 p.m., Monday-Friday. 10 a.m.-6 p.m., Saturday.

Caspian

Iron County Museum

Caspian
906-265-2617

Indoor-outdoor museum on former mine site with over 125 exhibits, including an 1890 homestead, depot, streetcar, barn, and home. 9 a.m.-5 p.m., Monday-Saturday. 1-5 p.m. Sunday, June-August. 10 a.m.-4 p.m., Monday-Saturday. 1-4 p.m., Sunday, May and September.

Copper Harbor

Brockway Mountain Drive

You'll find the start of the nine-mile scenic drive four miles west of Copper Harbor. High above sea level, the drive offers a panoramic view of the mighty Lake Superior, as well as neighboring woodlands.

Delaware Copper Mine

Kearsarge, on the Keweenaw Peninsula
906-289-4688

Tour an old copper mine. *See* Michigan at Work.

Fort Wilkins State Park
East US-41, Copper Harbor
906-289-4215

In addition to scenic drives, copper mine shafts, and the Copper Harbor lighthouse, the park houses the restored Fort Wilkins Historic Complex, built in 1844 as a U.S. Army post. The fort offers exhibits, period rooms, living history, and, audio-visual displays. Open 8:30 a.m.-9 p.m., daily, mid-May—mid-October.

Fayette

Historic Fayette Townsite
On CR-483, off US-2, Fayette State Park
Fayette (on Big Bay de Noc)
906-644-2603

Walk through the tall grass of this ghost town, once a thriving nineteenth-century iron smelting community. Restored buildings and modern exhibits tell the story of a town's rise and fall. Museum: 9 a.m.-7 p.m., daily, mid-May–mid-October.

Hancock

Arcadian Copper Mine Tours, Inc.
M-26, Hancock
906-482-7502

Travel 1/4-mile into an old copper mine to learn about the mining industry. *See* Michigan at Work.

Quincy Mine Hoist No. 2
US-41, Hancock
906-482-3101

A Keweenaw landmark, this mammoth hoist, designed to haul 10 tons of ore, operated through the end of the mining era in the 1930s. A short video and tour will give you a better understanding of the miner's life. 9:30 a.m.-5 p.m., daily, mid-June–Labor Day.

Iron Mountain

Cornish Pump and Mining Museum
Kent Street, Iron Mountain
906-774-1086

A collection of underground mining equipment and a video about the Ford gliders made in this area. 9 a.m.-5 p.m., Monday-Saturday. Noon-4 p.m., Sunday. May 15-October 31.

Iron Mountain Iron Mine
Nine miles east of Iron Mountain on US-2
906-563-8077

Tour an old iron mine. *See* Michigan at Work.

Menominee Range Historical Foundation Museum
300 East Ludington Street, Iron Mountain
906-774-4276

Children will enjoy the turn-of-the-century exhibits, which include replicas of a country store fur trapping and livery stable, Victorian parlor, and one-room schoolhouse. 10 a.m.-4 p.m., Monday-Saturday. Noon-4 p.m., Sunday, May-October.

Ironwood

Black River Drive
100 East Aurora Street, Ironwood
906-932-1122 (Chamber of Commerce)

Take the picturesque 18-mile drive north from Ironwood to Lake Superior, which winds near five waterfalls and ends in a beautiful harbor. The waterfalls are found at the end of footpaths at each marked turnoff.

Copper Peak Ski Flying Hill

CR-513, Ironwood
906-932-3500

Take a chair lift or elevator 240 feet above Copper Peak for a panoramic view of Canada, Lake Superior, and the three adjoining states of Michigan, Minnesota and Wisconsin. 10 a.m.-4:30 p.m., daily, Memorial Day-Labor Day.

Hiawatha, World's Tallest Indian

100 East Aurora, Ironwood
906-932-1122 (Chamber of Commerce)

This 50-foot tall molded fiberglass statue weighs 8 tons. Be sure to tell the kids that Henry Wadsworth Longfellow's poem "Song of Hiawatha," the story of the brave Indian chief who married the beautiful princess Minnehaha, took place near Lake Superior.

Mt. Zion Overlook

Off US-2 and Greenbush Street, Ironwood
906-932-4231

Drive to the top of Mt. Zion in the summer and enjoy a panoramic view of Lake Superior, Wisconsin, and the Porcupine Mountains. After Halloween, the area becomes a ski resort.

Ishpeming

National Ski Hall of Fame

610 US-41, Ishpeming
906-486-9281

This Copperstown of skiing fame honors skiing's pioneering athletes and greats. You'll be inspired by the short movie. 10 a.m.-4 p.m., daily, year-round.

Mackinac Island

You can tour the island many different ways—by foot, bicycle, horse, or horse-drawn carriage—but never by car. Leave your car in Mackinaw City and take the 30-minute ferry ride to the island.

Old Fort Mackinac

Mackinac Island
906-847-3328

The 300-year old fort and its 14 restored buildings, including a blacksmith shop, church, Indian dormitory, sally ports, and houses, offer children a lesson in living history. Costumed guides demonstrate cooking, spinning, musket firings, canon salutes, and military music. June 15-Labor Day: 9 a.m.-6 p.m., daily. May 15-June 14 and after Labor Day–Mid-October: 10 a.m.-4 p.m., daily.

Mackinaw City

While technically in the Lower Penninsula, Mackinaw City's location at the foot of the Mackinac Bridge makes it the gateway to the Upper Penninsula.

Colonial Michilimackinac and Mackinaw Maritime Park and Museum

Exit 339 off I-75 North, Mackinaw City
616-436-5563

Costumed staff and demonstrations make this reconstructed 1715 military outpost and fur trading village come to life. A small museum inside an old lighthouse exhibits nautical history. June 15-Labor Day: 9 a.m.-6 p.m., daily. May-June 14 and September: 9 a.m.-5 p.m., daily. October 1–mid-October: 10 a.m.-4 p.m.

Old Mill Creek State Historic Park

US-23, Mackinaw City
616-436-7301

A working sawmill, craft demonstrations, costumed guides, picnic sites, nature trails, and overlooks mark the site of a 1780s sawmill and dam. Archaeological digs are in progress mid-June–Labor Day. Park hours: June 15-Labor Day: 9 a.m.-6 p.m., daily. May 15-June 14 and after Labor Day–mid-October: 10 a.m.-4 p.m., daily.

Revolutionary War Sloop *Welcome*

Mackinaw City Marina, Mackinaw City
616-436-5563

Guides in authentic British Navy costumes take

visitors on a tour of the reconstructed 1775 British sloop. June 15-Labor Day: 9 a.m.-6 p.m., daily. September: 10 a.m.-5 p.m. daily. October 1–mid-October: 10 a.m.-4 p.m. daily.

Teysen's Woodland Indian Museum

416 South Huron Avenue, Mackinaw City
616-436-7011

Michigan Indian, fur trading, and lumber era artifacts. 7 a.m.-10 p.m., daily, May 1-October 25.

Manistique

Kitch-iti-kipi Spring and Raft

Palms Book State Park
Route 2, Manistique
906-341-5010 (Chamber of Commerce)

Take an unusual, slow-moving, glass-bottomed raft ride across the murky spring. The raft is large enough to hold several families.

Siphon Raft and Bridge

US-2, Manistique
906-341-5010 (Chamber of Commerce)

One of Ripley's Believe It or Not Mysteries, the road across this bridge is actually four feet below the level of the river, Don't ask me to esplain; it's just fun to drive over.

Marquette

Presque Isle Park

906-228-0460

A peninsula jutting into Lake Superior, this all-season park offers hiking and biking trails and a small children's zoo. Take the road circling the park shoreline and watch ore freighters at work.

United States Olympic Training Center Tours

Meyland Hall
Northern Michigan University, Marquette
906-227-2888

Take a look behind the scenes at the Olympic training site. *See* Michigan at Work.

Mass City

Windmill Farms
Mass City
906-883-3488

Farm visits with three-hour llama treks for families. Recommended ages for children: 5-13 years. Call several months in advance for reservations. No drop-ins.

Negaunee

Michigan Iron Industry Museum
73 Forge Road, Negaunee
906-475-7857

This new museum chronicles the story of Michigan's iron ore industry and the people who worked the mines. 9:30 a.m.-4:30 p.m., daily, May-October.

Paradise

Great Lakes Shipwreck Museum
North of Paradise on US-123
at Whitefish Point
906-635-1742

Shipwrecks never seemed so real or Lake Superior so frightening. This museum, located on the tip of a jutting bay, offers 170 years of shipwreck history in stunning displays and an evocative movie. 10 a.m.-6 p.m., daily, Memorial Day-October 15.

Tahquamenon Falls State Park
On SR-123, between Paradise
and Newberry
906-492-3415

Walk the trails of the Upper Falls and the Lower Falls and see the second largest waterfalls in North America (Niagara Falls is numero uno). Bring rain slickers; it seems to rain whenever we visit!

Pictured Rocks National Lakeshore

Children will not easily forget the crashing waves and jutting rock formations along the 42-mile Lake Superior shoreline that makes up Pictured Rocks National Lakeshore. Although there are several excellent lookouts, boat cruises offer the best view of the cliffs. Pictured Rocks Boat Cruises go out daily weather permitting. June: 10 a.m. and 2 p.m. July 1-August 31: 9 and 11 a.m., noon, 1, 3, and 5 p.m. September-mid-October: 10 a.m. and 2 p.m. Call 906-387-2379 for reservations. *See* Parks.

St. Ignace

Deer Ranch
West US-2
906-643-7760

Walk along a nature trail and feed or photograph native Michigan Whitetail deer in a natural setting. 9 a.m.-9 p.m., daily, Memorial Day-Labor Day.

Father Marquette Memorial and Museum
Straits State Park
720 Church Street, St. Ignace
906-643-9394, 906-643-8620

Learn about Father Marquette and Michigan Indian life in state-of-the-art audio-visual exhibits. The park offers a great view of the Mackinac Bridge. 9 a.m.-8 p.m., daily, mid-June-Labor Day. Reduced hours after Labor Day.

Marquette Mission Park and Museum of Ojibwa Culture
500 N. State Street, St. Ignace
906-643-9161

An Indian longbarn shares a city corner with a small museum dedicated to chronicling the Ojibwa way of life. 10 a.m.-8:30 p.m., daily, Memorial Day-Labor Day. Reduced hours to mid-October.

Sault Ste. Marie

Soo Locks

St. Marys Falls Canal, Portage Avenue
Sault Ste. Marie
906-362-3301 (Chamber of Commerce)

An observation platform overlooks the world's busiest and largest locking system, first built in 1855. The Visitor Center houses a film about the locks, artifacts, and a working lock model. Park is open 6 a.m.-midnight, daily, in the summer. Visitor Center is open 7 a.m.-11 p.m., daily, May-November.

Soo Locks Boat Tours

Dock 1 at 1157 East Portage Avenue
Dock 2 at 500 East Portage Avenue
Sault Ste. Marie
906-632-6301

Two-hour narrated tours travel through the locks and pass the St. Mary's Rapids. July-August: 9 a.m.-7 p.m., daily. May 15–mid-June and September 1-October 15: 9 a.m.-4:30 p.m., daily.

Soo Locks Train Tours

317 West Portage Avenue, Sault Ste. Marie
906-635-5912

Tour (1¼ hour) describes historic sites along the 15-mile route. Departures every half hour, on weekends, and every hour on weekdays, 9 a.m.-7:30 p.m.. Memorial Day–mid-October.

S.S. *Valley Camp*
and Marine Museum

Johnston and Water Streets, Sault Ste. Marie
906-632-3658

The world's largest Great Lakes maritime museum is housed in a massive Great Lakes freighter and includes aquariums, lifeboats from the sunken Edmund Fitzgerald, shipwreck displays, and other maritime displays. The site also has a gift shop, marina, historic home park, riverfront parks, and picnic sites. July 1-August 31: 9 a.m.-9 p.m., daily. May 15-June 30 and September 1-October 15: 10 a.m.-6 p.m., daily. Last ticket on sale one hour before closing.

Tower of History
Portage Avenue, Sault Ste. Marie
906-632-3658

Ride up 21 stories into Michigan's sky and see Michigan and Canadian wilderness for 20 miles in every direction from five observation platforms. 10 a.m.-6 p.m., daily, mid-May–mid-October. Last ticket on sale one hour before closing.

Shingleton

Iverson Snowshoe Factory
Maple Street, Shingleton
906-452-6370

Watch snowshoes being made. *See* Michigan at Work.

16
PROGRAMS FOR THE SCHOOLS
A Sampling of Traveling Programs

Michigan is full of talented actors, dancers, artists, and musicians who will bring their art into the schools. There are also traveling science and history programs, sponsored by area museums and individuals, which offer school children new ideas in an entertaining format. Here is a sampling of traveling programs available for school, church, synagogue, library, or civic organizations. Fees are not listed because they fluctuate with each booking, depending on the size of the group and traveling distance.

Theater

Actor's Alliance Theatre Company
Jeffrey M. Nahan
30800 Evergreen, Southfield
313-642-1326

Professional theater company offers touring musical and dramatic productions.

Storytelling

Ami D.
Ami Jackson
Detroit
313-934-8635

Multi-cultural storytelling, accompanied by piano, harp and vocals, with audience participation. Ami D. spins folktales and makes important characters from history come to life. Preschool-high school.

Science

Ann Arbor Hands-On Museum Outreach
219 East Huron Street, Ann Arbor
313-995-5439

The Ann Arbor Hands-On Museum offers comprehensive science-based workshops designed to enhance curricula through creative and interactive activities, including Human Biology, Magnetism and Sound, Mathematics, Michigan History, and Astronomy.

Music

Ann Arbor Symphony Orchestra
527 East Liberty, Ann Arbor
313-994-4801

A morning and afternoon, weekday concert is offered to tri-county school children in January and April. Teachers can call for tickets, preparatory materials, and to book a classroom visit by a symphony docent. Geared for upper elementary and middle school.

Puppets

Atlantis Expedition

Nancy Henk
313-881-3038

The Atlantis Expedition interprets classical music with unusual forms of puppetry, including giant puppets, masks, and shadow puppets. Their show is geared for grades 1 to 6 or family audiences and requires an auditorium setting. Also, workshops and residencies are available.

Theater

The Attic Theatre

7939 Third, Detroit
313-875-8286

The Attic Theatre Outreach program offers mainstage productions, artists-in-residence, one-act children's plays, as well as music, dance, comedy sketches, and oral history.

Drug Education

BABES

17330 Northland Park Court, Southfield
313-443-1676
1-800-54-BABES

Engaging puppets teach children about healthy living skills, and encourage them to feel good about themselves when they "say no" to drugs and alcohol. For grades preschool-12. Children can also become a member of the Babes Club and receive the monthly bulletin.

Storytelling

Barbara Schutz-Gruber

Ann Arbor
313-761-5118

Award-winning storyteller whose favorites include folk tales from around the world, tales from Michigan and the Great Lakes, medieval legends, ghost stories, and string stories—stories illustrated with figures and shapes created by a simple piece of string. Preschool-high school.

Storytelling

Becky Goodspeed

3030 Oak Hollow Drive SE, Grand Rapids
616-949-3867

Through imagination and vivid word pictures, the magical world of stories come to life. Goodspeed offers performances, residencies, and workshops.

Animals

Binder Park Zoo—Zoomobile Outreach

7400 Division Drive, Battle Creek
616-979-1351

A variety of thematic presentations incorporating role-playing, hands-on activities, and live animals, for preschool-middle school age children.

Drug & Crime Prevention

Blue Pigs

Detroit Police Crime Prevention Section
313-596-2520

Through a variety of songs and musical styles, three talented Detroit Police officers offer children information about child protection, drug abuse and awareness, and crime prevention. The approximately 45-minute show is tailored for elementary school audiences.

Theater

Boarshead: Michigan Public Theater

425 South Grand Avenue, Lansing
517-484-7800

Theatrical performances for grades K-6, include material derived from oral and written Michigan histories. Also, custom-designed acting and playwriting workshops and school residencies.

Theater

Bonstelle Theatre
Department of Theater,
Wayne State University, Detroit
313-577-3010

Bonstelle Theatre offers "Movin' Theatre," a touring performance of theatrical dance, various forms of stage movement, and period styles. For middle school and high school.

Puppets

Brad Lowe
Fantasy E-FEX
P.O. Box 717, Lake Orion
313-373-1717

Brad Lowe offers original adaptations of traditional stories, using music and hand puppets, as well as costume-character appearances and puppetry demonstrations and workshops.

Music, Values

Carol Johnson
P.O. Box 6351, Grand Rapids
616-243-6194

Using original material, Carol Johnson accompanies herself on guitar, banjo, or piano and sings of self worth, the environment, and living and loving joyfully. Appropriate for elementary schools and family events.

Music

Chamber Music for Youth
3000 Town Center, Suite 1335, Southfield
313-357-1111

The Lyric Chamber Ensemble visits middle schools and high schools, offering concerts and workshops.

Chemistry Is Fun

Dow Chemical Company
2020 Dow Center, Midland
517-636-2474

Dow Chemical chemists, engineers, and technicians travel to schools within the five-county area around Midland, offering a program of experiments designed to interest students in science careers. For grades 3-12. Also, "Recycle This," a rock music video about recycling, targeted to grades 7-12, is available to all Michigan schools, 1-800-441-4369.

Children's Theatre of Michigan

M'Arch McCarty
Drayton Plains
313-666-9139
313-666-3031

Janet and M'Arch McCarty offer original musical story-theater performances, including tall tales and silly stories, for children of all ages.

Cranbrook Institute of Science

500 Lone Pine Road, Bloomfield Hills
313-645-3210

Outreach program topics for grades K-8 include astronomy, anthropology, physics, and dinosaurs.

Crazy Richard the Madd Juggler

Route #1 Box 255A, East Jordan
616-536-7987

Crazy Richard offers a unique and lively show combining juggling, clowning, mime, and audience involvement.

Theater, Dance

Crossroads Productions

Donald V. Calamia
13120 Nathaline, Redford
1-800-348-8988

This entertaining and popular touring theater company offers a wide variety of performances targeted specifically for young children, families, and young adults. The touring schedule includes "Family Classics" (fairy tale theater), "Contemporary Social Dramas" (thought-provoking dramas about divorce, AIDS, and drugs), "Storytime Theatre" (folk tales and popular children's stories), and "Showcase Presentations" (special shows for special occasions). Also offers productions with O.J. Anderson.

Puppets

Daren Dundee, Entertainer

21175 Carson, Mount Clemens
313-463-1798

Puppeteer Daren Dundee offers a variety of programs for young children, and the whole family, incorporating story-telling, puppetry, and magic.

Science

Detroit Audubon Society

121 South Main Street, Royal Oak
313-545-2929

Schools can subscribe to a bi-monthly reader, "Audubon Adventures," all about birds, created by the National Audubon Society. Speakers with a slide presentation on changing topics are available to clubs and schools. Program with live reptiles is also available.

Dance

Detroit Dance Collective
739 South Washington, Royal Oak
313-544-5550

Detroit Dance Collective, a modern dance company made up of performers who are also dance educators, offers a variety of school performances, classes, and workshops for students. They will design programs to meet the special needs of any group.

Science

Detroit Edison—
School Safety Coordinator
Public Affairs Department
2000 Second Avenue, Detroit
313-237-9213

Audio-visual presentation explaining how electricity is made and transmitted, plus safety tips. For grades 4 to 6. Free. Call to schedule, 8 a.m.-4:30 p.m., Monday-Friday.

Art

Detroit Institute of Arts—
Art to the Schools
5200 Woodward Avenue, Detroit
313-833-7883

Call 9 a.m.-5 p.m., Monday-Friday, for an "Art to the Schools," request form. Scheduling is not handled over the phone. Free 45 to 60 minute art appreciation talks are available for grades 4 to 6, Tuesdays and Thursdays, October to May. The talks are based on the DIA's collection and are illustrated with slides and reproductions. The topics include "People of the World," "Learning to Look," "American Art," "Native American Art," "Modern Art," "Arts of Asia," "African Art," "Ancient World," and "European Art."

Values

Dolls for Democracy

B'nai Brith Women's Council of
Metropolitan Detroit
25160 Lahser, Suite 130, Southfield
313-356-8811

"Doll ladies" bring into the classroom 12-inch replica dolls of famous courageous people who have worked for the betterment of humanity. The presentation teaches brotherhood/sisterhood and the importance of perseverance over adversity. The approximately 45-minute biographical presentation is geared to grades 2 to 6. It's free, but donations are accepted.

Science

Ecology Center

417 Detroit, Ann Arbor
313-761-3186

Offers hands-on environmental education and ecology presentations to school children of all ages. Can also call to schedule visit to Recycling and Education Station, 2050 South Industrial Highway, Ann Arbor.

Dance

Eisenhower Dance

Laurie Eisenhower
P.O. Box 80876, Rochester
313-652-7198

Performance, demonstration, audience-participation programs and residency for K-12.

Storytelling/Values

The Fabricators

Ami D. and Milli P.
Detroit
313-934-8635

Original folktales about ecology and animals, for middle-high school audiences.

Nature/Recycling

For-Mar Nature Preserve

5360 East Potter, Burton
313-736-7100

One-hour program geared for K-8 offers lessons on the environment, recycling, nature, and animals.

Music

Gemini

2000 Penncraft Ct., Ann Arbor
313-665-0165

Twin brothers Sandor and Laszlo Slomovits, professionally known as Gemini, offer concerts for elementary to high school students. They offer boisterous fun, incorporating a wide range of musical traditions and instruments into their songs.

Theater

Goodtime Players

Jan Koengeter
Ann Arbor Community Education and Recreation
313-994-2300, ext. 227

Goodtime Players offer original musical comedies. Shows are approximately 30 to 45 minutes and geared for elementary children and families.

Science/Animals

Howell Nature Center

1005 Triangle Lake Road, Howell
517-546-0249

Naturalists bring permanently injured mammals and wildlife into the classroom and teach children about wildlife preservation.

Science

Huron-Clinton Metroparks
1-800-47-PARKS

Free slide and movie programs on southeast Michigan nature for grades K to 12. Brochures are mailed in September. Act quickly; the programs are booked on a first come, first served basis.

Science

Impression 5 Museum
200 Museum Drive, Lansing
517-485-8116

Entertaining science shows for grades K to 12 introduce children to the world of Science.

Theater, Dance

In Cahoots
P.O. Box 141, Oxford
313-693-0233

In Cahoots is a booking service offering several fine children's theater and dance troupes, including "Bobbi Lucas: Pirouettes & Pigs That Fly," "Eisenhower Dance Ensemble," "Other Things & Co.," "A Reasonable Facsimile," and "Hansen and Thompson Present Stories and Spices and Cats Chasing Mices." All groups are suitable for school and community programs.

Science

Independence Oaks Nature Center
Starlab
9501 Sashabaw Road, Clarkston
313-625-6473

Starlab, a portable, inflatable planetarium, travels to schools for naturalist-led astronomy shows, suitable for 1st grade and older.

Storytelling

Judy Sima
Southfield
313-644-3951

Judy Sima offers her audience a variety of traditional tales, including ghost stories, children's literature, and humor. Children are encouraged to participate. Storytelling workshops are available for middle school-age children to adults.

Ecology, Values

The Junior World Game
Upland Hills Ecological Center
2575 Indian Lake Road, Oxford
313-693-1021

Multi-media presentation involves students in a hands-on role playing game. A giant map, projected on the floor, becomes the game board and children role-play world leaders. For grades 4-9.

Archeology and Ecology

Kelsey Museum of Archeology
434 South State Street, Ann Arbor
313-747-0441

Hands-on kits include educational materials and specimen, available to elementary and middle school classrooms.

Puppets

Kids on the Block
United Cerebral Palsy of Metro Detroit
23077 Greenfield
Suite 205, Southfield
313-557-5070

Engaging puppeteers teach children about physical disabilities using almost life-size puppets. For third and fourth grade.

Storytelling

Linda Day
Livonia
313-478-6339

Linda Day weaves folk tales, scary stories, humor, and participation tales for elementary-adult audiences. High school workshops are also available.

Science

Living Science Foundation
40400 Grand River, Suite F, Novi
313-478-1999

Over 40 entertaining, hands-on science shows for grades K-12, including "Animal Family," "Life on Earth," "Nature's Law," "Where in the World," "Prehistoric Life," "Ocean's Edge," and "Exploring Space." The Living Science Foundation instructors are widely known for their razzle-dazzle demonstrations and fine teaching skills. Prefers classroom visits over school-wide assemblies.

History, Dance

Madame Cadillac Dancers
15 East Kirby, Detroit
313-875-6354

Madame Cadillac Dancers bring the French Colonial period and the history of Detroit's first settlers to life with the authentic dance, music, and costumes. Their repertoire includes "First Lady of Detroit—story of Marie Therese Guyon," "Jean Baptiste Pointe du Sable, Black Man in the Wilderness," and "Ezekiel Solomon, Michigan's First Jewish Fur Trader." Each show is 50 minutes and appeals to families and children of all ages.

Theater, Disability Awareness

Mad Hatters, Educational Theatre
P.O. Box 2, Kalamazoo
616-385-5871

Using audience participation, Mad Hatters helps children and adults understand people with special needs or disabilities. Other drama topics include substance abuse, non-traditional careers, aging, and communications/teamwork. Performances are geared to both children and adults.

Music

Marc Thomas
22549 Power, Farmington
313-478-0738

Thomas and his puppet, Max the Moose, offer sing-along fun for preschool audiences.

Theater

Meadow Brook Theatre— Costumes in the Classroom
Oakland University, Rochester
313-370-3316

Costumes in the Classroom offers a curriculum enrichment for drama, history, English, and art classes. Six to eight period costumes are brought into the classroom and modeled during an informal lecture.

Aviation History

Michigan Balloon Corporation
1380 Friel Street, Burton
1-800-882-6456

Michigan Balloon Corporation brings a hot air balloon to the schools, teaches children about the history of hot air ballooning from 1783 to the present, and ends with a hands-on demonstration of how a balloon is inflated. For grades K-12.

Music, Theater

Michigan Opera Theatre— Community Programs Department
6519 Second Avenue, Detroit
313-874-7850

MOT offers top-notch creative performances geared to children of all ages, plus special educational programs such as master classes and workshops that can supplement school curriculum. Performances are approximately 45 minutes. MOT also offers adult and family shows.

Mime

The Mime Ensemble
415 South Adams, Rochester Hills
313-375-1027

Using both classic and unique approaches to mime, and circus skills—juggling, balloon tying, and stilt walking—The Mime Ensemble delights both children and adults.

Science, Literature, Values

Mobile Ed Productions
26455 Five Mile, Livonia
313-533-4455

Mobile Ed Productions offers a variety of educationally exciting programs for K to 12, including "World of Robotics," "Amazing World of Light," "Wonder and Mystery of Chemistry," "Physics is Fun," "Reptiles are Cool," "Succeeding Without Drugs," "Adventures of Huck Finn," and "Living with Abe Lincoln."

Storytelling, Music

Naim Abdur Rauf
830 Calumet, Detroit
313-832-4986

Using traditional African instruments and wearing traditional African dress, Abdur Rauf offers stories and songs that introduce children to African culture and history.

Recreation

Oakland County Mobile Recreation Units
313-858-0916

Mobile recreation units offer sports equipment, games, puppet shows, moonwalk, mime troupe, and traveling music show.

Drug & Safety Education

Officer Ollie and Friends
Wayne County Sheriff
1231 St. Antoine, Detroit
313-224-2234

For grades K-1 Officer Ollie offers "Don't Go With Strangers." For grades 2-3, it's "Be A Winner, Say No To Drugs."

Mime

O.J. Anderson
c/o Fleming, Tamulevich and Associates
733-735 North Main, Ann Arbor
313-995-9066

A multi-faceted entertainer, Anderson offers mime performances and workshops for school age children and adults.

Music

Omni Arts in Education
Bill Mobley
Detroit
313-886-4277

Retired music teacher Bill Mobley runs a non-profit agency that brings professional musicians into the Detroit and Pontiac schools.

Music

Peter Madcat Ruth
Donna Zajonc Management
P.O. Box 7023, Ann Arbor
313-662-9137

An internationally acclaimed harmonica virtuoso, Madcat Ruth offers his original blend of folk music, blues, jazz, country, and rock an roll to children and adults of all ages.

Puppets

Pippin Puppets
313-533-5229

Robert Papineau presents live, interactive puppet theater offering original stories with something to learn. Preschool-6th grade.

Music

Possum Corner
3387 Reese Road, Ortonville
313-625-1227

Possum Corner books Michigan folk musicians, including Modesty Forbids, an Irish folk group, for school or community performances.

Puppets, Storytelling

The Puppet Connection
Marilyn O'Connor Miller
Birmingham
313-642-8912

Multi-media storyteller Marilyn O'Connor Miller weaves imaginative stories using masks, puppets, and a variety of character voices and accents.

Puppets

Puppets To Go
Nancy Henk
313-881-3038

Puppeteer offers shows for libraries, schools and private parties for children of all ages. Also, workshops for adults and children.

Theater, Music

Reasonable Facsimile
Anne and Rob Burns
P.O. Box 294, Rochester
313-651-2276

Specializing in music and theater from the Renaissance, Anne and Rob Burns offer children of all ages a humorous view of knights, dragons, rogues, and ladies. Dressed in Renaissance costume, they play multiple characters and a variety of musical instruments from the era, including cittern, mandora, recorders, fifes, shawms, and percussion. Reasonable Facsimile is available for Renaissance, dance, music, and theater workshops, festivals, assemblies, and concerts.

Puppets

Red Rug Puppet Theatre
Beth Katz, Puppeteer
East Lansing
517-332-8442

Puppeteer Beth Katz performs fairy tales, holiday theme shows, and customized shows for school celebrations. Her performances are geared to elementary schools; she also offers puppetry workshops for teachers.

Puppets, Ventriloquist

Rick's Puppet Theater
48607 Presidential, Mount Clemens
313-566-0888

Puppeteer Richard Paul offers a variety of comedy-ventriloquism acts or puppet shows with large handmade puppets, which include holiday shows for Halloween, Christmas, and Easter, plus a very effective traffic and stranger safety show. For all ages.

Magic, Education

Scheer Magic Productions

Doug Scheer
38664 Evonshire, Farmington Hills
313-553-4987

Doug Scheer and his many alter egos—Wizzy the Wacky Wizard, Uncle Sam, and Jingle the Magical Elf—perform history, science, reading, ecology, safety, and just plain magic shows for children of all ages.

Music

The SongSisters

Chris Barton and Julie Austin
P.O. Box 7477, Ann Arbor
313-677-3575

Julie Austin and Chris Barton perform children's music on a variety of instruments, including guitar, banjo, autoharp, hammered dulcimer, recorders, flute, and homemade rhythm and folk toys. Their concerts mix stories, humor, songs, movement, and educational concepts.

Magic, Education

Stevens and Associates

Bernie Stevens
747 West Maple, Suite 501, Clawson
313-288-0338

Bernie Stevens offers a fun-filled, 30 to 45 minute family magic show with colorful effects and balloon animals. For children 4 and older. He also offers imaginative and educational school programs on topics of reading, science, and substance abuse for K-8.

Creative Writing, Theater

Storybuilders

Sue Fraley or Tom Shaker
P.O. Box 20580, Ferndale
313-543-8300

Storybuilders will come into the classroom with improvisational skits to help motivate creative writing. If student stories are sent at least one week before Storybuilders' visit, they will bring those stories to life in light-hearted vignettes. Storybuilders also performs musicals and holiday shows, plus "Sherlock Holmes and the Case of Substance Abuse," "Explorer's Scrapbook," a geography show and "Blue Balloon," an environmental musical.

Storytelling

Story Peddlar

William Boyce
313-886-4932, 313-577-6296

William Boyce, Wayne State University professor of communications, is the Story Peddlar, spinning stories for children and young adults.

Storytelling, Music

The Storytellers

Robert Allison
P.O. Box 15405, Detroit
313-884-2780

The Storytellers present dramatic oral interpretations of literature and folklore while demonstrating over 20 musical instruments from all parts of the world, including balafones, steel drums, berimbau, vibraphone, m'biras, tabla, cuica, ocarinas, and shakere.

Puppets

String Puppet Theatre
301 West Kilbuck, Tecumseh
517-423-2414

Traditional fairytales and folktales are presented using 32-inch hand-carved marionettes with colorful costumes, and hand-painted scenery.

History

Time Travelers
Greenfield Village
20900 Oakwood Boulevard, Dearborn
313-271-1620, ext. 505

Costumed characters bring to life famous inventors like the Wright Brothers and George Washington Carver, or offer a glimpse into pioneer and farm life, and early industry. Programs are offered for grades K-2 and 3-6 and book up quickly.

Science

U of M Exhibit Museum
1109 Geddes Avenue, Ann Arbor
313-764-0478

An endangered species exhibit is available to classroom teachers.

Animals

Upland Hills Farm
481 Lake George Road, Oxford
313-628-1611

Farmer Webster takes the animals on the road with a wide variety of farm programs that teach children where food and fiber originate.

Theater

Wallace Smith Productions
Touring Chamber Theatre
2896 South Commerce, Walled Lake
313-471-7705
313-669-0696 (TDD)

Touring Chamber Theatre offers an eclectic program of narrative storytelling, mime, dialogue, music, and dance. Programs are 35 to 50 minutes and encourage audience participation. The company's emphasis is on conflict resolution, problem solving, and positive values. For grades preschool to high school.

Theater

Wild Swan Theater
1510 Shadford, Ann Arbor
313-995-0530

Wild Swan Theater performs children's theater for grades preschool to 6 in a storytelling style using masks, mime, music, and puppets. Their productions are also accessible for sight and hearing-impaired children through sign language interpretation and audio-description.

Science

Young Entomologists Society
Gary Dunn
Lansing
517-887-0499

Gary Dunn brings artifacts, collections, 3-D models, puppets, and live bugs into the classroom with a lively format that debunks insect myths. Preschool-high school.

THANK YOU, THANK YOU!

The artwork appearing on the Chapter openings was created by the following area students:

Cover art based on drawings by Erica Ligeski, Owen Elementary, Trenton; Robbie Thomas, Cromie Elementary, Warren; and Rachel Quinlan, Owen School, Trenton.

Chapter 1: Benjamin Senopole, St. Clair Shores, James Rodgers Elementary, grade 5.

Chapter 3: Angela Oliver, Warren, Cromie Elementary, grade 5.

Chapter 4: Anne Jeannette LaSovage, Detroit, Burton International, grade 8.

Chapter 5: Courtney Rose, West Bloomfield, Doherty Elementary, grade 2.

Chapter 6: Philip Jackson, Lansing, Post Oak Elementary, grade 5.

Chapter 7: Owen B. Simmons, Southfield, Schoenhals Elementary, grade 4.

Chapter 8: Kyle Willette, Novi, Novi Woods Elementary, grade 4.

Chapter 9: Andrea Muzzin, Trenton, Owen Elementary, grade 5.

Chapter 10: Tiffany Miller, Dearborn, Henry Ford Elementary, grade 4.

Chapter 11: Suzy Housey, Troy, St. Hugo of the Hills, grade 5.

Chapter 12: Steve Gill, Farmington Hills, Forest Elementary, grade 5.

Chapter 13: Jeffrey Krause, Birmingham, Meadow Lake Elementary, grade 1.

Chapter 14: Mike Kegler, Grosse Pointe Woods, Ferry Elementary, grade 5.

Chapter 15: Courtney Brown, Rochester, Meadow Brook Elementary, grade 3.

Chapter 16: Andrew Wilkes-Krier, Ann Arbor, Burns Park Elementary, grade 4.

INDEX

This index lists sites and activities, both specific and general. For a complete listing of sites by city, please see Chapter 2, A City Listing of Sites.

Titles in the Great Lakes Books Series

Detroit: City of Race and Class Violence, revised edition, by B. J. Widick, 1989

Detroit Images: Photographs of the Renaissance City, edited by John J. Bukowczyk and Douglas Aikenhead, with Peter Slavcheff, 1989

Hangdog Reef: Poems Sailing the Great Lakes, by Stephen Tudor, 1989

Orvie, The Dictator of Dearborn, by David L. Good, 1989

America's Favorite Homes: A Guide to Popular Early Twentieth-Century Homes, by Robert Schweitzer and Michael W. R. Davis, 1990

Beyond the Model T: The Other Ventures of Henry Ford, by Ford R. Bryan, 1990

Detroit Kids Catalog: The Hometown Tourist, by Ellyce Field, 1990

Detroit Perspectives: Crossroads and Turning Points, edited by Wilma Henrickson, 1990

The Diary of Bishop Frederic Baraga: First Bishop of Marquette, Michigan, edited by Regis M. Walling and Rev. N. Daniel Rupp, 1990

Life after the Line, by Josie Kearns, 1990

The Making of Michigan, 1820–1860: A Pioneer Anthology, edited by Justin L. Kestenbaum, 1990

Michigan Lumbertowns: Lumbermen and Laborers in Saginaw, Bay City, and Muskegon, 1870–1905, by Jeremy W. Kilar, 1990

The Pottery of John Foster: Form and Meaning, by Gordon and Elizabeth Orear, 1990

Seasons of Grace: A History of the Catholic Archdiocese of Detroit, by Leslie Woodcock Tentler, 1990

Waiting for the News, by Leo Litwak, 1990 (reprint)

Walnut Pickles and Watermelon Cake: A Century of Michigan Cooking, by Larry B. Massie, and Priscilla Massie, 1990

Life on the Great Lakes: A Wheelsman's Story, by Fred W. Dutton, edited by William Donohue Ellis, 1991

Copper Country Journal: The Diary of Schoolmaster Henry Hobart, 1863–1864, by Henry Hobart, edited by Philip P. Mason, 1991

John Jacob Astor: Business and Finance in the Early Republic, by John Denis Haeger, 1991

Survival and Regeneration: Detroit's American Indian Community, by Edmund J. Danziger, Jr., 1991

Steamboats and Sailors of the Great Lakes, by Mark L. Thompson, 1991

Cobb Would Have Caught It: The Golden Years of Baseball in Detroit, by Richard Bak, 1991

Michigan in Literature, by Clarence Andrews, 1992

Under the Influence of Water: Poems, Essays, and Stories, by Michael Delp, 1992

The Country Kitchen, by Della T. Lutes, 1992

The Making of a Mining District: Keweenaw Native Copper 1500–1870, by David J. Krause, 1992

Kids Catalog of Michigan Adventures, by Ellyce Field, 1993

Dear Reader

Still not sure of what to do with the kids? Call your neighborhood library for a list of free family programs, including storytelling, puppet shows, and movies. Or call the departments of parks and recreation and community education in your city. You'll find a wealth of seasonal events, workshops, classes, and sports programs listed in their brochures. Most cities also offer a variety of enrichment opportunities for children with disabilities.

I'd love to hear about your family's adventures and experiences. How has this book helped you? Have I missed any of your favorite sites? Have you found any of the information incorrect or confusing?

Your feedback will help me with the next edition of the *Kids Catalog of Michigan Adventures*. Write to Ellyce Field, P.O. Box 250490, Franklin, Michigan 48025-0490. Be sure to include your name, address, and phone so I can reach you for further clarification.

Author Ellyce Field.
Photo credit: *The Detroit News*

DATE	ISSUED TO